PRINCETON SERIES ON THE MIDDLE EAST

Bernard Lewis and András Hámori, Editors

Islam, Judaism, and Christianity

The Kaaba, the holiest shrine in Mecca

ISLAM, JUDAISM, AND CHRISTIANITY:
Theological and Historical Affiliations

HERIBERT BUSSE

Translated from German
by Allison Brown

Markus Wiener Publishers
Princeton

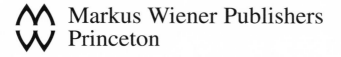

THE TRANSLATION OF THIS BOOK INTO ENGLISH
WAS SUPPORTED BY A GRANT FROM INTER NATIONES.

FOR INFORMATION WRITE TO: MARKUS WIENER PUBLISHERS
231 NASSAU STREET, PRINCETON, NJ 08542

BOOK DESIGN BY CHERYL MIRKIN
THIS BOOK HAS BEEN COMPOSED IN SEMITICA BY CMF GRAPHIC DESIGN

LIBRARY OF CONGRESS CATALOGING-IN-PUBLICATION DATA
BUSSE, HERIBERT
[THEOLOGISCHEN BEZIEHUNGEN DES ISLAMS ZU JUDENTUM UND CHRISTENTUM. ENGLISH]
ISLAM, JUDAISM, AND CHRISTIANITY: THEOLOGICAL AND HISTORICAL AFFILIATIONS/HERIBERT BUSSE; TRANSLATED FROM GERMAN BY ALLISON BROWN.
(PRINCETON SERIES ON THE MIDDLE EAST)
ISBN 1-55876-143-8 (HC: ALK. PAPER)
ISBN 1-55876-144-6 (PB: ALK. PAPER)
1. ISLAM—RELATIONS—CHRISTIANITY. 2. ISLAM—RELATIONS—JUDAISM.
3. CHRISTIANITY AND OTHER RELIGIONS—ISLAM.
4. JUDAISM—RELATIONS—ISLAM.
I. TITLE. II. SERIES
BP172.B8613 1997
297.2'8—DC21 97-40190 CIP

MARKUS WIENER PUBLISHERS BOOKS ARE PRINTED IN THE UNITED STATES OF AMERICA ON ACID-FREE PAPER, AND MEET THE GUIDELINES FOR PERMANENCE AND DURABILITY OF THE COMMITTEE ON PRODUCTION GUIDELINES FOR BOOK LONGEVITY OF THE COUNCIL ON LIBRARY RESOURCES.

PRINTED IN THE UNITED STATES OF AMERICA.

Contents

Introduction

Islam developed from Arab paganism. It is in no way surprising that traces of this tradition survived, openly or below the surface, amid the propagation of uncompromised monotheism. Monotheism, besides warning of a divine judgment, was also the starting point of Muhammad's activities as a prophet.[1] From the beginning, Islam was for obvious reasons closely tied to Judaism and Christianity. The Koran evolved over more than three decades, during which Muhammad was engaged in discussion with adherents of both religions. There is an abundance of documentation on this subject in the Koran, including statements about questions of dogma and practice, as well as narratives with a biblical background and various traditions, both written and oral, of Jewish or Christian origin. Muhammad used them to outline the salvation history *(Heilsgeschichte)* and to illustrate his teachings. Moreover, the Koran contains regulations as to the status of Jews and Christians in the Islamic community *(umma)*, and rules for Muslims to follow in coexisting with adherents of other faiths. This provided, in the course of the development of the Islamic state, the basis for laws that were enacted and behavior patterns that came into use with regard to Jews and Christians living together with Muslims, and with regard to the non-Muslim neighbor states, such as Christian Byzantium. Theoretically, all of this is still valid today, though in practice, modern thought has certainly brought about considerable changes. As re-Islamization in public and private life continues to spread, Muslims have proved willing to return to ancient regulations, or rather to rules regarded as ancient and therefore considered orthodox.

Whereas Jews and Christians in regions under Muslim control were not merely tolerated, but officially recognized on the foundation of laws revelatory in nature, the mutual relationship between Christian and Muslim states was marked over centuries by warlike conflict. Muslims viewed war against unbelievers *(djihād)* as a holy obligation much in the same way as Christians propagated the struggle against Islamic powers up to the beginning of the sixteenth century as a religious matter. In addition, efforts were undertaken on both sides to fight their opponents with spiritual weapons. Christians long thought they could win over Muslims through missionary activities. As each side started learning more about the other, a consciousness developed that acknowledged their common foundations and concerns. Thus the interaction shifted from belligerent confrontation and polemics to missionary activities and then to dialogue. This eased the situation between Christians and Muslims, whereas the attitude of Islam towards Judaism is at present dominated by the political situation in the Middle East. The logical final phase is a trialogue, wherein each of the three religions expresses and demonstrates a willingness to engage in discourse with each of the other two.

Muslims have always been concerned with these two religions, encouraged through Koranic statements and the presence of Jews and Christians in their living sphere. They could remain relatively unbiased in doing this, since they viewed Islam as the fulfillment and completion of the revelation. Throughout the Middle Ages and well into modern times, Christianity judged Islam in a bleak manner, often grotesquely distorted.[2] Not until the Enlightenment did the image of Islam start to change. In the nineteenth century, interest in the Middle East and the Middle-Eastern languages that had been linked to biblical sciences developed such that Islamic studies emerged as an independent academic discipline. This was significant in paving the way for discourse between religions, even though the early stages were all too frequently marked by misconceptions and misunderstandings. The "Academic Study of Judaism" (Wissenschaft des Judentums) that was flourishing at the time in Germany, which examined Judaism by subjecting it to criticism and modern methods of research, also laid the groundwork for the dialogue between Christianity and Judaism and, in the end, for the dialogue with Islam as well. Corresponding to the emphasis on historicism that was prevailing in the humanities, focus was placed on the question of the sources of the Koran and Islam. It was believed that researching Islam's dependence on the older revealed religions would lead to a better understanding of Islam itself. Scholars such as Julius Wellhausen (1844–1918) and Theodor Nöldeke (1836–1930) were pioneering in their research of the early history of Islam. Wellhausen's studies on ancient Arabic paganism, pre-Islam Medina, Muhammad's constitution of Medina,[3] and his relationship to external powers have retained their original validity.[4] Nöldeke created the foundation of the Koranic chronology.[5]

Wellhausen, whose background was in Protestant theology, restrained himself with respect to the question of the origin of Islam. Leaving open the question of whether the word "Koran" (Arabic *qurʾān),* the meaning of which is "recital, lecture," was transmitted to Muhammad by Jews or Christians, he claimed that a piece of poetry attributed to a Jew named Samaual and ideas found in the Koran have a common origin in the Hebrew-Arabic tradition. The two have so much in common that Samaual's poetry was suspected of being a contemporary forgery, intended to make Islam acceptable to the Jews.[6] Jewish scholars often came to the conclusion that Islam was to be viewed as an offshoot of Judaism,[7] whereas Christian scholars were on the look-out for Christian origins. Adolf von Harnack, famous historian of the early church, is known to have called Islam a Christian sect.[8] After World War I, numerous Christian authors supported the theory that Islam was rooted in Christianity. Among these were Wilhelm Rudolph,[9] Richard Bell,[10] Tor Andrae,[11] and Karl Ahrens,[12] to name only the most significant ones. Anton Baumstark, famous for his scholarly work on eastern Christianity, found similarities in style between the Koran and Christian liturgical texts.[13] Not all that long ago, Günter Lüling went so far as to postulate that a Christian prayer book was at the roots of the holy book of the Muslims.[14] Jacques Jomier was more reserved; with respect to the name Raḥmān in the Koran, he declared himself unable to answer the question whether it was of Judeo-Christian or Sabaean (Mandaean) origin.[15]

The results of the quest for the sources of the Koran were not always bound to the religious conviction of the respective scholar. Although not a Jew, Charles Cutler Torrey—Bible scholar, Semitist, and one of the founders of the American School of Archaeology in Jerusalem—opposed this phalanx of supporters of a Christian origin of the Koran with a theory that Islam was rooted solely in Judaism.[16] At the same time, however, there were also scholars who tried to offer a more balanced evaluation, including Joseph Horovitz[17] and Heinrich Speyer.[18]

Parallel to efforts seeking to elucidate the origin of the Koran, numerous biographies of the Prophet Muhammad were also written. Deserving of special interest are those by Frants Buhl,[19] Tor Andrae,[20] W. Montgomery Watt,[21] and Rudi Paret.[22]

Questions related to the direct influence of Judaism and Christianity on the Prophet, such as whether Muhammad had Christian teachers, as Theodor Nöldeke asked in 1858,[23] were replaced in the course of events by interest in exploring the environment in which early Islam developed. The poetry of Umayya b. Abī ṣ-Ṣalt (died 8/628–29 or 9/630–31), a contemporary of Muhammad (died 8 June 632) whose work is well-known and highly esteemed among Arabs, is overflowing with biblical motifs and themes treated in the Koran as well. This led Clement Huart to suggest that Umayya's poetry was a source used in preparing the Koran.[24] Since then, however, the authenticity of that poetry has been questioned.[25] Ideas propagated in the Koran were also assumed to have originated in southern Arabia, home of a highly developed pagan cult and at the same time—due to the changing political situation—influenced by Judaism, Christianity, and Zoroastrianism, the three dominant religions of the period. In 1906, Hubert Grimme, known for his biography of Muhammad, published an article in which he tried to show that a basic teaching of the Koran thought to be related to the Logos of Hellenistic tradition was actually based on a South Arabian model.[26] Fifty years later, Youakim Moubarac compiled a comprehensive list of divine names, titles, and attributes in the Koran that have correlations in South Arabian epigraphy.[27]

In reviewing scholarly attempts to trace the origins of Muhammad's teachings, it is important to take into account the person of the founder of Islam. The religion emerged in an environment that was extremely hostile to change. Especially in Mecca, site of the Kaaba sanctuary, the local aristocracy was resolved to maintain the status quo, cost what it may. It was Johann Fück who focused attention on Muhammad's originality: "It is significant to know how the Prophet used and treated the materials at his disposal, how he interpreted, altered, and selected them to serve his purposes. That he did this more intensively than any other great religious figure does not detract from his originality. On the contrary, it is essential that great thinkers gratefully use the material transmitted to them, filling it with new life."[28] Shortly after Fück, Gustav von Grünebaum praised Muhammad's leadership qualities while pondering the same issue: "Like scarcely any other apostle and reformer, Muhammad was an expert in taking full possession of the thinking and actions of his followers. No detail in conduct did he consider too small to be included in the religious system, after divine arbitration. Within an incredibly short time his ideas and the special terminology with which he presented them became indispensable and self-evident common property of everyday life and its specific language."[29]

Throughout the age of colonialism, Islam was viewed as a religion of inferior quality, an assessment not all that different from the judgment that had been passed in the Middle Ages. Consequently, propagation of the "righteous faith" was regarded as the necessary path to follow. Missionary activities in the lands of Islam were also imposed by the Second Awakening, which first appeared in the United States in the early nineteenth century. Conversion of the heathens and unbelievers was thought to speed the coming of the Last Judgment. It was in this spirit that Samuel Marinus Zwemer (1867–1952), well-known proponent of the Protestant Mission in the Middle East, referred to Islam as "a symbol of man's perversity and his preference for man-made religion."

The picture changed totally after World War II. Individual initiatives in Protestant as well as Catholic theological circles had laid the groundwork in the 1930s for the awakened interest in a dialogue with Islam. The goal of missionizing and converting was pushed into the background. Official initiative was first taken by the Catholic Church. In 1965, the Second Vatican Council issued the "Nostra Aetate," a declaration on the relationship of the Church to non-Christian religions. It expressed "deep respect" for Islam; the position of the Catholic Church toward Judaism was redefined as well. Other churches, as represented by the World Council of Churches, followed with similar official declarations; conferences, congresses, and seminars took place at various levels on the implementation of a dialogue. Theologians and Islamicists raised the issue of the common ground shared by the two, or three, religions. Joseph Henninger, who published a book of essays on Christian truths present in the Koran,[30] was the first of a number of authors of smaller and larger works on the subject. The most significant among them are Denise Masson,[31] Jacques Jomier,[32] Youakim Moubarac,[33] Adel Theodor Khoury,[34] and Ludwig Hagemann.[35] Walter Beltz,[36] as well, should be mentioned here. The two-way dialogue became a three-way encounter in the works of F. E. Peters[37] and Walter Strolz.[38] The list goes on.

The person of Jesus was always at the core of the controversies and the dialogue. The number of books and studies dealing with this subject is extensive. A bibliography published in 1977 lists no less than 726 works,[39] including only those works that had appeared in English or French since 1625 (also including some written by Muslims that had been translated from the Middle Eastern languages) and not including Koran translations.[40] There are, however, theologians who are skeptical of the dialogue, such as the New Testament scholar Heikki Räisänen.[41] Seeking what Muhammad said, what he meant, and why he said it as he did and not in another way, Räisänen outlined the life of Jesus based on the Koran, treated a number of relevant topics (the teachings and piousness of Jesus, his performing of miracles, and his being raised up to heaven, etc.) and closed with a description as it appears in the Koran of the dogmatic discourse on Jesus' essence and mission. The author limited his evaluation to a strictly text-based interpretation of Koranic statements, excluding the extensive material contained in the Hadith, the literary genre reflecting developments in

Islamic tradition, oral and written, on the life of Muhammad and the interpretation of the Koran.

This brief survey cannot be concluded without mentioning the theory put forward by Patricia Crone and Michael Cook.[42] They painted a totally new picture, based on Jewish and Christian sources including the very significant *History of Heraclius,* written shortly after 661 by the Armenian bishop Sebeos. Cook and Crone interpreted Islam as having developed as a link between a Jewish messianic movement and the Arabs, the latter claiming to be descendants of Abraham in the line of Hagar, as is well known. According to the authors' theory, the "religion of Abraham" represented the link between the Arabs, or Hagarians, and the Jews. At first the Muslims were extremely anti-Christian, but in order to break from the Jews and gain their independence, they assumed more pro-Christian attitudes. The Koran in its present form did not exist before the end of the seventh century, according to Crone and Cook. This is consistent with John Wansbrough's theory that the Koran was not compiled under the reign of Caliph ᶜUthmān (ruled 644–656), as is believed in Islamic tradition and as had been generally assumed by Western research up to now; instead, Wansbrough claimed it was compiled from scattered segments at a much later date.[43] This assertion has much in common with the generally accepted view in Western theology that the Jesus of the Gospels is not the historical Jesus, and that the Gospels reflect instead the opinions the early Christian community formed of its founder.

For now, we shall let Wansbrough's theory rest and assume that the Koran was completed during Muhammad's lifetime and that it took on its present form approximately fifteen years after his death. In addition to the Koran, the Islamic tradition regarding the life and teachings of Muhammad is important for our purpose here, i.e., the presentation of the relationship of Islam to Judaism and Christianity. It goes without saying that priority is given to the Koran, the Islamic tradition playing a secondary role. Early Arabic sources have been compiled in an Italian translation in the monumental work by Leone Caetani.[44] Ibn Isḥāq's biography, most important for our knowledge of Muhammad's life, was made available in revised form by Ibn Hishām (died 830). A translation by A. Guillaume includes all essential statements on

Muhammad's attitudes toward Jews and Christians, and provides background for correlating relevant Koran verses with certain concrete situations in the life of the Prophet.[45] The work was written in retrospect, of course, thus conveying to only a limited extent an accurate historical picture of Muhammad, making it comparable in that regard to the Gospels and the picture they depict of Jesus.

Finally, it must be noted that there is a tendency in modern critical scholarship to reduce almost everything Islamic tradition has to say about Muhammad to conveying a mere phantom of the Prophet himself.[46] It must be left to further research whether this turns out to be fully justified. For the pious Muslim, the Koran and the early Islamic tradition convey a true picture of the beginnings of Islam as much as the pious Christian finds the historical Jesus in the Gospels.

In the following, citations from the Koran are made primarily from the translation by A.J. Arberry.[47] The Bible quotations are generally cited from the Authorized (King James) Version, in a few cases only from The Jerusalem Bible.

I would like to thank Allison Brown for her excellent translation and the editorial effort she invested in the English language edition.

Mühlheim, Main
March 1998

The Religious Context on the Arabian Peninsula at the Time of Muhammad

Political and Religious Background

According to traditional sources, Muhammad was born in Mecca in 570 and died in Medina in 632. At the time he founded Islam, the inhabitants of the Arabian peninsula were pagans, adherents of the ancient Semitic religion. The region was, however, within the sphere of influence of a number of external religious currents that varied in kind and strength. Christianity had become the prevailing religion along the Mediterranean and had spread to eastern Africa, Mesopotamia, Persia, and India. Zoroastrianism had long since passed its peak by the time of Muhammad. It had experienced a renaissance under the Sassanids and became the state religion in Persia, which had broken through to the Mediterranean after conquering Syria and Egypt in 614; nevertheless, in 628—two years before Muhammad seized Mecca—Emperor Heraclius altered the situation by retaking the regions that had been lost and pushing forward up to Mesopotamia. The two empires devastated each other in these conflicts, thus paving the way for the Arabs. Zoroastrianism was not a missionizing religion. It was tied to Iranian culture and put on the defensive as the Sassanid Empire declined, finally sinking into oblivion in Persia in the course of developments that began with the Arab conquest and extended into the tenth century. Judaism had been present on the Arabian peninsula since time immemorial. Jewish communities of considerable size existed in Medina and other cities and settlements of the Ḥidjāz. The Jews had started facing serious difficulties after the Roman Empire had become Christian. Under the Sassanids, they had perhaps been less threatened. On the fringes, where Christianity had not yet gained unrestricted acceptance, Judaism remained a strength to be reckoned with.

In addition to the major religious communities, there were Gnostic groups and sects that had large spheres of influence and at times major followings. Among these was Manichaeism, which united different elements and still represented a great missionary strength. Isolated pagan cults also still existed in Mesopotamia. Sheltered in the marshlands of southern Mesopotamia, the Baptist sect of the Mandaeans survived the onslaught of Christianity and Zoroastrianism. The ideas and religious convictions of these groups and sects spread out over the Arabian peninsula with differing degrees of impact. They confronted a population that was still pagan yet on the verge of taking on a new religious orientation. This pertained most strongly to southern Arabia. As a result of political and economic upheaval, it was hit within hardly more than two centuries by Christian, Jewish, and Zoroastrian waves before finally turning to Islam.

The northern outskirts of the Arabian peninsula were ruled by Persia and the Byzantine Empire. Although the center with the Ḥidjāz was not in the mainstream, it was by no means isolated from the outside world. Mecca was located on a trade route, the famous "incense route" that Ptolemy had described. It ran parallel to the shores of the Red Sea, connecting southern Arabia with the region east of the Jordan River and Syria. A fork led from Petra to Gaza on the Mediterranean. Southern Arabian harbors provided sea connections to India and East Africa. Nadjrān, at the present-day border with Yemen, was an important center in the south. From there, a route branched off to the northeast along the Djabal Ṭuwayḳ (via present-day ar-Riyād) to the Shaṭṭ al-ᶜArab. There was an important Christian community in this city. Jewish communities existed in cities in the northern section of the incense route, though virtually nothing is known about their origins.[48] The most important ones, from north to south, were Taymāᵓ, Khaybar, and Yathrib/Medina. The Jewish community in Medina was organized in "tribes," three of which were to play a special role in Muhammad's life, namely, Banū Ḳaynuḳāᶜ, Banū ᵓl-Naḍīr, and Banū Ḳurayẓa. Not much is known about the internal affairs of these Jewish communities.[49] For example, it is not clear if they already had access to the Talmud, since the Babylonian Talmud had only been completed a short time earlier. There does not appear to have been an organized Jewish community in Mecca, though of course Jews participated at the markets that took place in and around Mecca in connection with the pilgrim festival. It also cannot be ruled out that Muhammad was adopting Jewish ideas when he taught that the Kaaba was built by Abraham.

The religious context in southern Arabia, as has already been indicated, corresponded to the political and economic changes that had taken place in the last few centuries prior to the emergence of Islam. In the early fourth century, Ethiopia invaded southern Arabia, facilitating the spread of Christianity. Nadjrān, mentioned earlier, had the most notable Christian community. From contemporary Greek and Syrian sources it is known that the population of Nadjrān was very cosmopolitan, comprised of several nationalities and denominations, including Greeks, Syrians, Ethiopians (Monophysites), and Nestorians.[50] According to Arabic sources, a cathedral was later built in Ṣanᶜāᵓ.[51] A Christian community that had some importance for the incense trade existed from the fourth century onward, on the island of Socotra.[52] Judaism was a powerful rival of Christianity in southern Arabia. It was favored by Persia, which reflected the power struggle between Persia and the Byzantine Empire, an ally of Ethiopia. In the early sixth century, the Himyarite ruler Ashᶜar Dhū Nuwās took the name Joseph and converted to Judaism, unleashing a period of Christian persecution that hit Nadjrān particularly hard and triggered another Ethiopian invasion.[53] Southern Arabia was ruled by Ethopian governors until 575, when the pro-Persian faction entered into negotiations with the Sassanids. The country then became Persian to at least a nominal extent until it was incorporated into the Islamic sphere of influence in 628. As a result of Persian supremacy, Zoroastrianism also spread into southern Arabia, but it probably did not extend beyond the narrow circle of Persian officials or merchants.

The two major powers to the north, Persia and the Byzantine Empire, refrained from direct political rule of the Arabs; they could not have carried this through in any case due to the rivalry between them that led to almost continuous warfare. However, the border between the two great powers was not a line dividing two totally different cultures. As is common, political borders did not separate ethnic groups, much less religions. In Syria and Palestine, there was only a very small Greek population, which belonged to the imperial church. The native residents were Monophysites, largely members of the Jacobite Church. There were also Jacobites in northern Mesopotamia. Their religious center was Takrit, the residence of the hierarch, who was responsible for all Jacobites under Persian rule. Southern Mesopotamia was characterized by Nestorian Christianity. Their religious leader resided in Seleucia-Ctesiphon (present-day al-Madāʾin, approx. 60 km south of Baghdad), the Sassanian capital. At the border between the two major powers, "phylarchs" had been established, i.e., Arab tribal rulers in the employ of the emperor, on the one side, or the Great King, on the other, and who served as their political agents in the adjacent desert. The Ghassanids were the Byzantine phylarchs. They were Monophysites and ruled the region east of the Jordan from Damascus to the Red Sea. The Lakhmids served the Sassanids. Their center was at al-Ḥīra on the Euphrates, near present-day Nadjaf. The Lakhmids were not Christians, but they favored Nestorianism. They ruled until shortly after 602. Organized Christian communities with bishops existed in Eilat at the Red Sea, Dūmat al-Djandal (al-Djauf, at the same latitude as Eilat, but 500 km farther east), and Taymāʾ. Their denomination is not definitively known, though there were most likely Christians of various denominations, as in Nadjrān.[54] In the Ḥidjāz, Muhammad's native region, organized Christianity had not yet been able to gain a foothold. Even though it has been claimed in Arabic sources that St. Bartholomew the Apostle held sermons there,[55] it seems certain that no systematic missionization ever took place in the Ḥidjāz. If any

Christians lived there, they were monks or hermits who lived in seclusion in the desert. Monasticism from its beginnings was closely tied to the desert. There were likely a large number of monks in Arabia who had had a falling out with their church for dogmatic or disciplinary reasons and had sought refuge in the desert. In addition to the monks and clerics, there were certainly isolated lay Christians of various denominations who settled along the trade routes as merchants. Perhaps there were even some who had been forced to leave their homelands for religious or political reasons. They promoted Christianity through their mere presence. Sources mention a large number of such Christians.[56] One "specialist" who worked temporarily in Mecca was a Coptic carpenter who built the roof of the Kaaba when Muhammad was approximately 35 years old and had not yet become a prophet,[57] i.e., around 605. Christian slaves in Mecca are mentioned in the biography of the Prophet. Muhammad is said to have frequently conversed with Djabr, a young Christian slave. Adversaries thus believed Muhammad took information from the Christian and proclaimed it to be a revelation. Muhammad dismissed the accusation with the following words: "And We know very well that they say, 'Only a mortal is teaching him.' (that which he proclaims as divine revelation). (But) The speech of him at whom they hint is barbarous; and this is speech Arabic, manifest." (sura 16:103/105). ᶜAddās, a Christian slave from Ninive, is supposed to have recognized Muhammad as a prophet when, before eating a bunch of grapes, he spoke the words, "in the name of God."[58] Finally, Bilāl must be mentioned in this context. He was an Ethiopian slave and certainly a Christian, and he became one of Mohammad's most loyal followers.[59] When Muhammad was at the height of his influence, a Coptic Christian entered his household; it was Maria, a slave who had been presented to him as a gift from Muḳauḳis, the Byzantine governor of Egypt. She bore a son to Muhammad.[60] There are also reports that a Christian named Sardjis served the Muslims as a guide in the desert during a military campaign east of the Jordan. He was apparently a native of the region. After returning he is said to have converted to Islam.[61]

Native residents could gather information about the Christian creed from Christians living in the Hidjāz. There were also Christians from abroad who came to Mecca for the annual pilgrim festival and market. There was a whole series of similar events surrounding the Meccan pilgrim festival. In the month of Shawwāl, i.e., two months before the *Ḥadjdj,* a market took place in ʿUkāẓ (70 km east of Mecca) with a ritual similar to the one in Mecca. The rocks there were the destination of pilgrimages, and pilgrims circumambulated them, similar to the practice at the Kaaba in Mecca. The pilgrims then moved on to al-Madjanna (several miles from Mecca) and remained there for twenty days of the following month, Dhūʾl-Ḳaʿda. Then they went to Dhūʾl-Madjāz (southeast of Mecca, near ʿArafāt), where they stayed until the Meccan pilgrim festival started on the ninth of Dhūʾl-Ḥidjdja. The entire journey lasted almost ten weeks, not including travel to and from the starting point. In the months preceding and following the pilgrim festival, general peace prevailed, so that the visitors could observe their religious practices and duties undisturbed. Tor Andrae suggested that itinerant Christian preachers, perhaps from southern Arabia, appeared at these markets and gave Muhammad important impulses for his preaching.[62]

Trading Activities of Meccan Merchants; Ethiopia

Meccan merchants traveling for trade purposes encountered Christianity and other religions in the surrounding countries. Muhammad's great grandfather Hāshim b. ʿAbd Manāf supposedly died at Gaza on such a trade journey. Hāshim's brothers also died in foreign countries: Al-Muṭṭalib in southern Arabia, and Naufal in Iraq. Muhammad's uncle al-ʿAbbās often took trips to Yemen to purchase spices to sell at the pilgrim festival in Mecca.[63] Another Meccan, Naḍr b. al-Ḥārith, had been in al-Ḥīra, residence of the Persia-oriented Lakhmids, and he knew the mythical history of the Persians that Firdausi later compiled in his epic *The Book of Kings.* Naḍr tried to use this knowledge to outdo Muhammad, whenever the latter told Bible stories or stories with a biblical background.[64] Muhammad himself is supposed to have traveled to Syria with his uncle and guardian Abū Ṭālib, who had raised the orphaned Muhammad. On this journey

Muhammad is said to have met the monk Baḥīrā in Bosra. The monk supposedly recognized Muhammad as the future prophet of the Arabs and protected him from the Jews, who had wanted to seize him.[65] The story was later elaborated upon, going so far as to claim that Muhammad had received instruction in Christian doctrine from the monk.[66] From the Islamic perspective this was intended to provide confirmation, by a Christian authority, of Muhammad's calling to prophethood. The narrative of Zayd b. ᶜAmr, who wandered throughout Syria and Mesopotamia in search of the true religion, is a variation of this story. In the region east of the Jordan he met a monk who foretold the appearance of a prophet in Arabia.[67] And finally, as regards the closest circle around Muhammad, his father-in-law Abū Bakr must be mentioned, who later became the first of the four "legitimate" caliphs. He was a knowledgeable merchant who is said to have been well-traveled.[68]

It cannot be ruled out that Muhammad himself took trips to Syria or other neighboring countries, especially since he was involved in trade prior to his prophetic calling, after he had married the wealthy merchant widow Khadīdja. Aside from the trip taken during his adolescence, no additional travels are mentioned in the sources, and the Koran includes no indications whatsoever of travel, even though a lot of attention is paid to autobiographical elements. Muhammad did take part in a number of military campaigns, though these did not extend beyond the borders of the Arabian peninsula. The northernmost point he reached during these campaigns was, as reported by Ibn Isḥāḳ, Dūmat al-Djandal, as mentioned above.[69] By this time, however, he already had a clearly outlined picture of Christianity, so there was little he could learn here, especially since he did not have any contact with the enemy during this campaign. There is no mention of travel prior to his becoming a prophet due to the fact that very little is known of his development period in general, as is the case with all the great founders of religions. Perhaps he did not want to offer any information about travels during his youth, since he might have then been accused of gathering his knowledge of Christianity and the Christian Holy Scriptures from remote regions. Even the few contacts he had with Christians in Mecca, as mentioned above, led contemporaries to suspect he did nothing more than retell Bible and other related stories. For the same reason, traditional Islamic sources interpret the expression *al-nabī al-ummī* (sura 7:157), translated by A. J. Arberry as "Prophet of the common folk," to mean that Muhammad could neither read nor write, and the source of his preachings was not books, but God. Muslims could cite the passage in the Koran where God said to Muhammad, "Not before this didst thou recite any Book, or inscribe it with thy right hand" (29:48).

Let us once again look toward the south. The Ethiopian vice king Abraha, who ruled Yemen before the Persians took power there, had a cathedral built in Ṣanᶜāʾ that was intended to rival the Kaaba and attract the Meccan pilgrims. After a Meccan desecrated the cathedral, Abraha decided to lead a military campaign to Mecca to destroy the Kaaba. He failed, however, because of a recalcitrant elephant accompanying his army. While retreating, the army suffered serious losses. This event was recorded in the Koran in sura 105, under the heading "The Elephant."[70] There might be some historical foundation to this legendary elaboration of the story.[71] According to Islamic tradition, Abraha's campaign took place in the year 570, which is referred to as the "elephant year." This is supposedly the year of Muhammad's birth. In any case, memories of Abraha's attack were able to discredit the Ethiopians in the eyes of the Meccans and later the Muslims. The same is true for the story that Ethiopian Christians saw the infant Muhammad with his foster mother and intended to take him away and bring him to their king, since the child was destined to have a great future. The foster mother supposedly then took the infant back to his mother Āmina.[72] The theme of this story corresponds to the one about the monk Baḥīrā, who, as mentioned earlier, prevented Muhammed from falling into the hands of the Jews as a child. Both narratives intended to show that the two older religions, Judaism and Christianity, perceived themselves as being threatened by Muhammad and thus they attempted to control the future prophet in order to thwart his prophetic mission and prevent the founding of Islam. Despite the negative image of the Ethiopians, which Muhammad was certainly aware of from the very beginning, as sura 105 is one of the early revelations,[73] Muhammad sent a group of his followers to exile in Ethiopia when he feared not being able to hold out in Mecca due to the strong resistance offered by his opponents. Later sources explain this decision by saying that Muhammad referred to Ethiopia as a friendly land, where the negus would not tolerate injustice.[74] But the hopes put in the negus were disappointed in the end. According to traditional sources, after the Muslims had demonstrated their "Christian" convictions by reciting sura 19, which tells the story of Jesus' birth, the negus refused to comply with the demand of the Meccan delegation, Muhammad's opponents, that the exiles be turned over to them. Apparently, however, the negus had problems with his subjects later on, when they accused him of false Christological teachings, pretending that he had been influenced by the Muslims. In any case, the Muslims failed in Ethiopia and returned to the Ḥidjāz, except for a single Muslim who converted to Christianity and remained in Ethiopia.[75]

It is not known whether the series of three groups sent to Ethiopia was intended to pave the way to resettle the entire community, including the Prophet himself. Only on the basis of later events could it be concluded that this had been planned. A short time later, Muhammad entered into negotiations with the inhabitants of Ṭāʾif, Mecca's neighboring city to the southeast. His desire to be accepted by them was not satisfied, however. After this rejection he turned to the inhabitants of Yathrib/Medina and began negotiations that ended with the Hidjra, the "emigration" of Muhammad and his followers from Mecca and their resettlement in Medina. In light of these developments it seems plausible that Ethiopia had been considered as a substitute residence for the community, perhaps with the intention of returning to Mecca when the situation improved. The choice of Ethiopia attests to the attempt to seek support among Christians. In deciding between Christians and Zoroastrians, i.e., between the Byzantine Empire and Persia, Muhammad had already chosen the Christians in the year 614. The famous passage in sura 30 ("The Greeks") alludes to the Persian victory, which marked the beginning of the fourteen-year period of Sassanid rule at the eastern end of the Mediterranean Sea. "The Greeks have been vanquished in the nearer part of the land; and, after their vanquishing, they shall be the victors in a few years. To God belongs the Command before and after, and on that day [when the Greeks are victorious] the believers shall rejoice in God's help; God helps whomsoever He will; and He is the All-mighty, the All-compassionate" (vv. 2–4).

The prophecy of the imminent defeat of the Persians reveals political far-sightedness. The Byzantines were defeated a year before the exiles were sent to Ethiopia, which explains why the Prophet sought refuge in the south rather than the north. The Ḥidjāz was surrounded by the Persians, since southern Arabia had been under Persian rule since 575. The Koranic decree in favor of the Christians also testifies to the certainty of the Prophet that God stood on the side of the believers. The status of the "People of the Book" *(ahl al-kitāb),* who were tolerated by Islam, was not granted until later, as we shall see.

Relationship to the Jews

The judgment of the Greeks/Byzantines in sura 30 testifies to considerable sympathy shown Christianity. Judaism, too, was within Muhammad's horizons at a very early point, even if nothing is mentioned of this in the sources; mention is made of the contact he had in Mecca with individual Christians, but not of his contact with Jews. Sura 17:1 is cited as expressing Muhammad's attitudes toward Judaism before he fled to Medina, making reference to the travel of the Prophet by night "from the Holy Mosque [i.e., from the Kaaba] to the Further Mosque *(al-masdjid al-akṣā).*" Islamic sources had, at a very early stage, identified the "Further Mosque" as the site of the Temple in Jerusalem, though this is not undisputed.[76] Muhammad seems to have first encountered Jews while in Medina. According to traditional Islamic sources, the first person whom he saw after arriving in Medina was a Jew.[77] We shall not discuss this further here. Muhammad had not planned Yathrib/Medina as the destination of the Hidjra because there was a large Jewish community there, perhaps the largest in Arabia. He had not wanted to attempt living with the Jews after having been disappointed by the Christians in Ethiopia and the pagans in Ṭāʾif. Before the Hidjra he had held lengthy negotiations with residents of Medina, who had become acquainted with him and his teachings during the pilgrim festival. They were prepared to support him. For this, they were to go down in history with the honorable title "helpers" *(anṣār)*. However, these people were not Jews prior to their conversion, but pagans. Muhammad was called to Medina as an arbitrator to resolve disputes that had erupted among various groups within the population there. Jews are mentioned in the "Constitution of Medina" he enacted after his arrival, but only as one group among several.[78] He surely tried to secure support from the Jews as soon as he arrived. To a certain extent, he repeated the Ethiopian experiment, though the starting conditions were very different. This time it was not the Christians who were his partners, but the Jews. Muhammad adopted some liturgical customs from them, since it was now possible to organize the religious life of the Islamic community without any outside interference. He introduced Jerusalem as the direction to face during prayer *(ḳibla)* in the mosque he had built after his arrival; this is assumed although not stated explicitly in the Koran. After seventeen months, the direction was changed. Instead of Jerusalem (the name is not mentioned in the Koran), the Kaaba in Mecca became the direction to be faced during prayer (2:142–150). We shall return to this point later on. Based on the Jewish model, the beginning of religious services was signaled by a trumpet blast. This was later replaced by a wooden clapper *(nāḳūs)*, an instrument of Christian origin.[79] Finally, the call to prayer *(adhān)* was introduced, as is still common today throughout the Islamic world.

Although Muhammad had made some appeals to the Jews in Medina, it was nevertheless clear that a break was to come. Changing the direction of prayer after scarcely a year and a half was only the first sign of the disaster that was to befall the Jews. It was a hopeless venture to want to convert the Jews to Islam, as Muhammad quickly realized. In contrast to the Christians, who had settled on the Arabian peninsula more by accident than by plan and who were hardly educated in theology and living far away from the theological centers of Christianity, the Jews were well-versed in their Scriptures and schooled in religious debate, even if perhaps they had not yet gained access to Talmudic scholarship. In Muhammad's biography, there is mention of a learned rabbi from Medina who was a wealthy owner of date palms, and there was a Jewish school or synagogue in Medina.[80] In view of the closed phalanx of a wealthy Jewish community that was well-educated in its tradition, Muhammad was in a poor position. He had come to Medina as an impoverished refugee at the head of a company of have-nots, with very limited and mostly second-hand knowledge of the Bible and Jewish rituals. According to Islamic sources, it is assumed that the subjects of debate between Muhammad and the Jews are summarized in sura 2:1–100.[81] In the battles that broke out against the Meccans shortly afterward, Muhammad was not certain of Jewish support. Muslims and Jews could not live side by side in the long term. Muhammad rid himself of the Jews in several stages. Two tribes were exiled from the city and the third was the victim of a massacre. If one can believe traditional sources, Muhammad continued to persecute the Jews well beyond his own death. In his will, he proposed to exile the Jews from the Ḥidjāz (and the Christians from the Arabian peninsula). ᶜUmar b. al-Khaṭṭāb, the second caliph (634–644), carried out the last will of the Prophet and drove the Jews out of Khaybar, where they had settled after being forced out of Medina.[82] It is of course known that Jewish communities have survived to the present day in southern Arabia. After the Jews, Christians were banished as well, and they disappeared from the Arabian peninsula entirely. Christianity has only recently returned to the region in connection with oil drilling, and its scope is limited to foreign workers employed there temporarily.

The Meccan Sanctuary

The transformation of the pagan Kaaba into the "House of God" *(baitu llāh)* was of paramount importance in establishing Islam in Mecca and on the Arabian peninsula. Muhammad achieved this by linking it with Abraham, founder of monotheism and alleged common forefather of Jews and Arabs. Abraham and the understanding of his function in the history of salvation was a central aspect of Muhammad's debate with Jews (and Christians). This will be discussed in detail later on. It can be assumed that Muhammad had already heard of Abraham in the early Meccan period. He believed that the Kaaba in Mecca was built or purged of idolatry by Abraham, assisted by his son

Ishmael. Contrary to the assumption of Snouck Hurgronje that Muhammad did not declare Abraham as the builder of the Kaaba until he came to Medina, in order to motivate the Muslims to fight against Mecca, it must be assumed that the Prophet had already supported this notion before going to Medina in exile.[83] Perhaps he even got the idea from the Jews. In the biography of the Prophet there is mention of rabbis who are supposed to have said that the Kaaba was the temple of their father Abraham, but they could not hold religious services there, because the pagans had placed idols in the temple and sacrificed animals there to worship them. In another passage in the same source, the pagan Arabs had supposedly recognized the precedence of the Kaaba over all other shrines in Arabia, since it was the temple and the mosque of Abraham, the friend of God *(khalīlu llāh),* as he is styled in the Koran (4:125).[84]

It is part of Muslim dogma that Abraham went to Mecca and, together with his son Ishmael, built the Kaaba or purged it of idols. This is the interpretation expressed even by modern Muslim authors who otherwise engage in a critical examination of the history of the Kaaba.[85] There have also been a number of attempts in Western research to prove a foreign origin of the Meccan shrine. In the mid-nineteenth century, Reinhart Dozy went the furthest in this regard. He believed that by linking biblical and Arabian information he could prove that the tribe of Simeon had been banished during the time of Samuel (cf. 1 Chron. 4:24–43).[86] According to Dozy, they went to Arabia and founded Yathrib/Medina. Mecca, too, was supposedly founded by the Simeonites. Dozy explained Hubal, the name of the idol put up in the Kaaba which was venerated by the pagan Arabs, as being a corruption of the Hebrew *ha-Baal.* He further claimed that the belief that Abraham founded the Kaaba was based on a misunderstanding; the name "Abraham's station" *(maḳām* Ibrāhīm, sura 2:119/125), which refers to the shrine and also appears in the Koran, originally meant "the station of the Hebrews."[87]

There have also been Christian claims to the Kaaba, according to a number of sources. Long before Muhammad's call to prophethood, a stone with an inscription was found in the Kaaba. The inscription was a Gospel quotation warning against false prophets (Matt. 7:16).

Similarly, a stone with a Syrian inscription was found during the reconstruction of the Kaaba, when Muhammad was still a young man.[88] Significant for our context is the ninth century description of the interior of the Kaaba written by al-Azraḳī, the Meccan historian.[89] According to his report, the columns were decorated with pictures of prophets, angels, and trees; there were pictures of Abraham with gaming arrows in his hand,[90] and pictures of Jesus son of Mary, his mother, and the angel. Perhaps this was a picture of Mary with the infant Jesus, surrounded by angels. After concluding this general report, al-Azraḳī included no less than nine individual reports on the same subject. According to the most specific site description, the pictures were located on the center column near the door. Reports vary about what happened to them after the conquest of Mecca. Some say that Muhammad had all pictures removed before he entered the Kaaba; other reports say he ordered their removal after having entered the Kaaba, but explicitly made an exception of the pictures of Jesus and his mother. There are reports that the pictures were wiped away using cloths dipped in water from the well of Zemzem. It appears that they had been painted with highly soluble paints.

It is difficult to say how to assess these reports. Was the story that Christian pictures were discovered in the Kaaba invented to allow Christians to participate in the pilgrim festival? Such an explanation is less plausible than the assumption that there actually were such pictures in the Kaaba prior to the Islamic period. Since the Kaaba was a shrine for people throughout a very large region, it had attracted diverse rituals that had previously been practiced elsewhere, including rituals not only for the god Hubal but also for the three goddesses mentioned in the Koran—al-Lāt, al-ᶜUzzā, and al-Manāt (sura 53:19–20). Muhammad is said to have destroyed 360 idols with his own hands when Mecca was conquered.[91] This number is not to be taken literally, but neither can it be ruled out that there had indeed been Christian symbols and images among them. Those who painted or worshipped such pictures were certainly not Christians closely connected to a church that would have ordered, or even permitted this. According to the sources mentioned above, it had even been said that the Ḳuraysh themselves had put the pictures in the Kaaba.

The counterpart to Dozy's theory of a Jewish origin of the Kaaba is provided by Günter Lüling. He claimed that the Kaaba was originally a Christian shrine,[92] and he attempted to prove it by referring to the architectural design and appropriate passages in old-Arabic literature. This is of course based on the theory he had previously introduced that the Koran had a Christian source. Even if the Kaaba was not a site of Christian worship in the sense that Lüling claimed it to have been, it cannot be ruled out that there might have been Christian symbols like those described above. It is perhaps not by chance that the picture mentioned is one of the Madonna. There is reference in the Koran to an odd understanding of the Trinity. God asked Jesus if he taught the following: "Take me and my mother as gods, apart from God" (5:116). Jesus answered negatively, of course. The obvious assumption here, that Muhammad made a mistake in listing the three persons of the one Godhead, can be countered with the assumption that the reference was to the Collyridians, a Christian sect that worshipped the Virgin Mary. Their existence in "Arabia" (i.e., the region east of the Jordan and the Sinai peninsula) was mentioned by Epiphanius of Salamis (died 403), archbishop of Cyprus who came from Palestine. As he wrote in his *Panarion* ("medicine box"), a description of 80 heresies, the name is derived from the shortbread *(kollyris)* that women prepared as an offering in their worship of Mary and then ate, apparently emulating the receiving of the eucharistic host. The Collyridians might be identical with the Philomarianites mentioned by Leontius of Byzantium (died 543–544), who dealt extensively with the question of the Trinity.[93] With respect to the cited Koran passage, Muhammad was most likely referring to such a Christian sect. This is in any case more plausible than assuming that the Prophet defined the Trinity in such an erroneous manner out of pure ignorance. The picture of the Madonna might also have been painted by an Arab. Al-Azraḳī wrote of a female visitor to the Kaaba who was a member of the Ghassān tribe. Upon viewing the picture, she is said to have called out: "My father and my mother be your ransom! You [Mary] are surely an Arab woman!"[94]

The Ḥanīfs

Reports of Jewish or Christian elements in and around the Kaaba reflect the religious pluralism that was present in Arabia at the time of the emergence of Islam. Jews and Christians living in the Ḥidjāz, and certainly those in southern Arabia as well, were non-Arabs and thus considered foreigners, even if, like the Jews of Medina, they had been living on the Arabian peninsula for many centuries and had adopted—to the extent their religions allowed—the language and lifestyle of their Arab environment. In northern Arabia, on the other hand, entire Arab tribes, such as the Banū Taghlib, had converted to Christianity. In the Ḥidjāz there were only isolated individuals who had given up paganism. According to later Islamic tradition, they were called *ḥunafāʾ* (sing. *ḥanīf).* The term was based on Muhammad's reference to the Patriarch Abraham as a *ḥanīf,* since he was neither Jew nor Christian (2:135/129, etc.).[95] Those traditionally referred to as a *ḥanīf* did not belong to any of the major revealed religions that were dominant in the surrounding areas and had became established in Arabia. Ibn Isḥāq mentioned four prominent *ḥanīfs* in his biography of Muhammad and described their fates.[96] The most well-known of these was Waraḳa b. Naufal, a cousin of Khadīdja, Muhammad's first wife. Waraḳa had read Christian Scripture and evidently recognized the revelation of Muhammad as genuine, after hearing of it from Khadīdja. He died a Christian. Two other *ḥanīfs* who were initially followers of Muhammad later converted to Christianity. One was in Ethiopia, where he had gone with others seeking asylum. The other entered the Byzantine service, whereby he was of course lost to Islam. Only one of the four, Zayd b. ʿAmr, remained a *ḥanīf.* He was a poet and, while traveling in the region east of the Jordan, as mentioned above, met a monk who prophesied the coming of a prophet in Arabia. His *ḥanīf* qualities are described as not worshipping idols, abstaining from eating blood and the meat of animals killed by strangulation, not eating any sacrificial meat, and rejecting the killing of (unwanted) children. He left Mecca in search of the "Ḥanīfiyya," the religion of Abraham.

The list of prohibitions that Zayd supposedly complied with is strongly reminiscent of the resolution of the apostle council, which released pagans who had converted to Christianity from having to comply with all the Jewish ritual laws, as has been passed down in the Acts of the Apostles, and demanded of them only those obligations serving to dissociate them from pagan ritual (Acts 15:29). It is also similar to the Noachian law with its ban on consuming blood and on killing (Gen. 9:1–6). In fact, however, the list reflects Koranic commandments, e.g., sura 2:173/168, which includes a list of foods that one is forbidden to eat: "carrion, blood, the flesh of swine, what has been hallowed [when it was slaughtered] to other than God." The prohibition of killing children alludes to sura 17:31/33: "And slay not your children for fear of poverty; . . . surely the slaying of them is a grievous sin." There was a clear intention to portray Zayd b. ʿAmr as a man for whom the only step to Islam still to be taken was his profession of faith, or to be more exact, the recognition of Muhammad as the Prophet of God. Zayd was to a certain extent an *anima naturaliter islamica.*

It is not clear whether people who turned away from paganism but had not yet affiliated themselves with a monotheistic religion lived according to the norms postulated for Zayd b. ʿAmr. It is apparent, however, that the *ḥanīfs* had more in common with Christianity than with Judaism. This also applied to a man named Abū Ḳays of Medina. He was also a poet, like Zayd, and recited his teachings in verse. In pre-Islamic times, which—corresponding to the reference in Acts 17:30—were referred to by Muhammad as the period of ignorance *(djāhiliyya),*[97] Abū Ḳays practiced an ascetic piety similar to that of monks.[98] He was a *ḥanīf* and became a Muslim after the Hidjra.[99] Such asceticism was also practiced by Muhammad himself. Once a year, according to traditional sources, he retreated to Mount Ḥirāʾ near Mecca, where he fasted and fed the poor. It is also here where he is said to have received his first revelation.[100] If this is true and one takes the traces of Christianity in pre-Islamic Arabia into account, it becomes clear how strong Christianity had become in regions that had originally been outside the domain of missionary efforts, and how desperately the Arabs had sought a new religious orientation.

Muhammad's Sources

Muhammad's knowledge of Judaism and Christianity is also reflected in the biblical materials he was familiar with and the manner in which he used them in the Koran. The narratives in which this information is used presumably came from Jewish or Christian sources. It also seems plausible that Muhammad had read neither the Old nor the New Testament, nor did he become acquainted with them through informants. Of the names of the books of the Old Testament, he knew only the Torah, or Pentateuch *(taurāt),* and the Book of Psalms *(zabūr);* he referred to the Scriptures of the New Testament cumulatively as "the Gospels" *(al-indjīl).*[101] There are very few quotations from the Old and New Testaments, even in a very broad sense.[102] The use of biblical materials, both in terms of content and extent, leaves much to be desired. Biblical stories were incorporated in the Koran rather at random; their only purpose was to illustrate the dogmatic and moral teachings of Islam. Apart from that, one has to assume that there was a connecting link between the Bible and the Koran, through which materials of the former were transmitted to the latter, though the nature of this link can only be speculated. Regarding the Old Testament, it could take the form of commentaries, translations, etc., as are known from Jewish post-biblical literature and Christian exegesis. Similar is true for New Testament materials. Aside from the New Testament Scriptures themselves, the Gospel harmonies (such as the Diatessaron of Tatian) and commentaries of the literary genre of catena might have played an important role. The Syrian Bible exegesis is particularly significant, represented by Ephrem the Syrian and other theologians, and there might also have been Ethiopian and Coptic Egyptian influence. Some Old Testament materials had already been influenced by Christianity when Muhammad learned of them. There is generally a dual relationship between Islam, on the one hand, and Christianity and Judaism, on the other. Muhammad either made his own judgments of Judaism or adopted those passed on it by Christians. Similarly, he adopted some Jewish materials directly from the Jews or learned of them within a Christian context. As J. Horovitz has shown, biblical names in the Koran are mostly those of the Aramaic or Ethiopic translations of the Hebrew text, whereas it sometimes remains open whether Muhammad had heard the names from Jews or Christians.[103]

In seeking the sources of Muhammad's knowledge of Christian and sometimes also Jewish doctrine, special attention must be paid to the liturgy. It has already been said that Muhammad adopted certain liturgical rituals from the Jews. The liturgical texts of Jewish and Christian religious services were taken mostly from the Bible, and it was for that reason that those texts were better known than others. Erwin Gräf compiled some examples in which Christian liturgy served as a Koranic source.[104] Some Koranic passages suggest the Psalms as well.[105] The Book of Psalms was the prayer book for both Jews and Christians, so it is sometimes difficult to know the exact source of allusions to that book. It has even been suggested that the Muslim creed, "There is no God but Allāh," so often cited in the Koran, and time and again recited by the believers, was taken from a Jewish prayer.[106]

Much biblical material was known on the Arabian peninsula in the pre-Islamic period and incorporated by poets into their work. Christian elements in pre-Islamic compositions have long been a subject of study.[107] The notion itself is controversial enough, and this is magnified by the questionable dating and authenticity of the works. A prominent poet who made use of biblical material was Umayya ibn Abīʾṣ-Ṣalt. He lived in Ṭāʾif, the highland sister city of Mecca, and was related to the Meccan patriciate of the Ḳuraysh. Umayya was a contemporary of Muhammad and is believed to have died in 630. As far as his religious attitudes are concerned, he was a *ḥanīf*. He professed faith in a single God, whom he imagined as the "Lord of the Servants." He used apocalyptic images to describe the residence of God, the household of the angels, the Last Judgment, Paradise, and Hell. Based on a biblical model, he told of the creation of the world and described important episodes of the history of salvation: the Flood, Abraham, Lot, Moses and the Pharaoh; he also included non-biblical judgments such as the destruction of the ʿĀd and Thamūd, who are also mentioned in the Koran. According to Umayya, the faithful individual has a responsibility to adhere to moral standards. Because of strong agreement between the poetry of Umayya and the wording of the Koran, there has been intense debate in Western research on the question of which came first. After considering all arguments, the most plausible answer is that Umayya and Muhammad, whose deaths were only two years apart, both used the same sources.[108]

Even though Muhammad may have used the same materials as Umayya (and other writers), he differed from the poet by his awareness of his prophetic mission. This enabled him to found a religion, whereas the poet merely wanted to teach through his words, at the same time entertaining his audience. The Prophet's subject matter and the content of his sermons were similar to the poet's words, as is confirmed by his efforts to dissociate himself from the poets. As Muhammad's compatriots believed, the Prophet differed from the poets in that he could bring about miracles, which was evidence of his mission. This is expressed in sura 21:5. However, Muhammad ruled out the working of miracles for himself and, in the subsequent verses, he referred to earlier divine judgments and the destruction of the unbelievers as setting precedents. He called himself a "messenger" *(rasūl)* and explicitly rejected the terms "poet" *(shāᶜir)* and "soothsayer" *(kāhin)* (69:40–42). No one taught him the art of poetry (36:69). Poets, as he said elsewhere, are inspired by Satan and have gone astray (26:224). They are possessed *(madjnūn)* and do not enjoy such great respect that the Arabs would abandon their religion for their sake (37:35/36). Being possessed put poets in almost the same category as soothsayers, as can be derived from sura 52:29. Muhammad wanted to have nothing to do with either of them. He distinguished himself formally from poets through his rhyming prose, a cross between verse and simple prose. The soothsayer, too, uses rhyming prose, and the fact that Muhammad mentioned the soothsayer in only two places in the Koran (52:29 and 69:42) demonstrates his fear of being regarded as one of them.

The People of the Book (ahl al-kitāb)

Unity and Diversity in Their Religion

Adherents of the older revealed religions that have Holy Scriptures are mentioned in the Koran under the general heading of "People of the Book" *(ahl al-kitāb)*. Muhammad believed that the faith and the contents of the Scriptures of the various revealed religions, including Islam and the Koran, were identical in principle and differed only in language. He knew that the Holy Scriptures of the Jews and the Christians were written in foreign languages, even though the languages are not explicitly named. Muhammad believed that the Scriptures are identical except for the language they were written in. This is based on the assumption that there is a heavenly proto-Scripture and that the Holy Scriptures of the different religious communities or nations (the two terms are used synonomously) are merely copies in the respective language of the nation. The heavenly proto-Scripture is called the "safely preserved tablet" (*al-lauḥ al-maḥfūẓ*, sura 85:22)[109] or "Mother of the Book" *(umm al-kitāb)* (13:39; 43:4). Muhammad believed he was called upon by God to make the contents of the heavenly proto-Scripture accessible to Arabs in the Arabic language. He called the Holy Scriptures, irrespective of religion, the "Book" *(kitāb),* insofar as the written version was meant, and "recitation" or "reading" (Koran, *qur'ān),* if the oral aspect was stressed.[110] The "barbarous [non-Arabic] Koran" *(qur'ān a'djamī),* which was how he referred to the recitation of the Jews, Christians, and others (41:44), is contrasted with the "Arabic Koran" *(qur'ān 'arabī)* (12:2; 20:113; 39:28; 41:4; 42:9/7; 43:3) or the "Arabic judgment" *(ḥukm 'arabī)* (13:37). He emphasized several times that he received and was preaching the revelation "in clear, Arabic tongue" (26:195; see also 16:103/105; 46:12).

In a number of Koran passages, the adherents of the religions which Muhammad dealt with are listed. In addition to Muslims, who are described as believers per se, Jews, Christians, and Sabaeans are also listed (2:62/59). By Sabaeans, he probably meant the Mandaeans, members of a Gnostic Christian sect in lower Mesopotamia.[111] The list in sura 5:69/73 differs from the one in sura 2 only to the extent that Christians are listed following Sabaeans. A third list, which records Sabaeans and Christians in the same order as in sura 5, appears in sura 22:17. Here it has been extended to include the Zoroastrians/Magians *(madjūs* from the Greek *magos);* the list ends with mention of the pagans. Thus the range extends from Muslims to polytheists, with members of the older revealed religions holding an intermediate position between the two extremes. The lists in suras 2 and 5 end with a conciliatory message: "whoso believes in God and the Last Day, and works righteousness—their wage awaits them with their Lord, and no fear shall be on them, neither shall they sorrow." This also confirms belief that the faiths of Jews, Christians, and Sabaeans (Mandaeans) are identical with Islam and that these followers, like Muslims, have claim to salvation. This is not the case with the list in sura 22. The six groups—Muslims, Jews, Sabaeans, Christians, Zoroastrians/Magians, and pagans—are interpreted as religious groups with different faiths. The tenor is generally negative. At the end of the list it is stated: "God shall distinguish between them on the Day of Resurrection." At this point, we can ignore the question whether here the Muslims and adherents of other revealed religions are seen as one group in contrast to the pagans; if so, that would imply a positive judgment of all religions with Scriptures. That is not intended here. We shall return to this point later on. In comparing the closing of the third list to that of the other two, it is apparent that Muhammad had changed his position and dissociated himself from the People of the Book.

Followers of the Mosaic religion are mentioned in the Koran under two names: the Children of Israel *(Banū Isrāʾīl)* and Jews *(yahūd).* They are referred to as the Children of Israel in all stories using biblical subject matter. The Bible story of Jacob wrestling with the angel in Peniel, which led to his receiving the name Israel ("God wrestles") (Gen. 32:25–32), is not included in the Koran. The name Jacob (Yaʿqūb) is mentioned several times, but Israel appears only once (19:58). "House of Jacob," the counterpart to "Children of Israel," appears twice (12:6; 19:6), and "seed *(dhurriyya)* of Jacob" once (29:27). Occasionally, Jacob's descendants are also called "the Tribes" *(al-asbāṭ),* without any further specification (2:136/130; 3:78/72; 4:163/161). Most common is "Children of Israel," without any direct reference to the identity of Israel or Jacob. This is what they were called even before they received the Torah (3:93/87). The name appears most often in the stories of Moses and the Pharaoh and the receiving of the Ten Commandments on Mount Sinai (2:83/77; 5:12/15, etc.). In the stories about the birth and life of Jesus, the Jews are still called the Children of Israel, and Jesus addresses them as such (3:49/43; 5:72/76). With respect to its content, sura 2:40/38–44/41, addressed to "Children of Israel!," could be a sermon of Jesus, although it closes with mention of Islamic prescripts, prayer *(ṣalāt)* and alm tax *(zakāt).* Speyer sees a relation between the closing sentence and Matthew 23:3, where Jesus denounces the hypocrisy of the Pharisees and the scribes.[112] "Children of Israel" was the preferred self-reference of the Jews in post-biblical times; it was a name with theological content. In the New Testament, the name is usually used to refer to the Jews.[113] Muhammad referred to his Jewish contemporaries in this way: "Surely this Koran relates to the Children of Israel most of that concerning which they are at variance" (27:76/78). Less often, members of the Mosaic faith who were contemporaries of Muhammad are called "Jews" (2:113/107; 3:67/60, etc.) According to the Koran, the Jews were nothing more than unbelieving Israelites: Jesus addressed the Children of Israel; these were divided into two groups, the Christians *(naṣārā),* who believed in Jesus, and the others, who were unbelievers. The latter were henceforth called Jews.

The Christians are consistently referred to in the Koran as *naṣārā* (sing. *naṣrānī).* The name is from the Syrian *naṣrājē,* as Christians were called in Persia, and can be traced back to the Greek Nazoraioi. In Acts 24:5, the high priest Ananias speaks of the Christians as the "sect of the Nazarenes" to the Roman governor Felix in Caesarea.[114]

The Koranic ideal is religious unity: one God, one proto-Scripture from which all revealed Scriptures were derived, one community *(umma),* one prophet as the preacher of God's word. The opposite has come to pass in the history of humankind. The division of the Children of Israel into Jews and Christians corresponds to a principle that in Muhammad's view was at work from the very beginning of the salvation history. Initially there was only a single religious community: Adam was not only the forefather of all humankind; as a receiver and preacher of divine revelation, he was also a prophet and founder of a community *(umma)* that was united in its belief. The same applied to Noah, who brought about a new beginning. But the effect of the speeches of the Prophets was that the communities they were sent to were split into believers and unbelievers. New prophets then appeared, and God "sent down with them the Book with the truth, that He might decide between the people touching their differences; and only those who had been given it were at variance upon it, after the clear signs had come to them" (2:213/209).[115] The clear signs might be a reference to the miracles that served to validate the bearers of the revelation. Sura 42:13/11–14 clearly illustrates the sequence of prophets by listing some of them by name: Noah, Abraham, Moses, Jesus, and Muhammad himself. Their sermon was the following: "'Perform the religion, and scatter not [into different groups] regarding it.' . . . They scattered not, save after knowledge [i.e., revelation] had come to them, being insolent one to another." The dissidents still exist and have not long since been destroyed through God's judgment, as is written at the end of 42:15/14, because God has allowed them a period of grace. They will be judged at the Last Judgment and at that time truth will justify the believers.

Jesus' call for unity is mentioned in several passages (21:92;

23:52/54; 43:63–65). The selection of disciples (cf. Matt. 10:1–4, etc.), referred to as "helpers" *(anṣār)* in the Koran, and their being sent forth (which is not mentioned explicitly in the Koran) led to division: "And a party of the Children of Israel believed, and a party disbelieved." (61:14). Muhammad was facing the same problem as preacher of God's word to the pagan Arabs. He emphatically admonished the believers not to divide into separate groups (3:103/98). Although humanity is still divided into different religious groups, according to the Koran the ideal of unity is achieved in Islam: "Had the Lord willed, He would have made mankind one nation; but they continue in their differences excepting those on whom thy Lord has mercy [i.e., the Muslims]. To that end He created them" (11:118–119).

The above wording reflects the doctrine of predestination, that is, that God wanted different religious communities to exist. The Muslims, to whom God showed his mercy and compassion by granting them the proper faith and unity, were predestined to receive God's mercy even before they were born: "To that end [i.e., to receive mercy] He created them." This represented a new model of religious pluralism, according to which the division was not the fault of human beings, but was desired by God (6:35; 6:149; 13:31). If God wills it, then it must be accepted by humanity. "If God had willed, he would have made you one nation; but [He divided you into groups] that He may try you in what has come to you [i.e., the revelation]." (5:48/53). The sentence can also be understood in the present tense: "wills" rather than "had willed," "divides" rather than "divided," etc., which would then describe the ongoing state. Since all that comes from God is good, the diversity of religious communities must be accepted. The acknowledgment of each and every profession of faith based on revelation can be found in the passage directly preceding the one quoted above: "To every one of you We have appointed a right way and an open road" (5:48/52). The reason for religious pluralism is always seen as a way for God to test humanity. In religious pluralism the believers are supposed to recognize the will of God and his wisdom, even if it is not totally apparent.[116] Within the scope of what is required by the faith, the individual should do what is good. People are supposed to be quietistic toward other religions. The decision as to who has the true faith will be made by God on Judgment Day. "So be you forward in good works; unto God shall you return, all together; and He will tell you of that whereon you were at variance [in this world]." (5:53/48 end).

Thus religious pluralism developed either as a result of the lack of faith of humanity or because it is God's will. A third possible explanation for this phenomenon is based on the ethnic diversity of humanity. At the beginning of this chapter we already saw that Muhammad considered himself the prophet of the Arabs. He believed he was called upon to preach God's word to the Arabs in their language, and to grant them access to the revelation, which other peoples already had access to. The principle of linguistic spheres of responsibility is clearly expressed in the following statement: "We have sent no Messenger save with the tongue of his people, that he might make all clear to them" (14:4). The same is meant when Muhammad referred to a prophet who was sent to a certain people as that people's "brother," thus stressing the affiliation of a prophet to a people. Hence, Hūd was the brother of the ʿĀd (7:65/63), Ṣāliḥ was the brother of the Thamūd (7:73/71), Shuʿayb was the brother of the Madyan (Midianites) (7:85/83), and Lot was the brother of the residents of Sodom, the name of which is not mentioned in the Koran (it is called "the city," *al-madina,* or *al-muʾtafikāt,* "the (cities) turned upside down," i.e., Sodom and Gomorrah, 9:70; 69:9). Analogous to this, Noah was also called the brother of the people to whom he had been sent (26:105), even though the Flood, according to Koranic doctrine as well, was considered a universal judgment; correspondingly, Noah must be viewed as the prophet of all of humanity before it underwent division. The characterization as "brother" is totally superfluous in this case, since the ethnic affiliation of Prophet and people must be presupposed. The confusion of the languages as a result of the building of the Tower of Babel, incidentally, is not included in the Koran. Ethnic pluralism, like many other things that are difficult to understand, is explained through the omnipotence of God (25:56/54).

Referring to the Prophet as "brother" calls to mind Deuteronomy 18:15, where God proclaims to Moses the raising up "of a Prophet from the midst of . . . thy brethren." This promise is taken up again in the speech by Stephen before he was stoned, this time with reference to Jesus (Acts 7:37). In the Koran, reference to a prophet as a man "from among them" means the same thing as "brother." Muhammad always used this expression to refer to himself: God "has raised up from among the common people [i.e., the Arabs] a Messenger from among them, to recite His signs to them [in Arabic], to purify them, and to teach them the Book and the Wisdom [in Arabic]" (62:2; see also 2:129/123; 2:151/146; 3:164/158).

This begs the question as to the chronological order of the three explanations of religious pluralism. The explanation based on ethnic diversity is without a doubt the oldest, since it presupposes total harmony among the religions and peoples, with the exception of the pagans. When Muhammad developed this theory he was still convinced that he was not preaching anything different than the Prophets who came before him, and he believed that Judaism, Christianity, and Islam were identical with regard to religious doctrine and the Scriptures. This belief was, by the way, due to Muhammad's lack of information on the true nature of the older religions. The two lists of religions discussed above, in sura 2:62/59 and 5:69/73, are part of this phase. The explanation of the diversity as a result of sin and rejection of the prophetic mission then replaced the irenic model based on ethnic diversity. In this second phase, Muhammad was determined to create unity, with force if necessary. His willingness to use force can be seen by the measures he used against the Jews of Medina. As his sphere of power grew and his political horizons were broadened, he saw a need for more pragmatic attitudes towards Jews and Christians. The Zoroastrians had also entered his field of vision by this time, as apparent in the expanded list of religions in sura 22:17. In this third phase he saw salvation in tolerance, without making the slightest of concessions regarding dogma. This new position meant nothing more than leaving the final judgment up to God and postponing it until the Judgment Day.

Jews and Christians

Muhammad's attitudes toward the "People of the Book" changed from unqualified approval to fundamental dissociation. This is evident in the terminology he used in naming groups. In discourse about the other revealed religions, reference is made almost exclusively to Jews and Christians. At first they are jointly called the "People of the Book." As Muhammad's knowledge grew, Jews and Christians are later clearly distinguished. This distinction is also a sign of the later dissociation, first from the Jews and later from the Christians. At the end there is total severance. Accusations and reproach that had been aimed at one or the other are now applied to both, thus paving the way to return to the consolidating terminology of "People of the Book," as had been used originally. Of course, this development took place slowly over time. There were periods of transition between each of the three stages, in which both specific (i.e., calling each religion by its own name) and general terminology were used.

The first stage coincides almost entirely with Muhammad's period in Mecca from his calling around 610 until the Hidjra twelve years later. The beginning of the period in which he showed openness toward Christians can be set at 614, marked by the defeat of the Byzantines by the Sassanids, in which Muhammad clearly supported the Byzantines (i.e., the "Greeks") and thus Christianity, as documented in sura 30:1–5/4. Impending conflict with the pagans of Mecca is evident in the statement of support for the Byzantines/Greeks. This conflict became more severe in the following period, reaching a climax in the refusal directed against the pagans, as documented in the short sura 109: "'O unbelievers, I serve not what you serve. . . . To you your religion, and to me my religion!'" As Muhammad's small community became increasingly threatened, the Prophet turned to Christian Ethiopia and sent a group of his followers there. It is not clear what his purpose was in doing that, nor are the criteria known, according to which the exiles were chosen.[117] It can nevertheless hardly be doubted that he had complete trust in the Christians at that time.

In his conflict with the pagans, Muhammad sought approval and acceptance among both Jews and Christians. In Mecca he could expect such support, since at that time Islam was still in an initial stage and had not yet formed clear contours, at least for outsiders. Compared with the attitudes and customs of pagans, Muhammad's views must have seemed to the Jews and Christians to coincide at least in part with their own, especially since the Prophet himself believed that his faith did not differ significantly from the established religions of revelation and he saw the Koran simply as an Arabic Bible. The following statement might have corresponded to this situation: "Those to whom We gave the Book before this believe in it and, when it is recited to them, they say, 'We believe in it; surely it is the truth from our Lord. Indeed, even before it we had surrendered.'" (28:52–53; similarly, 29:47 and 3:199).

For the pagans, the fact that the Koran was based in some way on the Bible took on a very different meaning. Muhammad's image of himself as the bearer of a revelation was countered by the pagan claim that the Koran was nothing but a plagiarism of the Bible. "The unbelievers say, 'This is naught but a calumny he has forged, and other folk have helped him to it.' . . . They say, 'Fairy-tales of the ancients that he has had written down. . . .'" (25:4–5). Other examples have been discussed earlier (cf. above, p. 27). Toward the end of the Meccan period, the harmony between the Muslims and adherents of the older revealed religions started to wane. Jews and Christians tried to stave off the Prophet's attempts to embrace them. Conflicts with Jews and Christians ensued, but Muhammad was still prepared to remain objective: "Dispute not with the People of the Book save in the fairer manner, except for those of them that do wrong; and say, 'We believe in what has been sent down to us, and what has been sent down to you; our God and your God is One, and to Him we have surrendered *(muslim).*'" (29:45–46). The fact that wrongdoers are explicitly excluded testifies to the division between the Jews and Christians, on the one hand, and the Muslims, on the other. This is also apparent in other passages, where distinctions are made among the different "Peoples of the Book": Only a segment of them are assumed to read and interpret the Scriptures correctly, i.e., "with true recitation" (2:121/115); some of them acknowledge only segments of the Koran (13:36); and a segment of the people with access to the Scriptures are simply declared unbelievers (3:100/95).

The second stage in Muhammad's relationship to the "People of the Book" started with the Hidjra in September 622. Whereas in Mecca he dealt only with isolated Jews and Christians, in Medina he was faced with three separate "tribes" of Jews; Christians played only a minor role at this time. At first, Muhammad put all his effort into winning over the Jews by making overtures to them. This included, as mentioned earlier, adopting liturgical rituals of theirs such as turning toward Jerusalem for prayer. The abandoning of this practice in February 624—shortly before the first major battle against the Meccans, at Badr—marked the end of this chapter in Islamic-Jewish relations. Up to this time, all conflicts had been carried out verbally, but the new period was characterized by the use of brute force, since it became obvious that the Jews could not be won over to fight in the war with Mecca. Two Jewish tribes were exiled from Medina, the Banū Ḳaynuḳāᶜ as early as 624, and the Banū Naḍīr in August 625, shortly after the battle of Uḥud. This battle ended poorly for the Muslims and they only narrowly avoided catastrophic consequences. The Banū Ḳurayẓa suffered even more, shortly after the "trench war" that took place in April 627.[118] Almost without exception, the men were massacred, women and children forced into slavery, and their property distributed among the Muslims.[119] This marked the beginning of the third stage in Islamic-Jewish relations. It was characterized by a wait-and-see policy on the part of Muhammad. Jews were declared unbelievers, but they were nevertheless tolerated under certain conditions. The judgment was left up to God; the conflict between Jews and Muslims was to be resolved on the Judgment Day.

The phase of rapprochement included, along with the practice of facing Jerusalem for prayer, an attempt to introduce fully complementary dietary laws and allow marriage with the Jews. The stipulations are listed in sura 5. According to verse 3, the only meat that Muslims were permitted to eat was that of animals slaughtered in the proper way, i.e., with an invocation of the name of God. Consuming the meat of sacrificial animals of pagan rituals, cadavers, pork, and blood was not allowed. Prohibition of the drawing of lots with arrows served to abolish a pagan custom that had played an important role in the lives of the Arabs.[120] A clear reference is made to Jewish dietary laws in verse 5/7: ". . . and the food of those who were given the Book is permitted to you." The phrase immediately following, "and permitted to them is your food" must have outraged the Jews, since Muhammad, of course, was not authorized to enact dietary laws for the Jews. In the polemics against the Jews that soon developed, Jewish dietary laws played an important part, as we shall soon see. Verse 4/6 was perhaps inserted at a later time. It reflects the original sentiments of Muhammad, which were not influenced at all by Jewish dietary laws. In this verse, namely, everything is permitted: "The good things are permitted you." In subsequent verses, game killed by hunters—reference here was certainly to falcons—was declared permissible provided the name of God was invoked before the meat was consumed. This was considered abominable by the Jews, since their law banned hunting in general. Nimrod and Esau appear in the Bible as hunters and rebels opposing God. More than that, the falcon is an unclean bird to the Jews. The Jews were probably also dissatisfied with the regulations in verse 5/7 regarding marriage. Therein, male Muslims were allowed to marry not only women who were believers, i.e., Muslim women, but also "women of them who were given the Book before you." However, if the regulation is interpreted in a narrow sense, Jewish men were not permitted to marry Muslim women.

If such regulations were indeed enacted shortly after the Hidjra,[121] they could have served to threaten the harmony with the Jews. This also applies to the change in the direction to face during prayer, from Jerusalem to Mecca. This measure, together with preaching that Abraham was the first Muslim and built the Kaaba (or purged it of pagan worship), were part of efforts postulating the inheritance of the Scriptures and the prophethood from Abraham down to Muhammad. It is stated several times in the Koran that the Scriptures were passed down as an inheritance, without explicitly stating who inherited it from whom (7:169; 35:32/29; 42:14). On the other hand, it is very explicit in sura 40:53/56 that the Children of Israel inherited the Scriptures from Moses. The revelation and the prophethood are seen as passed from generation to generation in the same way as, for example, the Israelites inherited the land from the Egyptians (26:59) and Solomon was David's heir (27:16). Abraham marked the beginning of this succession of inheritance, as can be seen in Jesus' genealogy, traced all the way back to Adam in sura 3:33/30. Whereas Adam and Noah are mentioned as individuals and individual prophets, Abraham is spoken of as "the House of Abraham" *(āl Ibrāhīm).* (Reference is later made to the House of ᶜImrān, which was Jesus' genealogical line.) Abraham was a believer (19:41–48) and, therefore, he was given Isaac and (later) Jacob: "and each We made a Prophet" (19:51). The angels had already announced at Mamre that Isaac would be a prophet (37:112). The further development is explained in sura 29:27: "And We gave him [i.e., Abraham] Isaac and Jacob, and We appointed the Prophecy and the Book to be among his seed." Besides Isaac, Ishmael must also be mentioned, since Arabs see him as their progenitor. The line of heirs is presented as a list of prophets: Abraham, Ishmael, Isaac, Jacob, "the Tribes" *(al-asbāṭ,* meaning of course the twelve sons of Jacob as the progenitors of the twelve tribes comprising the "Children of Israel"), Moses, Jesus, and the Prophets (2:131/125–132/126; 3:84/78; 4:163/161, part one). In sura 42:13/11 the list is reduced to Abraham, Moses, and Jesus, and in sura 87:19, only Abraham and Moses. The latter sura speaks of the "scrolls" of Abraham and Moses, which shows that Muhammad was convinced that Abraham had already received a Scripture based on revelation.[122]

Muhammad included himself in the list of heirs by declaring that the Arabs are decendants of Abraham. Not only did Abraham supposedly build (or purify) the Kaaba (2:125/119, 127/121), but God gave him "the place of the House" (i.e. the Kaaba) as a residence (22:26). The legend continues, incorporating Ishmael: He helped to build, or purify, the Kaaba and took up residence in Mecca. Muhammad was a descendant of Ishmael. This will be discussed in greater detail below.

The elaborately designed structure representing the inheritance of Scripture and prophethood, with Ishmael as the progenitor of the Arabs is based on the biblical story of the casting out of Ishmael and his mother Hagar, and his life as an archer in the desert (Gen. 21); when Abraham died, Ishmael reconciled himself with Isaac and the two brothers buried their father in the cave of Machpelah. The descendants of Ishmael, divided into twelve tribes in analogy to the tribes of the

Israelites, lived in "settlements and encampments" in the northern part of the Arabian peninsula (Gen. 25:16 JB). This biblical information could support Muhammad's theory that Ishmael was the progenitor of the Arabs. However, there is nothing in the Bible that supports the notion that Abraham (and Ishmael) built the Kaaba, nor are there any pagan Arabs of the pre-Islamic period who were named after them.[123]

In Western research, contradictory theories have been presented regarding Muhammad's view of Abraham and his connection to the Kaaba. Christiaan Snouck Hurgronje represented the opinion that Muhammad introduced Abraham's building of the Kaaba in order to motivate the Muslims to reconquer Mecca and reestablish monotheistic religious services at the Kaaba.[124] There is some reference to such a motivation in the Koran (e.g., 2:217/214), but it must be assumed that Abraham had some connection to the Kaaba even before the Hidjra. Also, one has to keep in mind that the Koran is not primarily a source of errors that Muhammad can be shown to have made if his statements are compared with those of the Bible; rather, the Koran is a source of attitudes and teachings that existed on the Arabian peninsula during Muhammad's time. The counterposition to Snouck Hurgronje was taken by Youakim Moubarac, who assumed that Abraham's presence in the Ḥidjāz is to be taken as a historical fact and that Abraham played an important role for Muhammad from the very beginning of his prophetic activities. Moubarac saw the story of Abraham's building the Kaaba as more than merely a legend serving ulterior motives.[125] With that, Moubarac was accommodating the uncompromising faith that Muslims show in the historical truth of Koranic statements. Between the two extremes is the opinion of Edmund Beck, who recognized Abraham's significance in Muhammad's teachings prior to the Hidjra, but questioned the truth of the Patriarch's presence in Arabia.[126]

The story of Abraham as the first Muslim and the builder of the Kaaba is only one element in Muhammad's teachings of the inheritance of the Scriptures and prophethood. Primarily, it served efforts to prove to the Jews of Medina that Muhammad was a legitimate prophet, called upon by God, since the Arabs were descendants of Abraham through Ishmael.

The Transgressions of the Jews

Muhammad did not find an open ear among the Jews of Medina. They rejected his teachings, which sounded exotic to them, and were not prepared to support him in realizing his plans with respect to Mecca and the pagan Arabs. A hiatus probably took place shortly after the Hidjra. Discourse between Muhammad and the Jews was marked from that point on by animosity. This is apparent in many Koranic passages. Accusations made against the Jews can be divided formally into three categories: (1) complete Bible stories which Muhammad used to justify his opinions. These will be dealt with in context in the next chapter; (2) lists of the sins of the Israelites, usually in connection with Bible stories; (3) individual statements, some of which were taken from the Bible or related sources and some of which were based on contemporary events or the teachings and rituals of the Jews. Arguments used against the Jews had partly Christian origins, already finding expression in the New Testament, liturgical texts, and works of early church theologians that could be used against the Jews.

A list of sins compiled from the Bible appears in sura 2:49/46–61/58. God recalls his good deeds and compares these to the ingratitude of the Israelites. This ingratitude is followed by God's forgiveness, which is in turn followed by a new transgression. The list begins with the saving of the Israelites from the clutches of the Egyptians and the drowning of the latter in the Red Sea, "while you were beholding" (vv. 49/46–50/47). The goodness shown in their being saved from drowning is followed by the good deed of the revelation from God on Mount Sinai, but the Israelites built the Golden Calf and reverted to idolatry (vv. 51/48–52/49). This is repeated in different forms in the next few verses (vv. 53/50–54/51). Then the Israelites demanded of Moses: "'Moses, we will not believe thee till we see God openly'" (v. 55/52). In this example, the initial good deed of God is not stated. Without a doubt, it could have been added that Moses came down from Mount Sinai with the stone tablets with the Ten Commandments and demanded that the Israelites accept the Law as a revelation from God, whereby they answered as in verse 55/52. Their punishment for this was a thunderbolt. The Israelites fell to the ground, dead, but they were brought back to life, which is to be interpreted as the due forgiveness. This is followed by the deeds of God during their wanderings in the desert: the cloud, the manna, and the quails. The cloud offered shade. Its declared function was not to guide the Israelites, as is told in the Bible (Exod. 13:21f., etc.), but to protect them from the blaze of the sun like a tent. The food is presented with the instructions: '"Eat of the good things wherewith We have provided you."' But the Israelites were ungrateful and unruly, "And they worked no wrong upon Us [God], but themselves they wronged." (v. 57/54). The Koran does not say what constituted the wrongful deed.[127] The Jewish dietary laws are probably meant; elsewhere it is stated that the Israelites had imposed these on themselves, which supposedly means that all foods were allowed before they received the Torah (3:93/87). The instructions that came with the food in the desert, to eat of the good things that God had given them, thus invalidated the Jewish dietary laws, with their complex set of rules. The Israelites were then told to "Enter this township, and eat easefully of it wherever you will," etc. (v. 58/55). This refers to the commandment from God reported by Moses to enter the Promised Land with force (cf. 5:21/24–26/29).[128] All foods were allowed in the Promised Land. This is the same authorization as was tied to the meals in the desert—manna and the quail. Since the Israelites refused to conquer the Promised Land, their punishment was to wander through the desert for forty years (5:26/29; cf. Num. 14).

The list of God's good deeds and the transgressions of the Israelites in sura 2 closes with the miracle of Moses getting water from the stone in the desert (Exod. 17:1–7) and the discontent of the people with the food God had given them (Num. 11:4–6). The closing verses of the list are an accusation summarizing that the Israelites were unbelievers, that they killed the Prophets, were unruly, and had violated God's commandments. The punishment they were given is summarized in verse 61/58: "And abasement and poverty were pitched upon them, and they were laden with the burden of God's anger." Without a doubt this refers to the destruction of the Temple and the dispersion of the Jews among the nations of the world.

There is a similar list in sura 4:153–162/160. The reason for it is the Jews' demand that Muhammad let a book *(kitāb)* come down from heaven to confirm his message. The Prophet answered with the accusation already familiar from the first list, that the Israelites had demanded of Moses, "Show us God openly." And after that they worshipped the Golden Calf, though God pardoned them (v. 153). Then came God's declaration of his covenant with them on Mount Sinai and God's commandment to enter the Promised Land and honor the Sabbath. The Israelites broke the covenant, were unbelieving, slew the Prophets, and even dared to blame God for their sins: "Our hearts are uncircumcised" (v. 155/154).[129] The list is continued with the transgressions against Mary and Jesus. They calumniated against Mary because she gave birth to Jesus but could not present a husband (v. 156). Here Muhammad could have taken the opportunity to specify the charge that the Israelites slew the Prophets by accusing them of sharing the blame for the Crucifixion of Jesus, but this is not done. The transgression of the Jews did not lie in the fact that they killed Jesus, according to verses 157–158, but in their claiming to have done so. We will return to that idea later. Muhammad said at this point that when Jesus was accepted into heaven, he was taken out of reach of his enemies (v. 158). The list ends with a series of transgressions that follow along the line of statements in the New Testament: they barred many from God's way, collected interest, and consumed the wealth of the people in a deceitful way (vv. 160/158–161/159). This and the killing of the Prophets call to mind Jesus' lamentation about the scribes and the Pharisees: "for ye shut up the kingdom of heaven against men: for ye neither go in *yourselves,* neither suffer ye them that are entering to go in . . . for ye devour widows' houses; . . . that ye are the children of them which killed the prophets." (Matt. 23:13–33). Jesus called out over Jerusalem in condemnation: "O Jerusalem, Jerusalem, *thou* that killest the prophets, and stonest them which are sent unto thee. . ." (Matt. 23:37, Luke 13:34).

Whereas the punishment for the transgressions listed in sura 2 consisted of the abasement of the Jews and their living in poverty (v. 61/58), the punishment in sura 4 was seen as God's having "forbidden them certain good things that were permitted to them" (v. 160/158). This wording brings the strict Jewish dietary laws to mind. We have just seen that Muhammad believed that all foods were allowed to be eaten prior to the receiving of the Torah and that the Israelites had imposed the dietary laws upon themselves without this having been commanded by God. Here the dietary laws were interpreted as the punishment for sins. This is the message of another passage as well: at the end of a listing of meats that Jews were not allowed to eat, it says: "that We [i.e., God] recompensed them for their insolence" (6:146).

In addition to the transgressions that appear in lists, there are some mentioned individually that are in part identical with those in the lists. A lot of emphasis was placed on passages charging the Jews with improper and unlawful use of Holy Scriptures. It was repeatedly said that they concealed the Scriptures, the clear signs *(bayyināt),* and the truth (2:159/154, 174/169), although "they recognize it as they recognize their sons" (2:146/141; 6:20, etc.). It also states that they did this despite the fact that God commanded them to make the Book ". . . clear unto the people, and not conceal it." (3:187/184). It seems that the secrecy applied only to a certain segment of the Scriptures. In one instance it is stated that they wrote the Scripture on parchments and revealed it to the people, but they also concealed a lot (6:91). Perhaps the accusation of keeping the Scripture secret referred to the ark in the synagogue where the Torah scrolls are kept, which is attested as early as in the Talmud and which was certainly practiced by the Jews in Medina.[130] Another explanation is also possible, namely, that Muhammad repeated a Christian accusation against the Jews. This charge came from the fact that the Christian canon of the Old Testament is more comprehensive in the version passed down in the Septuagint than the Hebrew version that was canonized after the Septuagint was already in circulation. The early church interpreted the Apocrypha as "concealed" Scriptures kept from the public, the contents of which were considered heretical and thus not recognized. Hieronymus (died 419–420) carried this name over to the books of the Old Testament that were not included in Jewish canon, without intending to debase these books. Nevertheless, the Jews were repeatedly accused of keeping these Scriptures secret, since they do not appear in Jewish canon.[131] This would correspond to Muhammad's reproach that they publicized only a portion of the Scriptures and concealed the rest. However, he also said that they knew the Scriptures "as they recognize their sons," which would mean that they knew what was part of the canon and what was not, just as they knew if someone were their son or not. The secrecy was thus based not on ignorance, according to Muhammad, but intention, which was no less than deliberately withholding information.

The accusation that the Jews distorted the Scriptures is less clear: "We cursed them and made their hearts hard, so that they perverted words of the scripture by moving them from the location where they belonged" (5:13/16; similar 4:46/48). It is also stated that some Jews "heard God's word, and then tampered with it, and that after they had comprehended it, wittingly" (2:75/70). The charge of Scripture falsification *(taḥrīf)* later became a part of the standard repertoire of Islamic polemics against the Jews (and the Christians), as will be shown below. By comparing biblical texts with the Koran it could be argued that Jews and Christians had deviated from the teachings of their prophets, who had taught pure Islam. Perhaps Muhammad was thinking of what is referred to as *keri* and *ketiv* in Hebrew, the common Jewish practice of reading a word written in the margin instead of the one in the text, or of making changes in the text to eliminate expressions that were offensive or which detracted from God's majesty. However, that would presume that Muhammad had delved deeply into the details of Jewish scholarship. In that case he certainly would have recognized the extensive effort made by the scribes to pass on the texts in unabridged and unadulterated form.

More plausible than the accusations mentioned thus far is the one that the Jews sold the Scriptures cheaply: "So woe to those who write the Book with their hands, then say, 'This is from God,' that they may sell it for a little price; so woe to them for what their hands have written, and woe to them for their earnings." (2:79). Sura 2:174/169 expresses a similar notion, where the charge of selling the Scriptures goes hand in hand with that of concealment. Being damned to hell is considered befitting their greed: "they shall eat naught but the Fire in their bellies."[132] Perhaps Muhammad was referring to the commercial production of tefillin, leather strips with boxes containing slips with scriptural passages. He thought the tefillin were amulets, which he considered highly offensive. This misconception regarding the function of tefillin might have been widespread, even in Jewish and Christian circles. In the New Testament, the word *tefillin* is rendered by the word *phylacteries* (Matt. 23:5), which literally simply means "protection," assigning the tefillin a magical function.[133] Pious Jews were repulsed by such an interpretation, and even Muhammad detested any form of magic, which gives humans power over forces that God alone can determine.

The Jews were also accused of other transgressions: arbitrary interpretation of the Scriptures, which led to their unlawfully driving people from their homes (2:84/78); failing to honor the Sabbath (2:65; 7:163–166; see also 5:60/65); charging interest (4:161/159); embezzlement of entrusted possessions and justifying such actions with the claim that they are permitted against pagans (3:75/68). The charge of stealing people's wealth through deception (4:161/159; 9:34) was raised against Jewish scholars *(aḥbār)* (as well as Christian monks). With respect to the Pharisees and scribes, this accusation already appeared in the New Testament (Matt. 23:14). The same was meant by the accusation that Jews consumed unlawfully acquired wealth (5:42/46) and that the rabbis and scholars did not intervene (5:62/67). Perhaps more serious than violating bans was the charge that Jews declared actions allowed (in God's name) that were actually forbidden: "They forbade not one another any dishonour that they committed; surely evil were the things they did." (5:79). This might refer to the dietary laws, which—as explained above—Muhammad thought were arbitrarily introduced by the Israelites.

Not only did the Jews act immorally, according to Muhammad, but their dogma allegedly also included errors: They declared that damnation to hell was not eternal but could be limited in duration (2:80/74; 3:24) and they declared that God suspended his generosity: "God's hand is fettered." (5:64/69).[134] The Jewish understanding of themselves as the Chosen People played only a minor role in Muhammad's polemics: they claimed to be "friends of God" (62:6) and that Paradise (literally: Last Abode with God) belonged to them personally (2:94/88). Muhammad commented on this arrogance with the ironic statement that they should seek death (2:94/88) in order to go to the paradise reserved for them as quickly as possible.

Muhammad repeatedly spoke of the punishments imposed on the Jews because of their transgressions. He mockingly compared those who have the Torah but neither understand nor observe it with an ass carrying books (62:5). It was stated a number of times that the strict laws of the Jews were payment for their sins. This included the strict dietary laws (6:146) as well as the commandment to honor the Sabbath (16:124). The curse placed on them by God carried much more weight. According to the Koran "So for their breaking their compact We cursed them" (5:13/16). They were cursed since they did not honor the Sabbath (4:52/55; 5:60/65), they kept Scriptures secret (2:159/154), and practiced idolatry (4:51/54). The Bible itself spoke out against them. Muhammad followed Christian tradition in taking David and Jesus as witnesses: "Cursed were the unbelievers of the Children of Israel by the tongue of David, and Jesus, Mary's son; that, for their rebelling and their transgression." (5:78/82). David's curse might refer to Psalm 109 (JB), "An Appeal Against Enemies" which contains a curse on David's enemies; according to St. Augustine, Psalm 68 contains a reference to the Crucifixion of Jesus and a curse on the Jews.[135] As a people who have been cursed, Muhammad placed them on the same level as polytheists (4:118; 7:38/36), the unbelieving people of ʿĀd (11:60/63), the Pharaoh (11:99/101; 28:42), and even the devil, the enemy of all humanity (15:35–38; 38:78). Anyone befallen by a curse of God is damned to hell in the Last Judgment (11:18/21; 13:25; 33:57; 40:52/55).

The curse on the Jews marked the peak of agitation against them. It can be assumed that this occurred around the time of the massacre of the Banū Ḳurayẓa. Later, Muhammad once again assumed a more moderate position and left the judgment of the Jews up to God. This restraint was the result of pragmatic politics that Muhammad felt compelled to assume after his sphere of influence had grown and it became necessary to declare a pact, not only with the Jews, but with Christians and Zoroastrians as well. The truce with Mecca in March 628 gave Muhammad the opportunity to expand northwards. In May-June of the same year he conquered Khaybar, the oasis town northwest of Medina mentioned earlier. He made a contract with the majority Jewish population there, whose numbers had increased even more with the Jews who had been driven out of Medina. The pact assured them the right to continue residing on their estates, but they were made tenants of the Muslims. It seems that Muhammad took this more lenient path only after some hesitation, initially having intended to drive the Jews out.[136] Economic considerations certainly also played an important role, since for the Muslims a contract was of course more profitable than owning an oasis stripped of inhabitants. Muhammad had long since realized that the Jews could not be forced to convert to Islam. Thus, accompanying the tenancy contract, the Jews had to be guaranteed religious freedom. This paved the way for future policies toward all peoples with revealed Scriptures, regardless of denomination. It assured religious freedom and at the same time obliged them to pay a tax to the Muslims, usually in the form of a poll tax *(djizya)* (9:29).[137] The policy became more concrete as—in addition to Khaybar—other oasis cities with Jewish populations were conquered. Further expansion to the north (Eilat, Dūmat al-Djandal, etc.) and south (Nadjrān) led to the need to make agreements with Christians and Zoroastrians as well.

Muhammad's Assessment of the Christians

Muhammad's position toward the Jews assumed its final form in the contracts concluded with them. The "Jewish issue" was thus resolved.[138] The "Christian issue" was linked with it in some ways, but this conflict had a less dramatic development than that with the Jews. Muhammad was originally on good terms with the Christians. The harmony already showed some signs of strain in Mecca, since it could not be avoided that the Prophet was confronted with dogmas he could not accept. This pertained to Christian forms of devotion such as monasticism, which were extreme in manifestation and behavior; Muhammad had difficulty accepting these since he tended toward moderation. In Medina, once the Jews showed themselves to be obstinate, Muhammad contrasted them with the Christians, who were presented as a prime example of good conduct, even if Muhammad had already learned to differentiate among the various Christian doctrines. His certainty in being able to win over the Christians was seriously shattered when the last exiles returned from Ethiopia and he had to admit defeat. This occurred around the time when Khaybar was conquered. After the Hidjra, Muhammad's contact with Christians virtually disappeared. In the "Constitution of Medina" that he enacted after his arrival, Jews were mentioned but not Christians. He did not confront Christians again until—at the latest—the "year of the delegations," after Mecca was conquered. In addition to the delegations of the Arab tribes, Christian delegations from southern Arabia also appeared in Medina. This is when the ultimate division took place, though it was mitigated through the precedent set by the agreement with the Jews. Whereas the Arabs subjected themselves and accepted Islam, the Christians were not prepared to take this step, and concessions had to be made to them. From this point on, they received religious freedom and were obliged to pay taxes, similar to the treatment of Jews. This represented the third stage in the development of Muhammad's stance toward the "People of the Book": Jews and Christians were once again summarized into this common category.

In sura 57:26–27, where the salvation history is outlined, the judgment of Christians is benevolent. Noah, Abraham, and Jesus preached God's word, which was accepted by some people, but rejected by most. "And We set in the hearts of those who followed him [i.e., Jesus] tenderness and mercy." A statement about monasticism follows, saying it was not based on divine law, but was an institution created by humankind. Muhammad let this pass, but not the corruption of the monks, when he said: "but they [i.e., the monks] observed it not as it should be observed." We shall see that they were charged with the same transgressions as the scribes and Pharisees. This section might have been added later. Muhammad's assessment of monks and priests was still totally positive in sura 5:82/85–83/86, where Christians were contrasted with Jews and pagans, whereby the Christians were judged most favorably: "Thou wilt surely find the most hostile of men to the believers are the Jews and the idolaters; and thou wilt surely find the nearest of them in love to the believers are those who say 'We are Christians'; that, because some of them are priests and monks, and they wax not proud." And more than that: according to Muhammad, when Christians hear how Muslims recite the Koran they recognize that the

Koran and the Gospels are identical and declare themselves to be devout Muslims: "They say, 'Our Lord, we believe; so do Thou write us down among the witnesses [of the truth].'"

Muhammad also compared Jews and Christians in sura 3:110/106-115/111. He accepted the generalized reference to the "People of the Book" and judged their attitude toward Jesus' preaching, as can be understood from the context. One group was characterized as unbelievers; they rejected Jesus' message, and "they will be laden with the burden of God's anger, and poverty shall be pitched on them; that, because they disbelieved in God's signs, and slew the Prophets without right" (v. 112/108). This group was obviously the Jews. Separate from this group were those who accepted the message and were judged favorably, namely, the Christians. "Some of the People of the Book are a nation upstanding, that recite God's signs [i.e., the Gospels] in the watches of the night, bowing themselves" (v. 113/109). This is doubtless an allusion to the nocturnal religious services of the monks and vigils that were held on the night before a religious feast, including prayer and recitation of Scripture. Muhammad saw the profession of faith of these devout Christians as identical to Islam: "believing in God and in the Last Day, bidding to honour and forbidding dishonour, vying one with the other in good works"[139] (v. 114/110).

But the harmonious relations could not last long. The break came when Muhammad entered into discourse with the Christians, and his understanding of Jesus was confronted with theirs. Muhammad believed that Jesus was a messenger *(rasūl)* (5:75/79), the word of God *(kalima),* and spirit *(rūḥ)* of God (4:171/169), without making any concessions to Christian Logos doctrine, with all its consequences. These were nothing more than expressions Muhammad adopted to portray Jesus' prophetic qualities.[140] He saw Mary as a "just" woman *(ṣiddīḳa)* (5:75/79), which is the word commonly used in the Koran to connote biblical patriarchs, saints, and devout persons.[141] To Muhammad, Jesus was nothing more than a mortal who, without any male intervention, was put in Mary's womb by God's word of creation "be," just as Adam had also been created of dust by God (3:59/52; 19:35). Contrary to the "begot, not created" of the Creed of Nicaea and Constantinople, Jesus was "created, not begot," according to Muhammad's doctrine. God could have also created angels of mortals as their successors, a new generation (43:60). According to Muhammad, Jesus was neither God nor an angel, but a man, a clear indication of which was the fact that he ate food (5:75/79).

Central to Christianity is the doctrine of redemption, which goes hand in hand with the dogma of the original sin. The latter is unknown in Islam. According to Islam, Adam was expelled from Paradise, together with Eve, because they had sinned, but their sin was not inherited by their descendants. Redemption is effected, according to Christian teaching, by the death of Jesus on the cross. Since redemption in the Christian understanding does not exist in Islam, the Crucifixion of Jesus was not a major point in Muhammad's controversy with the Christians. Contrary to the clear statements in the Gospels, he simply denied it, saying that someone resembling Jesus was crucified in his place (4:157). Muhammad felt it was not possible for Jesus, as a human being, to "ascend" to heaven, as Christians believe. Jesus was raised up into heaven (3:55/48) (literally: "God said, 'Jesus, I will take thee to Me and will raise thee to Me'"). In other passages, however, Muhammad agreed with the Christian interpretation, for example, that Jesus lives in heaven, as does his mother, as is shown by the following wording: "'Who then shall overrule God in any way if he desires to destroy the Messiah, Mary's son, and his mother, and all those who are on earth?'" (5:17/19). This is reminiscent of Mary's assumption into heaven. The statement that Jesus is a sign of the "knowledge of the Hour [of the Judgment]" (43:61) can be interpreted in an eschatological sense that Jesus will come down from heaven and defeat the anti-Christ (cf. 2 Thess. 2:3–11). At the Last Judgment he will not be a judge, however, but a witness in the court. This will be discussed later in greater detail.

Although Muhammad's interpretations partly coincided with Christian opinions regarding Christology and Mariology, Muhammad felt there was no common ground with respect to teachings about God. He countered belief in the Trinity with an uncompromising conception of monotheism. His criticism of Christians and their teaching of Jesus as God is harsh: "They are unbelievers who say, 'God is the Messiah, Mary's son.'" (5:17/19) and "They are unbelievers who say, 'God is the

Third of Three.' No god is there but One God." (5:73/77). Christian doctrine of Jesus as the son of God is rejected with reference to God's omnipotent creative powers. According to Muhammad, all that has been created belongs to God and he does not need a son; he creates simply by uttering the word "Be!" (2:117/111; similarly 4:171/169; 43:84), but he does not beget. The latter thought is expressed most impressively in sura 112, which belongs to the early Meccan period. It probably developed in discourse with the Christians on Jesus' essence: "Say: 'He is God, One, God, the Everlasting Refuge, who has not begotten, and has not been begotten, and equal to Him is not any one.'"[142] Muhammad introduced his own personal faith, based on knowledge gained by revelation, as proof of the dogma of the absolute unity of God, which he saw as threatened by the assumption that there is a son of God: "Say: 'If the All-merciful has a son, then I am the first to serve him.'" (43:81). According to Muhammad, it was inconceivable that a prophet, who of course was nothing more than a mortal, proclaim to be God: "It belongs not to any mortal that God should give him the Book, the Judgment, the Prophethood, then he should say to men, 'Be you servants to me apart from God.'" (3:79/73). Jesus kept to this principle when he said, "'Children of Israel, serve God, my Lord and your Lord.'" (5:72/76). In this way, the Christian doctrine of the divinity of Jesus was refuted by Jesus' own words. When the Christians presented Scriptures as proof, they were lying, according to Muhammad: "And there is a sect of them twist their tongues with the Book, that you may suppose it part of the Book, yet it is not part of the Book; and they say, 'It is from God,' yet it is not from God" (3:78/72). He might have been referring to the Christian Creed promulgated in Nicaea and Constantinople, which consisted largely of scriptural quotations, but also included passages that are not part of the Scriptures, or are only suggested in them. On the other hand, it is doubtful that Muhammad had delved so deeply into Christian theology to be able to distinguish between scriptural texts and council resolutions. The charge that Christians distorted the wording of the Scriptures and claimed passages to be scriptural that are not was also used against the Jews, as has been discussed earlier.

Muhammad made use of a number of kinds of proof in his campaign against the doctrine of the divine nature of Jesus. One of these was a syllogism, whereby the qualities of God—uniqueness, creative omnipotence, incorporeity—served as the premises: God does not eat. Jesus eats. Therefore, Jesus is not God. Another form of argumentation was to draw conclusions from major to minor events, from the difficult to the simple, a method also often used by Jewish scribes: If God created Adam from dust, how much easier was it for him to create Jesus in the womb of Mary. The third kind of evidence was scriptural. Whenever Christians mentioned scriptural passages that could be used to prove that Jesus was God, Muhammad declared them to be falsifiers of the Scriptures. And if all else failed, regardless of the reasoning and evidence employed, he resorted to a common oath, a practice that was already commonplace among Arabs in pre-Islamic times. An example of this can be found in sura 3:61/54. After the Christians evidently rejected argumentation along the lines of major to minor—from the creation of Adam to the creation of Jesus—Muhammad called upon them to swear an oath: "Come now, let us call our sons and your sons, our wives and your wives, our selves and your selves, then let us humbly pray and so lay God's curse upon the one who lie."[143] Such an oath, taken in company, had the same impact as a divine judgment. According to Islamic tradition, this oath must be seen within the context of Muhammad's negotiations with the Christian delegation from Nadjrān, which went to Medina for the purpose of drawing up a contract, as was discussed above.

Followers of an exotic doctrine with respect to Trinity believed that the Trinity consisted of God, Mary, and Jesus (5:116). Other Koran passages refer to this doctrine as well. The argumentation that Jesus cannot be God since he ate food also excluded his mother Mary from having a divine nature (5:75/79). Also, it was said that God could have allowed Jesus and his mother to perish if he had so wished (5:17/19). It can be concluded from this that Muhammad had heard of Mary's bodily assumption into heaven. It must be kept in mind that this doctrine was represented by Modestus, the patriarch of Jerusalem (died 634), a contemporary of Muhammad and a prominent theologian.[144] Modestus administered the patriarchy of Jerusalem starting in 614, replacing the patriarch Zechariah, who was deported to Mesopotamia by the Persians, along with a large part of the congregation. It has already been noted that Muhammad was aware of the Persian victory over the Byzantines.

The interpretation of Mary as part of the Trinity, whose essence is equivalent to that of Jesus, and her continuing to live together with her son coincides with the teachings of the Collyridians and Philomarianites, who have been mentioned earlier.

Severance with the People of the Book

Discourse with the Christian delegation from Nadjrān that was sent to Medina in the year 630–31, at the height of Muhammad's influence, must have opened his eyes to the fact that the Christians, like the Jews, were going their own way and adhered to a faith that could not be reconciled with Islam. All hope had been eliminated. Muhammad had to make a pact with the Christians as he had done with the Jews, since they did not respond to his call to Islam. Jews and Christians were then once again referred to jointly as the "People of the Book." As such, they formed a group that, together with the pagans, were regarded as unbelievers in contrast to the Muslims. Sura 3:18/16–22 can be understood within this context. The section begins with the solemn profession of faith in the one God, as is attested threefold: from God, the angels, and the Muslims ["men possessed of knowledge"] (v. 18/16).[145] "The [only] true religion with God is Islam" (v. 19/17); those who have received the Scriptures, i.e., Jews and Christians, as well as pagans, are called upon to accept Islam. Force is not used, however, nor is it threatened. By calling upon them to convert, Muhammad fulfilled his mission (v. 20). Whoever does not follow the invitation would have to suffer the consequences, that is, punishment in the Last Judgment (vv. 21–22).

Joint reference to Jews and Christians as "People of the Book" served to accuse both groups of having committed sins that only one of the groups had previously been charged with. At the close of the chapter just mentioned, the three sins of unbelievers who must reckon with punishment are listed: (1) they disbelieve in the signs of God; (2)

they unjustly slay the Prophets; (3) they slay men who bid for justice (3:21). No distinction is made as to whether these sins were committed by Jews, Christians, or pagans. The sins might apply to all three groups, which might in fact be the case regarding the first one listed. Regarding the other two, as we have seen above, it was specifically the Jews who had been referred to as murderers of prophets. There are also passages in the Gospels where Jesus accused the Jews of precisely this (Matt. 23:30, Luke 11:47) We have also seen that the Jews saw themselves as the Chosen People and assumed the exclusive right to salvation. Jews and Christians cumulatively were now accused of both of these sins: "Say the Jews and Christians, 'We are the sons of God, and His beloved ones.'" (5:18/21).[146] "And they say, 'None shall enter paradise except that they be Jews or Christians.'" (2:111/105).

Both Jews and Christians are rebuffed, too, in sura 9:30–36. Their sins were seen as twofold, namely, heretical doctrine and moral transgressions. The heretical doctrine, according to the Koran, consisted of the Jews declaring ᶜUzayr to be the son of God and the Christians declaring Jesus to be the son of God. ᶜUzayr is the Arabic name for Ezra, reformer of the law and Jewish scholar, as is later mentioned. It has been assumed that Muhammad was alluding here to a Jewish or Judeo-Christian sect that worshipped Ezra as the son of God. It can also refer to 4 Ezra 14:9 or the Apocalypse of Ezra 1:7, where Ezra withdrew himself from the mortals and was taken up into heaven.[147] This is all very unlikely, as we shall see below. Such a doctrine put Jews and Christians into the same camp as the pagans, which is why Muhammad cursed them with the phrase: "God assail them!" (v. 30). "They have taken their rabbis *(aḥbār,* sing. *ḥibr)* and their monks, and also Jesus, the son of Mary, for lords beside God" (v. 31). It is remarkable that monks are assumed here to have served the same function as the Jewish scholars. They were both teachers of the law and religious leaders of the people. The name Jesus was added following, so the comparison of *aḥbār* and *ruhbān* would not be interrupted. Muhammad called upon Jews and Christians to profess their faith in the one God and presented himself as the messenger sent by God to help Islam become victorious, "that He may uplift it above every religion, though the unbelievers be averse." (v. 32–33). It is obvious that the Prophet was at the height of his power at the time he said this. The moral transgressions of the Jews and Christians were seen as the deceitful actions of scholars *(aḥbār)* and monks *(ruhbān)*, who "consume the goods of the people in vanity" (v. 34). This is the sin that Jesus accused the Jews of—i.e., the scribes and Pharisees—in the Gospels. The passage ends with the description of the punishment for those "who treasure up gold and silver, and do not expend them in the way of God" (vv. 34–35). This refers solely to the Muslims and their obligation to pay alms tax *(ṣadaḳa* or *zakāt)*. The greed of Jewish scholars and Christian monks was held up to them as a bad example. Muslims were not to behave in such a way!

The examples discussed above show that Muhammad obviously had difficulty finding moral transgressions he could charge the Christians with. He had no recourse than to transfer to the Christians the same sins he had already accused Jews of committing. It cannot be ruled out totally that at the time there were Christians who were opposed to monasticism and had extended Jesus' reproach of the scribes and Pharisees to the monks. In such a case, Muhammad might have agreed with these critics—perhaps Christians—who had converted to Islam. On the other hand, Muhammad transferred the Christian doctrine of the divine nature of Jesus to ʿUzayr/Ezra, which means that, in his opinion, the Jews were culpable of the same kind of heresy as the Christians. The mere fact, however, that Muhammad attributed this doctrine to the Jews in general, and not to a specific group or segment of them, arouses doubts as to the foundation of this charge. According to 4 Ezra (or 2 Esdras) 14:9: Ezra was taken up to heaven, "to live with . . . those who are like you," after he completed his mission. There is a big difference, however, between being raised up into heaven and the belief that the person is ascended into heaven as the son of God. Elijah also went to heaven (2 Kings 2:1–18), but the Jews would not have attempted to worship him as God. The only explanation is the presumption that Muhammad, in the heat of debate, wanted to accuse the Jews of heretical doctrine on a par with the heresy of the Christian doctrine that teaches the divine nature of Jesus. In doing so, he could take advantage of the high esteem granted Ezra in Judaism.[148]

Jews and Christians were severely criticized, but Muhammad left their judgment and punishment up to God. Occasionally he considered them among the pagans, and at times he gave them an intermediate status between that of believers and unbelievers (cf. 4:150). He made agreements with them in order to regulate coexistence with the communities into which the "People of the Book" were organized. Individual Muslims were discouraged from having personal contact with them: "O believers, take not Jews and Christians as friends; they are friends of each other." Those who became friends with Jews or Christians were no longer regarded as Muslims. Jews and Christians were considered sinners and God denied them proper guidance (5:51/56).

When Islam penetrated southern Arabia, Muhammad also came into contact with Zoroastrians, called "Magians" *(madjūs)* in the Koran. There might also have been Zoroastrians in Khaybar and further north, where they settled as merchants along trade routes. After the Prophet had made pacts with the Jews and Christians, he saw no problem in treating the Zoroastrians in a similar manner and acknowledging them as "People of the Book." They evidently realized that it was to their advantage to present themselves to Muhammad as followers of a religion that had, in certain matters, common ground with Judaism and Christianity. They could refer to their monotheistic faith, as they had a founder Zoroaster (or Zarathustra) who could be seen as equivalent to Moses and Jesus; and they had the Avesta, a book of holy writings they believed Zoraoaster received as a revelation. There were certainly practical reasons why Muhammad considered the Zoroastrians on a par with Jews and adherents of other religions with Scriptures. No more detailed information is available; they are mentioned in the Koran only once, i.e., in the list in sura 22:17 already discussed above, where they appear along with Jews, Sabaeans, Christians, and pagans ("idolaters"). Muhammad's known position toward the "People of the Book" is presented here as well; namely, that "God shall distinguish between them on the Day of Resurrection; assuredly God is witness over everything."

The Religion of Abraham

As we have seen, Muhammad's attitudes toward the "People of the Book" went through several phases. First he sought recognition, then he strove toward cooperation, and finally he took severe measures against the Jews. In the end he made a pact first with the Jews and then with other groups. This necessarily meant he acknowledged them as independent communities with their own rights, distinct from his own. Politically, they were subject to the authority of the Muslims. Today one would refer to such conditions as religious autonomy. Muhammad's severance with the "People of the Book" went hand in hand with his efforts to draw a continuous line from Abraham to his own prophetic mission and to declare Jews and Christians as having deviated from the religion of Abraham *(millat Ibrāhīm).* As explained above, the story of Abraham as the founder of the Kaaba served the purpose of proving Muhammad and the Arabs to be heirs to the prophecy and recipients of the promises made to Abraham and his descendants. The patriarch Abraham was made the starting point of a tradition that was abandoned by Jews and Christians and finally taken up again by Muhammad.

Abraham was a *ḥanīf* and not a pagan (2:135/129; 3:95/89; 4:125; 6:79, 161; 16:120–123). Since pagans are polytheists *(mušhrik,* literally: one who places other gods with God), a *ḥanīf*—the opposite of a pagan—can be understood only as someone committed to monotheism. Muhammad seemed at times to have held the opinion that a revelation is not necessary to profess faith in monotheism. Abraham recognized the one God while gazing at the star-filled heavens, as we shall see in the following chapter. The faith of the *ḥanīf* is in "God's original upon which He originated mankind. There is no changing God's creation. That is the right religion" (30:30). According to the Koran, this "natural religion" is identical with Islam and Abraham was the first Muslim. The revelation relevant here is that Abraham was commanded by God to "surrender," i.e., to profess his faith in "Islam": "When his Lord said to him, 'Surrender,' he said, 'I have surrendered me to the Lord of all Being.'" (2:131/125). From him, this faith was passed down to his descendants, since such instructions were passed from one generation to the next: "And Abraham charged his sons with this and Jacob likewise: 'My sons, God has chosen for you the religion; see that you die not save in surrender *(muslim).*'" (2:132/126). While in prison, Jacob's son Joseph professed his faith in the religion of his fathers Abraham, Isaac, and Jacob, and he preached faith in the one God to his fellow prisoners (12:38–39).

Whereas Joseph professed his faith in the religion of Abraham, the "Tribes," i.e., the descendants of the sons of Jacob, broke with this tradition. At Mount Sinai, the Jews received the Torah, a complex law stating many obligations on the part of the Jews, as punishment for their sins or which they imposed upon themselves, as shown above. The religion of Abraham was free of all law. The Prophet called to the Muslims: "He has chosen you, and has laid on you no impediment in your religion, being the creed of your father Abraham" (22:78). It is also mentioned in other passages that Islam would relieve "them of their loads, and the fetters that were upon them," i.e., burdens placed on the Jews and Christians in the Torah and the Gospels (7:157; cf. also 2:286). Perhaps this was a reference to the Judeo-Christians, who are also mentioned elsewhere in the Koran. On the other hand, the Gospels confirm the Mosaic law in its entirety (cf. Matt. 5:17–19).

Muhammad explicitly stated that the religion of Abraham had come to an end among the descendants of the Patriarch and the tradition was no longer passed down: "That is a nation that has passed away." There was no longer a connection between the House of Abraham and the Arabs, Muhammad's contemporaries, such that one would be responsible for the other or that one must represent the other before God (2:134/128, 141/135). The certainty of salvation for the Jews based on their being descendants of Abraham was thus rejected. Since the tradition of passing monotheistic faith from generation to generation had been interrupted, it was necessary to repeat the commandment to worship only one God; this was revealed to Muhammad. "Then We revealed to thee: 'Follow thou the creed of Abraham, a man of pure faith and no idolater.'" (16:123). The difficult passage of 4:51/54–55/58 should perhaps be interpreted within this context. It states that "those who were given a share of the Book," i.e., the Jews, believe in demons *(al-djibt)* and idols *(aṭ-ṭāġūt).*[149] "Those are they whom God has cursed." It has already been discussed that the Jews had been cursed. According to Muhammad, the Christians, too, had abandoned pure monotheism as a result of their doctrine of the Trinity. Thus, Jews and Christians were distinguished from followers of the religion of Abraham not only on the basis of the law; rather, a defection took place in all aspects.

Tracing history back to Abraham was also done in the theology of Paul the Apostle. It is worthwhile to take a look at this without jumping to rash conclusions. In chapter 4 of the Epistle to the Romans, Paul spoke of the justification of Abraham on the basis of faith and not works; i.e., not the law, since this did not yet exist at the time of Abraham. Circumcision did not yet exist either, when Abraham faithfully accepted the promise that he would be the father of many peoples, even though this was clearly precluded by his life situation. The children of Abraham were declared to be all those who have faith. Faith creates life, just as life grew from Abraham's body even though he was past the fathering age, because he had faith. This is why Christians are justified by believing in the works of redemption through Christ's Crucifixion and resurrection. The law was replaced by faith, as Paul wrote in the Epistle to the Galatians: "And if ye *be* Christ's, then are ye Abraham's seed, and heirs according to the promise" (Gal. 3:23–29). The law "was added because of transgressions" (Gal. 3:19). The verb "added" clearly indicates that the religion of Abraham did not have a law and was a religion of faith. In any case, it did not include any law comparable to Jewish ritual law. As we have seen, Muhammad, too, said that the religion of Abraham was free of heavy burdens and the law was imposed upon the Jews as punishment for their transgressions. Abraham is called "the friend of God" in the Koran (4:125), as well as in the Old Testament (Isa. 41:8) and the New Testament (James 2:23), though it is not possible to determine which source Muhammad used. His anti-Jewish polemics often used Christian reasoning, especially in the debate on the significance and role of Abraham. Perhaps the same applies here as that claimed earlier about the sins of the Jews being shifted onto the Christians—namely, that the history was traced back to Abraham first with respect to the Jews and only later were the Christians incorporated, without taking into account the special nature of their relationship to the biblical patriarch.

Narratives from the Old Testament

An Overview

Muhammad's attitudes toward Jews and Christians are reflected in the Bible stories he selected and the way he adapted them to serve him in his teachings. Old and New Testaments and Jewish and Christian canon and non-canonical writings formed a unit for him. As has already been suggested, he was first introduced to some parts of Old Testament canon through Christianity. For purely practical reasons, we shall examine first the Old Testament narratives and then those from the New Testament. Most of this material is scattered throughout the entire Koran, since the longer suras are usually not dedicated exclusively to one topic.[150] There are several exceptions to this generalization, e.g., sura 71 with the heading "Noah" (Nūḥ) contains only the story of the Flood; sura 12 with the heading "Joseph" (Yūsuf) is dedicated primarily to the story of Joseph. Most suras offer a mosaic of fragments comprising a variety of literary genres, in which Bible stories make up only a small part of the total.

There are only a few instances in which a series of narratives, each having its main focus, appear in the same sequence as they do in the Bible. Sura 7 covers the entire period from Genesis to the exodus of the Israelites from Egypt, their wanderings in the desert, and their settling in the Promised Land. This includes the creation of humankind and the Fall (vv. 11–25); announcements to the children of Adam (specific to the Koran) (vv. 26 and 31/29); Noah and the Flood (vv. 59/57–64/62); the judgment of the ʿĀd and Thamūd (specific to the Koran, analogous to the story of the Flood) (vv. 65/63–79/77); the judgments of Sodom and the Midianites (the latter of which is specific to the Koran) (vv. 80/78–93/91); a general view of the divine judgments (vv. 94/92–102/100); the story of Moses, the exodus of the Israelites from Egypt and the wanderings in the desert (vv. 103/101–162); and the story of the transgressors of the Sabbath in the "township bordering the sea" (vv. 163–166). The narratives in sura 11:25/27–99/101 and, in a similar albeit shorter form, sura 54:9–42, also cover events from the Flood to the exodus from Egypt.

The period from the Flood to the Last Judgment is treated in the narratives in sura 21, whereby the order is sometimes inaccurate: the Flood (vv. 76–77); Abraham's conversion and his descendants (vv. 51–73); the judgment of Sodom (vv. 74–75); the story of Moses (vv. 48–50); David and Solomon (vv. 78–81); Job, Ishmael, Jonah, etc. (vv. 83–88); Zachariah and John the Baptist (vv. 89–90); Mary and Jesus (vv. 91–94); and the Last Judgment (vv. 95–105). The order is even more distorted in sura 19, where the stories of Zachariah and John (vv. 1–15), Maria and Jesus (vv. 13–36), and the Last Judgment (vv. 37–40) are at the beginning, followed by a block with the stories of Abraham (vv. 41–50), Moses (vv. 51–53), and other prophets (vv. 54–57).

In the consecutive narratives on the beginnings of the world, emphasis is placed on the Creation, the Garden of Eden, and the Fall. The story of Cain and Abel, however, is told only once (5:27/30–32/35), within the context of justifying the commandment against killing and exceptions to this law. The narratives on the Flood and the period from Abraham to David and Solomon make up the largest share in terms of quantity. The story of the two kings represents the conclusion to the subject of the Israelites. This corresponds to the Jewish view of history as depicted in the New Testament, for example, in the speech of the proto-martyr Stephen, whose outline of the salvation history starts with Abraham and ends with David and Solomon (Acts 7:2–53). Within these narratives, the following sequence can be identified, in decreasing order in terms of quantity: Moses and the exodus of the Israelites from Egypt; Noah and the Flood; the story of Abraham; Lot and the destruction of Sodom. These stories served Muhammad primarily as self-affirmation and have generally been reinterpreted by him such that they deal with prophets who spread the word of God and suffer affliction, whose lives are endangered, and who are generally saved along with the believers through the annihilation of their enemies in a divine judgment. According to this view, anyone who received a divine revelation and spread its message is a prophet.[151] The names of the scriptural prophets of the Old Testament were unknown to Muhammad, with the exception of Jonah (Yūnus) (21:87–88; 37:139–148). Nevertheless, certain passages are reminiscent of texts of scriptural prophets, such as the story of bones that are brought to life, in sura 2:259/261 (cf. Ezekiel 37). Others mentioned briefly in the Koran are Elijah (Ilyās) (6:85; 37:123–132); Elisha (al-Yasaᶜ) (6:86; 38:48), and Job (Aiyūb) (4:163/161; 6:84; 21:83–84; 3:41–44).

The Creation, Paradise, and the Fall

There are two versions of the story of the creation of humankind in the Bible, one within the framework of the creation of the world in six days (Gen. 1:1–2:4), and the other as a separate narrative wherein the first couple is granted access to the Garden of Eden and forbidden to eat fruit from the "tree of knowledge" (Gen. 2:4–25). This is followed by the story of the Fall and their expulsion from Paradise (Gen. 3). Both of these versions also appear in the Koran. The former often consists merely of a brief sketch, for example, in sura 6:1–2: "Praise belongs to God who created the heavens and the earth and appointed the shadows and light; . . . It is He who created you of clay." This is condensed even further in sura 4:1, where it mentions only the creation of the world in six days and the creation of humankind, making an allusion to Eve (though her name is not mentioned in the Koran): "Mankind, fear your Lord, who created you of a single soul, and from it created its mate, and from the pair of them scattered abroad many men and women." One can sense traces of Genesis 1:28, where God blesses the human beings and commands them to be fruitful, to multiply, and to replenish the earth.[152]

The story of the creation of humankind and its subsequent Fall is told several times. In sura 2:30/28–39/37, the story appears in three parts:

(1) God calls a council in heaven and proclaims to the angels his plans to create human beings. God counters the angels' reservations that humans will be sinful and there will be bloodshed by referring to his omniscience (perhaps a reference to the planned act of salvation). He teaches Adam the names of all things, whereby Adam surpasses the angels in knowledge (vv. 30/28–33/31);

(2) God commands the angels to bow down before Adam. All obey except for the devil, "and so he became one of the unbelievers." (v. 34/32);

(3) God allows the first couple to reside in the Garden of Eden and permits them to eat of all the fruit except for that of one particular tree. This is followed by the story of temptation by the devil, the violation of God's instructions, and the subsequent expulsion from Paradise (vv. 35/33–39/37).

The following table offers an overview of where the different parts of the story are mentioned in the Koran (including sura 2), indicating the main focuses:

sura	2	7	15	17	20	38	95
1	30/28–33/3	11	126–27			71–72	4
2	34	11–18	28-48	61/63–65/67	116	73–85	
3	35/33–39/37	19–25			117–123/121		5

The story serves to explain the existence of evil in the world without resorting to dualism. The devil was a fallen angel who refused to obey God's command. The first part, which tells of the consultation in heaven and the creation of humankind, is not handled very intensively. On the other hand, part two of the story is obviously the most important and it appears in five other places aside from sura 2. This second part, the conflict between God and the rebellious angel, is treated in detail in sura 7. The devil refused to bow down before Adam, since he considered himself superior to the mortal. He was banned from heaven, but managed to retain the ability to tempt humanity until the Last Judgment. His first victims were the progenitors of the human race, and their story follows (vv. 19–25). A more comprehensive version of the negotiations between God and the devil, with a theological interpretation involving the principle of free will, can be found in sura 15:31–43. To avenge the fact that God let him fall into sin, the devil wanted humanity to be seduced by all the temptations of the world and to live a life of sin. God did not stop him, but imposed the restriction that "over My servants thou shalt have no authority, except those that follow thee, being perverse" (vv. 41–42). These will be condemned to hell.

In the Bible, the story of the Fall of humanity and expulsion from the Garden of Eden is followed directly by the story of Cain and Abel and fratricide. In the Koran, it ends with a conciliatory gesture. Humanity lost Paradise and was given over to the tribulations of life on earth, but there is a promise of future salvation: "Thereafter Adam received certain words from his Lord, and He turned towards him; truly He turns, and is All-compassionate. We said, 'Get you down out of it, all together; yet there shall come to you guidance from Me, and whosoever follows My guidance, no fear [of the Judgment] shall be on them, neither shall they sorrow [after the Judgment].'" (2:37/35–38/36; similarly, 20:122–124). The "guidance" *(hudā)* is Islam.[153]

As is the case with many narratives, the story of Paradise and the Fall also appears in a shorter version, in sura 95, which must have been one of the earliest suras, as is evident by the shortness of length and the form of an oath at the beginning (vv. 1–3):[154] "We indeed created Man in the fairest stature then [however] We restored him the lowest of the low" (vv. 4–5). The story could not have been told any more concisely. This succinctness was only possible since Muhammad could assume that his listeners knew the story and needed only key words to recall it.

Cain and Abel

The story of Cain and Abel (Gen. 4:1–16) is told in sura 5:27/30–34/38. It is divided into two parts: the story itself (vv. 27/30–31/34) and the law derived from the story (v. 32/35-34/38). The story itself was considerably shortened in comparison with the version in the Bible, though some details were also added. Names are not mentioned explicitly. Cain and Abel are referred to as the "two sons of Adam." The fact that Cain was a farmer and Abel a shepherd is also not mentioned in the Koran.[155] Each of them, individually, made a sacrifice: "It was accepted [by God] of one of them, and not accepted of the other." Cain threatened to kill his brother, who answered with the argument that God accepts sacrifices only from those who are godfearing. Abel offered this as an apology, but also as an explanation for God's disfavor toward Cain, whose intentions were violent. Abel remained passive in response to Cain's threats. ""Yet if thou stretchest out thy hand against me, to slay me, I will not stretch out my hand against thee, to slay thee." Moreover, he announced that Cain would be damned to hell (if he commited murder): "That is the recompense of the evildoers." After Cain killed his brother, a raven scratched at the ground to show him that he should bury his brother. The proper measures to be taken in dealing with corpses were not yet known to Cain. This part of the narrative ends with the murderer expressing repentance: "And he became one of the remorseful."

The law derived from this story is the absolute prohibition against killing in Jewish law. Muhammad referred to two exceptions: "who slays a soul not to retaliate for a soul slain, nor for corruption done in the land, shall be as if he had slain mankind altogether; and whoso gives life to a soul, shall be as if he had given life to mankind altogether."

Excluding the two exceptions named, this law against killing was taken from the Mishnah, as Abraham Geiger and, most recently, Norman Stillman remarked.[156] It appears as a commentary to Genesis 4:10: "And he said, 'What hast thou done? the voice of thy brother's blood crieth unto me from the ground.'" "Blood" is used in the plural *(deme),* which according to the Mishnah implies that not only the blood of Abel is meant, but that of any future descendants as well. The Mishnah text ends with the sentence cited. Exceptions to the commandment against killing also appear in the Bible (cf. Exod. 21:13) and of course the Talmud. Muhammad made reference to Jewish law in citing the exceptions, which were "prescribed for the Children of Israel." Blood feud is sometimes permitted, according to the Koran, and sometimes forbidden.[157] Muhammad most certainly learned of the story as a whole, including the law derived from it, from Jewish scholars. He used it as a weapon in his conflict with the Jews of Medina, attempting to show them on the terms of their own tradition that violent force was allowed under certain circumstances. The Israelites did not all accept the words of the prophets who came to them: "then many of them thereafter commit excesses in the earth." It could be concluded from this that force could be used against them, since one of the two exceptions from the law against killing referred to "doing corruption [i.e., commiting excesses]."

This narrative must be seen within a larger context. It begins with the salutation: "People of the Book" in verse 19/22 and clearly ends with verse 34/38, since the salutation "O believers" in verse 35/39 introduces a new section. The section addressing the People of the Book is divided into three parts, not counting the introduction (v. 19/22):

(1) The story of Moses and the Israelites, who refuse to comply with the command to enter the Promised Land and are destined to wander in the desert for forty years as punishment (vv. 20/23–26/29);

(2) the story treated here of Cain and Abel, listing the exceptions to the law against killing (vv. 27/30–32/35);

(3) a list of punishments for those who "fight against God and His Messenger": death (by crucifixion), mutilation (chopping off of, alternately, foot and hand), or banishment from the land (vv. 33/37–34/38).

The narrative in part (1) offers evidence that believers must go to war if God commands it through the mouth of the prophet. The story of Cain and Abel in part (2) confirms that killing is permissible under certain circumstances; the narrative was told in such a way that the exceptions to the law against killing were directed against the Jews.

The meaning of part (3) is inherently clear. The entire section, from verse 19/22 to verse 34/38, was obviously targeted against the Jews of Medina. As mentioned above, some of them were exiled and some annihilated. It is not clear whether all three subsections appeared simultaneously or whether they were put together at a later time. There are several reasons to believe the latter assumption. Part (3) sounds like a commentary to (2): those who "commit excesses in the earth" are those "who fight against God and His Messenger."

The Flood and Other Divine Judgments

Noah (Nūḥ)

The biblical narrative on the Flood (Gen. 6:1–9, 17) deals with the extermination of sinners and deliverance of the pious. In the Koran, on the other hand, the story tells of a prophet who preaches God's word and is persecuted by the unbelievers. Noah and his followers were saved, since the unbelievers were drowned. The purpose of the Koranic narrative is twofold: it is a confirmation of the fact that God punishes sinners and it shows that the prophet who was commanded to spread the word of God can rely on God's support. God does not abandon his servants. This reinterpretation of the biblical narrative, aiming primarily to prove that God saves the righteous and punishes the sinners, provides a solution for a difficult problem, namely, what happens if the mere act of spreading God's word becomes dangerous for the prophet chosen by God. The prophet cannot avoid a God-given task. This question was very important for Muhammad himself when he was put under such severe pressure by the unbelievers in Mecca that in the end he feared for his life.

The story is told in the Koran at least ten times, more or less in detail (7:59/57–64/62; 10:71–73; 11:25/27–48/50; 21:76–77; 23:23–30; 26:105–121; 29:14–15; 37:75/73–82/80; 54:9–16; 71:1–28). Sura 71, with the heading "Noah," is one of the few suras dedicated exclusively to one subject. The story is also told in its entirety in sura 11. Noah preached monotheism to the believers and prophesied that the judgment would come if the people did not accept God (vv. 25/27–26/28). The conflict with his enemies is treated in detail (vv. 27/29–34/36). In verse 35/37, the narrative is interrupted by an insertion, wherein Muhammad rejected the accusations of his enemies that the story was invented. Noah was commanded to build the ark. He boarded it with his family and every species of animal (vv. 36/38–43/45). After the Flood, the ark came to rest atop Mount al-Djūdī (El-Judi) (v. 44/46).[158] Noah left the ark and received God's blessing (v. 48/50), perhaps echoing the Noachian covenant mentioned in the Bible (Gen. 9:1–17). There is a story intertwined in sura 11 that does not appear in the Bible: Noah's son refused to enter the ark. He wanted to retreat onto the mountain, where he believed he would be safe, and he drowned (vv. 42/44–43/45). God rejected Noah's prayers, in which he pleaded that the son be saved since he was part of the family (vv. 45/47–46/48). This intended to show that not blood relations, but faith alone has an impact on salvation. If Noah's son had believed in the judgment prophesied by his father and had acknowledged the ark as the only safe place of refuge, he would have been saved.

Of the various episodes, the words of the Prophet and his controversy with the adversaries are told in particular detail. The subject was suited for Muhammad to present his image of himself and interpret his own mission. Sura 71 is dedicated almost exclusively to Noah's speech. For better comprehension, some discussion of the outline and formal structure of this sura is in order. It can be divided into seven sections, based on criteria regarding form and content:

(1) heading, identifying the subject: warning of impending judgment (v. 1);

(2) call to have faith and prophecy of the judgment (vv. 2–4);

(3) Noah turns to God and justifies himself, saying that he repeatedly spread the word of God as the merciful Creator, but his efforts were in vain (vv. 5–14);

(4) continuation of (3), that God is the Creator of the world; that he created mortal human beings who die and rise (vv. 15–20);

(5) Noah turns to God and tells of adversaries who called upon the people to retain the idolatry of the forefathers. The names of five old-Arabic gods are listed (they were thus already worshipped during

Noah's time!);[159] Noah asks God to harden the hearts of the sinners so they would not avoid punishment (vv. 21–24);

(6) the aftermath of the Flood: the sinners are drowned and damned to hell in the judgment (v. 25);

(7) Noah asks God to rid the earth of unbelievers: "Surely, if Thou leavest them, they will lead Thy servants astray, and will beget none but unbelieving libertines" (perhaps a reference to the sons of God and daughters of men in Gen. 6:1–4) (vv. 26–27); Noah asks God for forgiveness for himself, his parents, and all believers, and asks that the "evildoers" not be saved (v. 28).

Analysis shows that this sura is a combination of what was originally at least three separate parts. The first part comprises chapters 1–4 (perhaps to be further divided); the second is made up of sections 5 and 6, whereby the story of the Flood itself is omitted. Section 6 describes only the outcome. The third part is section 7; it marks the beginning of a new story, since Noah was obviously still at the beginning of the events.

The thrust of Noah's prophecy varies in the three sections. In the first part he prophesied the impending judgment as a "warning," as it is referred to in verse 1. The judgment would be delayed if the people accepted God. In the end, however, the dead are resurrected and the Last Judgment comes. This subject is closely tied to proclaiming God as the Creator. The second part is about belief in the one and only God and the struggle against the old-Arabic gods. These are precisely the two subjects that Muhammad dealt with in the early stages of his mission: monotheism and the Last Judgment, whereby the order of the two subjects in the preachings of the Prophet is not fixed. The third part is only a fragment, though the situation is evidently similar to the one in part two. In any case, the second and third parts coincide in that Noah prayed for the demise of his enemies, the unbelievers. These sections are thus in the tradition of the psalms in which David, who was persecuted and just, prayed for salvation (cf. Psalms 3, 7, 35, etc.).

Noah came under pressure because of his prophecy. He was threatened with stoning (26:116); Stephen was subjected to this means of death, according to the New Testament, since he supposedly spoke blasphemous words against Moses and God (Acts 6:11), which constituted an attack on the religion of the fathers. Noah prayed for salvation: "so give true deliverance between me and them, and deliver me and the believers that are with me." (26:118; similarly, 21:76; 54:10). The extermination of the unbelievers served a dual function: the persecuted prophet was saved and disaster was brought upon the sinners.

Noah's enemies were the aristocracy, whereas his supporters were recruited primarily from the lower classes (11:27/29; 26:111). This is a classification of supporters and adversaries that might have been taken from the Gospels: Jesus received the poor, whereas the wealthy, the priests, and the Pharisees were his enemies. Certainly, this also reflected Muhammad's situation in Mecca, where his enemies were mainly notabilities and wealthy merchants. Just as Paul the Apostle resolutely asserted his economic independence and emphasized in his speech to the heads of the community of Ephesus that he demanded no reward for his preaching, but rather subsisted on work done by his own two hands (Acts 20:33–34), Noah, too, did not demand any remuneration (10:72; 11:29/31; 26:109). Muhammad's enemies had evidently accused him of seeking material gain from his preaching. Noah followed only God's commands (7:62/60). Just as Muhammad preached the Arabic Koran to the Arabs, Noah was a prophet "from among" his people and not a stranger (7:63/61). Like Muhammad (and Jesus), he was a mere mortal (11:27/29) and did not possess any divine powers. Nor was he an angel (11:31/33), although if God had so wished, he could have sent angels rather than a mortal to preach his word (23:24). Noah was also not "bedevilled" or "possessed" (23:25; 54:9), a charge that Muhammad often had to face.[160]

Other Judgments, Pseudo-Biblical Narratives

The most well-known biblical judgments are the Flood and the destruction of the city of Sodom. The Flood is also understood in the Koran as a universal judgment, but Muhammad needed an example of a partial judgment that he could apply to Mecca. The story of Lot and the destruction of Sodom satisfied this condition. In the Bible, Lot was a just man who was saved along with his family, while the people of Sodom perished because of their sins (Gen. 19:1–29). The story corresponded exactly to that of the Flood, except that the judgment was limited to one city. Muhammad reinterpreted the narrative, raising Lot to the status of a prophet, just as he had also made Noah into a prophet. Lot preached and had a following, and was saved when God commanded him to leave the city. In the Bible, the story appears in connection with the three angels visiting Abraham under the oak of Mamre. The angels set off for Sodom to carry out a judgment after Abraham's attempt to negotiate the punishment with God had failed (Gen. 18–19). Actually, the angels were already on their way to Sodom, the destruction of which had already been decided, and they had rested at Abraham's to announce the birth of Isaac. The Bible story serves a dual function, i.e., it is intended to show both that the just are blessed and that sinners are punished. Abraham was promised descendants and at the same time the thread of life of the sinners was cut.

The story of Lot and Sodom is embedded in the story of Abraham's promise in the Koran as well. In sura 11, the promise made to Abraham is reported (vv. 69/72–76/78), followed by the story of Lot and the destruction of the city—it's name is not mentioned explicitly in the Koran (vv. 77/79–83). The same is true of sura 51:24–37; in both instances, the focus is on the story of Lot and Sodom. In both sura 11 and sura 51, the narrative is included within a list of judgments that are told consecutively, starting with the Flood. This list also includes the story of Lot, though it could not yet be isolated from the story of Abraham and the angels at Mamre. Not until later did the two narratives become independent of each other. Isaac's promise appears on its own in sura 19:49–50 (cf. also 37:100/98–101/99 and 37:112f.) and the destruction of Lot's city is told as an independent story in sura 7:80/78–84/82 (cf. also 26:160–175 and 54:33–40).

In addition to the stories of the Flood and the destruction of Sodom, there are also narratives about judgments that are not based on biblical narratives. These are old-Arabic tales that were altered to correspond to the biblical models and reinterpreted theologically in keeping with the Koranic understanding of God and the world. They can be referred to as "pseudo-biblical" narratives. The story of the demise of the Midianites (Madyan) is somewhere in between; it is known from the Bible though there is no mention there of a judgment. The prophet of the Midianites was Shuʿayb, who can be identified with the biblical Jethro, Moses' father-in-law and priest of Midian (Exod. 2:16). The pseudo-biblical stories deal with the old-Arabic peoples of ʿĀd and Thamūd and their prophets, Hūd and Ṣāliḥ, and of the Sabaeans and their city al-Ḥidjr. They, too, perished since they did not obey the word of the prophets and stubbornly remained unbelievers. These are also stories of salvation, since it is shown how the prophets and their supporters became threatened and were saved through the destruction of the unbelievers.

Almost no individual contours distinguish the different peoples or cities befallen by a judgment. The speeches and actions of the prophets hardly differ from those of Noah, except for two examples that will be discussed shortly. The ʿĀd were characterized by their "broad stature" (7:69/67) and the fact that they lived beside sand dunes (46:21). On every prominence (the expression is not very explicit) they erected signs and hoped to achieve immortality through their buildings (26:128–129). They followed the command of "every froward tyrant" (11:59/62). Their habitations were now deserted just like those of the Thamūd (29:38). The Thamūd hewed houses out of the mountains (26:149); this was also claimed of the inhabitants of al-Ḥidjr (El-Hijr) (15:82). In another passage, however, it is said that the homes of the Thamūd had fallen down (27:52), which does not fit very well to homes hewn from mountains. Ṣāliḥ, prophet of the Thamūd, owned a camel. He stressed the importance of its care to the people, but it was maltreated and even hamstrung by the unbelievers (7:73/71; 11:64/67, 26:155). Nine men made a vow to oppose him with the intention of murdering him and his family and foiling the resulting blood feud by refusing to bear witness (27:48–49). The incomplete information provided by the Koran has inspired the creation and spread of legends. Considerable efforts have been made to localize the events. The rock tombs in the northern Ḥidjāz are thus called Madāʾin Ṣāliḥ ("Cities of Ṣāliḥ") or al-Ḥidjr, comparable to those in Petra, the biblical Sela in Edom (southern Jordan). A tomb claimed to be that of Ṣāliḥ can be seen both in southern Arabia and on the Sinai peninsula. Hūd is also associated with several locations.[161] Old-Arabic inscriptions that can be found throughout the Arabian peninsula are called "Thamudic."

Compared to the ʿĀd and the Thamūd, more is known about the Madyan—the biblical Midianites, descendants of Abraham through his marriage with Keturah (Gen. 25:1–2). They were cattle breeders and merchants in the northern Ḥidjāz who had close contact with Palestine.[162] They are mentioned as merchants in the Bible: Midianite merchants brought Joseph to Egypt (Gen. 37:36). In the Koran, they are warned to fill the measure and balance and not cheat (7:85/83; 11:84–85; 26:181–182). Starting as a small people, they were "multiplied" (7:86/84), which might be an allusion to the oppression of the Israelites by the Midianites—as is described in the Book of Judges—until they were beaten by Gideon. They are also referred to as the "men of the Thicket" *(aṣḥāb al-ayka)* (26:176, etc.),[163] and they did not live far from the people of Lot (11:89/91).

The Koran is not any more informative regarding the Sabaeans. Their story is told in sura 34: They owned "two gardens, one on the right and one on the left" (v. 15). Then the dam broke, the flood destroyed the gardens, and all that remained was a desert with sparce vegetation (v. 16). This catastrophe, perhaps referring to the breaking of the well-known Maʾrib Dam, was interpreted by Muhammad as punishment for the ingratitude of the Sabaeans (v. 17). The narrative in sura 34 continues that the Sabaeans were involved in trade as far as Palestine (v. 18),[164] and that they wanted to expand their trading territory out of greed; their punishment was the annihilation of their entire people (v. 19).

A biblical judgment is very significant in this context, i.e., the story of the Israelites being saved by passing through the sea when it parted, whereas the Egyptians were drowned. In the Koran, the "seven stories" are mentioned (15:87, cf. also 39:23); this is assumed to refer to the stories about judgments, though there is some uncertainty.[165] In any case, there are a series of lists of judgments in the Koran that are told consecutively, starting with the Flood. A complete series can be found in sura 11, for example: the Flood (vv. 25/27–48/50); the judgments of ʿĀd (vv. 50/52–60/63), Thamūd (vv. 61/64–68/71), Sodom (vv. 74/77–83, together with the story of the promise made to Isaac), and the Midianites (vv. 84–95/98). A similar series appears in sura 7:59/57–93/91 (the Mamre story is omitted here, but that is irrelevant in this context) and sura 26:105–191.[166] The sequence in sura 29 is slightly different: the Flood is mentioned first (vv. 14–15), followed by Abraham and Lot (vv. 16–35), the Midianites (vv. 36–37), and then ʿĀd and Thamūd (v. 38).

The judgment of the Midianites leads up to the time of Moses. According to both Bible and Koran, Moses sought temporary refuge in Midian (Exod. 2:11–22; sura 28:22–28). Consequently, the narrative in sura 11, which tells of the death of the Egyptians (vv. 96/99–99/101), directly follows the story of the death of the Midianites (vv. 84–95/98). Sura 7 is similar in this regard, except that between the story of the Midianites (vv. 85/83–93/91) and the story of Moses and the Egyptians (103/101–162) a summary is inserted, including general ideas about the cities and their "history," i.e., the speeches of the prophets, their rejection, and the judgment (vv. 94/92–102/100).

The series of judgments does not end with the death of the Egyptians. In sura 7, this (vv. 136/132–137/133) is followed by the story of the wanderings of the Israelites in the desert and their receiving the Ten Commandments on Mount Sinai (vv. 138/134–162). Then the story is told of the "township bordering the sea" and the transgressors of the Sabbath who were turned into apes as punishment (vv. 163–166), though details are difficult to make out. Whenever the Sabbath is mentioned, reference is to the Israelites or Jews. This indicates that the commandment to honor the Sabbath, which was an important aspect of the Decalogue received at Mount Sinai, was violated by the Israelites, i.e., the Jews, and their punishment is described. Immediately following this story, it is proclaimed that they will suffer hardship until the end of time: God "would send forth against them, unto the Day of Resurrection, those who should visit them with evil chastisement" (sura 7:167).

In the course of development of the Koran, the narratives about the judgments, told in varying detail, were gradually reduced to lists consisting merely of key words. For example, in sura 22:42/43–44 it is stated "If they [the unbelievers] cry lies to thee [Muhammad], so too before them the people of Noah cried lies, and Ad and Thamood, and the people of Abraham, the people of Lot, and the men of Midian; to Moses they cried lies. . . . and I reproved the unbelievers."[167] In sura 10, following the detailed story of the Flood (vv. 71–73), the subsequent partial judgments are so condensed that names of the peoples, cities, and prophets are not even mentioned: "Then we sent forth, after him [i.e., Noah], Messengers to their people, and they brought them the clear signs; but they were not men to believe in that they had cried lies to before. So We seal the hearts of the transgressors" (v. 74).[168] The generalized descriptions are followed by the story of Moses, in which emphasis was placed on the death of the Pharaoh and the Egyptians (vv. 75–92).

Abraham (Ibrāhīm)

The Prophet of God's Word, Distress, and Salvation

The story of Abraham in the Bible starts with his exile and the promise of progeny (Gen. 12). There is virtually nothing in the Bible about Abraham's life prior to his exile. Only in Joshua 24:2 is there brief mention that the fathers of the Israelites "dwelt on the other side of the river in old time" (i.e., Ur in the Chaldea, beyond the Euphrates) and "served other gods." From rabbinical and Christian sources it was already known that Abraham was subjected to persecution prior to his exile, as verified by Hieronymus.[169] This was Muhammad's source; therein he found statements that confirmed his own experience, i.e., that Abraham acknowledged monotheism, received his calling to prophethood, proclaimed his faith, suffered distress, and was then delivered by God. He was able to avoid further affliction since he was commanded to go into exile to a land that offered him safety.

Abraham found his way to believe in God the Creator by gazing at the stars in the sky. Believing that only an unchanging God could be responsible for the constant changes in the heavens (6:75–79), he abandoned his pagan beliefs and became a *ḥanīf* (6:79). According to Muhammad, the knowledge Abraham acquired rationally was then supplemented and completed by knowledge revealed to him by God; there was no doubt that Abraham was a prophet (19:41). His beliefs led him to become socially isolated. Whereas the Bible merely says that he left his father's home, the Koran tells the story of the conflicts with his unbelieving father. They are described in detail in sura 19, where Abraham told his father of his revelation: "Father, there has come to me knowledge such as came not to thee." He demands that his father have faith (vv. 41–43) and warned him of the punishment of damnation (vv. 44–45). Abraham's father reprimanded his son, threatening to stone him, and sent him away (vv. 46–47). Abraham prayed for his father (vv. 47–48).

In the conflict between Abraham and his father, the threat posed by the father's beliefs was reflected through the new religion. The question was raised whether obedience to God takes priority over obedience to one's father. We shall deal with this issue, which obviously carried a lot of weight in the considerations of Muhammad and his young congregation, again later. Rebelling against parental authority is considered deserving of punishment; according to the Ten Commandments: "Honor thy father and thy mother: that thy days may be long upon the land which the Lord thy God giveth thee" (Exod. 20:12). This does not apply, however, when faith is at stake. Abraham was rewarded with faithful progeny for the disobedience he showed his father for the sake of his beliefs (19:49–50).

Abraham also prophesied the word of God outside of his family and was thereby caught up in severe conflicts (6:80–82). This is usually described together with the dispute with his father (21:51–57; 26:69–82; 37:83/81–87/85; 43:26–28). The story about the king who claimed divine powers and was confounded by Abraham, who demanded that he make the sun rise in the west, must be seen within the context of Abraham's profession of faith (2:258/260).[170] An episode told several times within the scope of Abraham's struggle with the unbelievers is the destruction of the idols (21:58–67; 37:90/88–96/94). He was so hated that his enemies decided to burn him at the stake. However, he is saved when God intervened from the flames (21:68–70; 29:24; 37:97/95–98/96). This element actually comes from a very different story, namely, the deliverance of the three men from the burning fiery furnace (Dan. 3:24–30), but it was already told in this form in the Talmud.[171]

The story of Abraham's exile with Lot marks the point where the

Koran ties into the biblical representation, which does not start until this point: "So Abram departed, as the Lord had spoken unto him; and Lot went with him. . ." (Gen. 12:4). "and We delivered him, and Lot, unto the land that We had blessed for all beings" (21:71). Abraham's exile is also mentioned in another passage, though this is not immediately obvious: "He [i.e., Abraham] said, 'I am going to my Lord; He will guide me'" (37:99/97). Paret's [and to some extent Arberry's] translations are weak at this point and misleading as well. Abraham's statement, "I am going to my Lord," presupposes that God had previously issued a command. "To my Lord" means to Jerusalem, i.e., the Promised Land, where God had taken residence on Mount Zion. "He will guide me" should instead be "He [God] will show me the way," in keeping with Genesis 12:1, where God commands Abraham to leave his country and go "unto a land that I will show thee."

In the Bible, Abraham is promised numerous progeny several times. The first time is in connection with the command to leave his homeland (Gen. 12:1–3), and it is repeated after his separation from Lot (Gen. 13); the third time is after his meeting with the priest Melchizedek. God promised Abraham, who had been childless up to that point, numerous progeny: "'Look now toward heaven, and tell the stars, if thou be able to number them: and he said unto him, So shall thy seed be.' And he believed in the Lord; and he counted it to him for righteousness" (Gen. 15:5–6). This is followed by the covenant and the inheritance of the land, together with a theophany: God appeared to Abraham and, to prove the truth of his promise, he divided a heifer, a goat, and a ram. He laid the two halves next to each other. At night, "behold a smoking furnace, and a burning lamp that passed between those pieces. In that same day the Lord made a covenant with Abram" (Gen. 15:17–18). The fourth time the promise of numerous progeny and the covenant with God are mentioned is in Genesis 17.

Sura 2:260/262 is reminiscent of the puzzling form of the covenant mentioned in Genesis 15. Here, Muhammad used the story to demonstrate the resurrection of the dead. "Abraham said, 'My Lord, show me how Thou wilt give life to the dead'" and God answered "'Take four birds, and twist them to thee [and slaughter them?], then set a part of them on every hill, then summon them, and they will come to thee running. And do thou know that God is All-mighty, All-wise."[172]

The promise of progeny and the covenant spoken of so often in the Bible is taken up in sura 2:124/118. This is the only passage in the Koran dealing with the subject. Abraham was tested by God with words, as is stated at the beginning of this verse. Some scholars see the challenge in God's commanding Abraham to sacrifice his son Isaac; others see it in Abraham's being promised progeny although he had already reached old age.[173] In the former case, it would be a test of obedience; in the latter, a test of faith. The latter is more likely, as shall be shown below. Abraham was tested by being promised progeny through God's word, although both he and Sarah had long since passed an age in which they could conceive a child. The promise of progeny is not explicitly referred to as a challenge in Genesis 12, on the occasion of the first promise, but it is indeed suggested in Genesis 15:3, where Abraham complained of his being childless and feared that one of his servants would have to be his heir. The challenge is described clearly in Genesis 18, during the visit of the three angels at Mamre and the announcement of Isaac's birth, where Abraham made reference to his and Sarah's age. Sura 2:124/118 continues, "and he [i.e., God] fulfilled them," i.e., the words (of the promise), and thus he gave Abraham progeny, which is not explicitly stated. The following verse is not related to the previous one, as progeny is no longer the subject under discussion, but rather the people and their relationship to Abraham: "He [i.e., God] said, 'Behold, I make you a leader *(imām)* for the people.'" *Imām* is the leader, the model.[174] This is related to people in general, not specifically Abraham's progeny; Abraham was supposed to be a model for them. Therefore, he immediately asked "'And of my seed?' He [i.e., God] said 'My covenant shall not reach the evildoers.'" The covenant was based on the fact that God made Abraham into a model for humanity with respect to the faith he showed regarding the promise of progeny, and that all who believe as Abraham did are righteous.

Thus two issues are dealt with in sura 2:124/118: the promise and the covenant. In the Bible the covenant refers to land (cf. Gen. 15:18–21). In the Koran this is interpreted as the claim to salvation on the basis of faith. Here, Abraham is seen through a Christian interpretation. Jesus argued with the Jews, who insisted on asserting their heritage and their assurance of salvation (Matt. 3:9ff.). Being a descendant of Abraham does not mean anything in the absence of faith, however. According to Paul: "Abraham . . . is the father of us all [who have faith]" (Rom. 4:16). The covenant that God made with Abraham refers to the believers, not the biological offspring. In the Koran, the subject is interpreted accordingly: Abraham did not apply the covenant to his naturally born progeny since he was supposed to be a model "for humanity." Since he was concerned about his biological heir, he wanted to be assured that the heir, too, would be part of the covenant. Abraham received this assurance. But the sinners remained excluded! Humanity, of which Abraham was the leader *(imām)*, are the righteous and the believers, which can include Abraham's own children. His children form a group of believers, but they are not any more entitled than the others. Faith is what makes them righteous, not their being direct descendants of Abraham.

Under the Oak of Mamre; the Sacrifice of Isaac

The story of Abraham at Mamre and the visit of the three angels is told several times in the Koran, following closely the story as it is told in the Bible (Gen. 18), though in a more condensed form (11:69/72–73/76; 15:51–56; 51:24–30). With the exception of sura 37:100/98–101/99 and 112–113, it is part of the story of Lot and the judgment of Sodom, whereby emphasis is placed on the latter. This has already been discussed in the section on the prophets and judgments and need not be repeated here.

Whereas other events in Abraham's life are mentioned several times, sometimes with numerous variants, the story of the sacrifice of Isaac appears only in sura 37, within the context of a biography of Abraham. It includes several sections:

(1) Abraham's speech and his being saved from the fire (vv. 83/81–98/96);

(2) his exile (v. 99/97);

(3) his request for a son and tidings of the birth of Isaac, whose name, however, is not mentioned. This is a condensed version of the narrative about the appearance of the angel at Mamre (the location is

mentioned explicitly neither here nor in other Koran passages): "Then We gave him the good tidings of a prudent boy" (vv. 100/98–101/99);

(4) the story of the sacrifice of the son and his being saved. This episode corresponds closely to the story as it appears in the Bible, though considerably abridged and with a number of significant changes (vv. 102/100–110). Here as well, the name of the son is not mentioned. The intended sacrifice was not Isaac, but Ishmael, according to most Muslim Koran commentators. This interpretation is based on the fact that the announcement of Isaac comes after this story:

(5) "Then We gave him the good tidings of Isaac, a prophet, one of the righteous" (v. 112).[175]

The story told in section 5 is identical to that told in section 3, the announcement of a son, although his name is not mentioned. Both sections deal with the same event, i.e., the appearance of three angels at Mamre and the announcement of the birth of Isaac. It cannot be concluded from section 5 that the story told in section 4 is about Ishmael.

In addition to the question whether it was Ishmael or Isaac who was supposed to be sacrificed, the site of the event is also unclear. The Bible speaks of Abraham's going to the land of Moriah; the sacrifice was supposed to be offered at one of the mountains there (Gen. 22:2). According to 2 Chronicles 3:1, Mount Moriah was the site of the Temple built by Solomon. The Koran makes only vague references to the site. At the beginning of the narrative it is stated that Abraham received the commandment to sacrifice his son, when "he [i.e., the son] had reached the age of running *(saᶜy)* with him" (v. 102/100). Paret suggests a translation in which *saᶜy,* albeit marked with a question mark, refers to the ritual running between the two hills near the Kaaba, al-Ṣafā and al-Marwa, which mark the site of idols from pagan times. Running between the two hills seven times, after circumambulating the Kaaba seven times, is part of the pilgrim rituals. This interpretation of *saᶜy* would place the sacrifice in the vicinity of the Kaaba. A rock in Minā, near Mecca, was evidently already considered the site of Abraham's sacrifice in early times. In the tenth century, however, there were still Muslims who rejected this, supporting instead the Jewish tradition which placed Abraham's sacrifice on Mount Moriah, i.e., in Jerusalem.[176]

The reference to *saʿy,* or to Abraham's son's ability to carry out the ritual running, could also mean that the son was mature enough to make his own religious decisions. In the Bible, he asked his father where the sacrificial animal was, since he did not see one, although the flint and wood they brought with them were indications that a sacrifice was being prepared. Abraham's answer was evasive, as if to a child too young to understand, and of course in order not to make Isaac feel afraid (Gen. 22:6–8). In the Koran, however, Abraham told his son about God's commandment, although the child never asked, and the son gave himself up to the will of God without any resistance whatsoever: "He said, 'My father, do as thou art bidden; thou shalt find me, God willing, one of the steadfast.'" (v. 102). He was old and mature enough to recognize the full consequences of that which Abraham was ordered to do. By expanding on the biblical narrative, Muhammad's intention was to show that Abraham's son, too, was a Muslim, i.e. that he "surrendered *(aslama)* to God." Because of this focus, the question of the site was of minor importance. Abraham, as we recall, refused obedience to his father, since for him obedience to God took priority. He was rewarded with a son who was obedient not only to God, but to his father as well.

The Builder of the Kaaba and Progenitor of the Arabs

The story of Abraham building the Kaaba has no basis in the Bible. In fact, the Kaaba is not mentioned in the Bible at all. At most, a biblical reference can be sought in the construction of altars, which are mentioned frequently in connection with promise and covenant. One possibility is the altar at Bethel, the "House of God" (Gen. 12:8), since the Kaaba is also called "House" *(bayt)* (i.e., House of God). Chronologically, the building of the Kaaba was later than the birth of Isaac and the casting out of Hagar and Ishmael (Gen. 21), since it is stated in the Koran that Isaac was already born when Abraham was in Mecca (14:39) and Ishmael helped to build the Kaaba, as shall be discussed below. Nevertheless, it is difficult if not impossible to assign a precise date to the erection of the Kaaba within the chronology and topography of the biblical story of Abraham. The Koranic narrative, however, contains so much biblical material that it is justified to treat it within the context of the Old Testament narratives in the Koran.

The best place to start the discussion is with sura 3:95/89–97/91: The command to take on the religion of Abraham, a *ḥanīf,* (v. 95/89) is followed by the statement that "the first House established for the people was that at Bekka,[177] a place holy, and a guidance to all beings." (v. 96/90). It is then stated that reference was to the house at the station *(maḳām)* of Abraham, and that anyone who entered the station (or the house) was "in security," and that all are obliged to make a pilgrimage to the house "if he is able to make his way there" (v. 97/91). The Kaaba is thus synonomous with the "station of Abraham." The station of Abraham was the place where the Patriarch prayed (or offered a sacrifice) to God; in other words, it is closely related to the altars built by Abraham that are mentioned in the Bible.

Another relevant passage is in sura 2:125/119, following the promise and the covenant, which have already been discussed. It is stated that God "appointed the House to be a place of visitation for the people, and a sanctuary." He commanded: "Take to yourselves Abraham's station for a place of prayer." The Kaaba is a site of visitation, since it is the destination of the pilgrimage. As was already said in 3:97/91, it is also a place of safety. This can be interpreted as alluding to the peace that is kept during the four holy months of the pilgrimage (cf. 9:2; 9:36). There is no mention of the time or the people to whom God addressed the command to erect a shrine at the station of Abraham. "Station of Abraham" must be understood as the name of the site seen in retrospect, since the next verse suggests that God's command was addressed to Abraham and Ishmael: "And We made covenant with Abraham and Ishmael: 'Purify My House for those that shall go about it and those that cleave to it, to those who bow and prostrate themselves.'" These are the most important rituals of the services at the Kaaba, but even more significant is the fact that reference is made to a purification of the Kaaba. This implies that the site was holy, but had been desecrated. The "first House etablished for the people" in Bekka in sura 3:96/90 should perhaps also be seen as a house of worship that existed prior to Abraham's time. There is no mention there of who built it. According to Islamic tradition, the founding of the Kaaba was later traced all the way back to Adam.[178]

At one point, the Koran mentions the building of the Kaaba by Abraham and then later refers to its purification. Sura 2:127/121 clearly says that Abraham "raised up the foundations." Sura 22:26, however, refers again to the fact that he purified it. The question remains which is the older of the two versions. We can assume that Muhammad first believed Abraham to have built the Kaaba and he later corrected his opinion, concluding that Abraham purified the Kaaba rather than having built it. The latter interpretation corresponded more to Muhammad's own situation, since he himself felt called upon to purify the Kaaba—which was still in pagan hand and desecrated through the worship of idols—and return it to its original use to worship God.

Ishmael was involved in either the building or purifying the Kaaba. He is the key figure in the genealogical link connecting the Arabs to Abraham. According to the Bible, Sarah was responsible for casting out Ishmael and his mother Hagar after the birth of Isaac. Mother and son wandered through the desert of Beersheba, as told in the Bible, and suffered severe hardship, but they were miraculously saved. Hagar received the same promise of progeny for Ishmael as Abraham had received for his (as yet unborn) son Isaac (Gen. 15:4). Ishmael grew up to be an archer and lived in the desert of Paran (Gen. 21:8–21). This was a useful starting point in working Ishmael into the story of the Kaaba (and the Arabs). Abraham often appears alone when the Kaaba is spoken of, though in the story of its purification, both Abraham and Ishmael are mentioned (2:125/119); in 2:127/121, which speaks of Abraham as the builder of the foundation walls of the shrine, the name Ishmael could have been added later.

Not only did Abraham build the Kaaba or cleanse it of idolatry, he also introduced the notion of the pilgrimage *(ḥadjdj)*. The obligation to go on a pilgrimage is laid down in sura 3:97/91. The rituals are described in detail in sura 22:26–33. Of course these are based on pagan rituals, but the meaning was changed with reference to Abraham and the command he received from God. The pilgrimage festival and its rituals were altered to serve the worship of the one God; only the name of Allah was allowed to be mentioned over sacrificial animals. Believers were warned to "eschew the abomination of idols" and to "eschew the speaking of falsehood, being men pure of faith unto God, not associating with Him anything" (vv. 30–31).

Just as Solomon recited a prayer when the Temple was inaugurated (1 Kings 8:14–61), Abraham also recited a prayer when the Kaaba was completed (or when it was reconsecrated). Traditional sources refer to three versions of this prayer.

In the first version, Abraham spoke alone. "'My Lord, make this [i.e., the site of the Kaaba] a land secure, and provide its people with fruits, such of them as believe in God and the Last Day.' He [i.e., God] said, 'And whoso disbelieves, to him I shall give enjoyment a little, then I shall compel him to the chastisement of the Fire—how evil a homecoming!'" (2:126/120).

Both Abraham and Ishmael spoke in the second version. "'Our Lord, receive this from us; Thou art the All-hearing, the All-knowing'" (2:127/121). This refers to the Kaaba, the foundations of which were laid by both men. Prayers for acceptance were usually made when offering a sacrifice. Abraham's choice of words bring such an occasion to mind. This is likely if the building of the Kaaba is seen in relationship to Abraham's practice of building altars, as explained in the Bible, since altars were built for sacrificial purposes. Abraham and Ishmael then prayed for righteous faith for themselves and their descendants, and for divine instructions for the rites of the pilgrimage festival (v. 128/122). The concluding verse is a prophecy of Muhammad and Islam: "And, our Lord, do Thou send among them a Messenger, one of them, who shall recite to them Thy signs, and teach them the Book and the Wisdom, and purify them; Thou art the All-mighty, the All-wise." (v. 129/123).

The third version is an erratic block without any apparent connection to the context in sura 14:35/38–41. Once again, Abraham spoke alone: "'My Lord, make this land secure, and turn me and my sons away from serving idols (v. 35/38) . . . . Our Lord, I have made some of my seed to dwell in a valley where is no sown land by Thy Holy House; Our Lord, let them perform the prayer.'" The prayer ends with a petition for the daily bread ("fruits"), with recognition of God's omniscience, and with thanks to God for the gift of progeny: "Praise be to God, who has given me, though I am old, Ishmael and Isaac." At the end Abraham requested righteous action for himself and his descendants and he asked for forgiveness for his sins and those of his parents and all believers at the Last Judgment (v. 37/40–41).

Next to the erection or purification of the Kaaba, the most important outcome of Abraham's stay in Mecca was the establishment of a settlement of believers. It is not immediately apparent who the members of this community were. Initially, only residents were spoken of; God was asked to make the settlement a safe place and to grant the residents fruits, i.e., subsistence. This request was qualified insofar as it was intended to apply only to the believers; merely residing in Mecca was not enough to assure salvation (2:126/120). Then Abraham himself was given the house, i.e., the location or site of the Kaaba, as his residence (with the obligation to serve the one and only God and to purify the House). Abraham was evidently supposed to remain living there (22:26). Finally, it was said that Abraham let his descendants "dwell in a valley where is no sown land by Thy [God's] Holy House," i.e., the Kaaba. They were supposed to conduct services to God there. The region was evidently already populated, since the request followed "and make hearts of men yearn towards them," i.e., let them be welcomed by the neighbors. Abraham also asked for subsistence (literally: fruits), since the valley was infertile (14:37/40). It followed that the Meccans were descendants of Abraham since he asked that a prophet be raised from the midst of his descendants, which of course refered to Muhammad (2:129/123). At the time Abraham was staying at the Kaaba, Isaac had already been born, since the Patriarch thanked God for giving him Ishmael and Isaac (14:39). The only way to deduce that the Meccans, or Arabs, are descendants of Ishmael is through his participation in building or purifying the Kaaba.

Joseph (Yūsuf)

The story of Joseph represents the link between the story of the patriarchs and that of the Israelites in Egypt since it tells how the Israelites came to settle in Egypt. It is one of the few biblical stories treated in the Koran in a block, comprising a major part of sura 12 (vv.

1–102). It is entitled "Joseph" (Yūsuf) and referred to as the "fairest of stories" (v. 3).

The stories as told in the Koran and the Bible (Gen. 37–50) are very similar, but the Koran version is shorter and deviates from the Bible narrative in a number of points. The following episodes are included:

(1) Joseph tells his father Jacob (Yaᶜqūb) of a dream he had in which eleven stars and the sun and moon fell before him. Jacob interprets the dream as a sign of Joseph's being chosen, and warns Joseph about his brothers (vv. 4–6).

(2) Joseph's brothers throw him into a cistern and lie to Jacob, telling him that Joseph died and presenting Joseph's blood-drenched shirt as proof. Traveling merchants happen upon Joseph and sell him to a man in Egypt, who gives him to his wife as a house slave. No names are mentioned (vv. 7–21).

(3) The woman tries to seduce Joseph, but he resists her advances. The master of the house investigates the case and based on circumstantial evidence he exonerates Joseph of all guilt. The woman invites her women friends over and presents Joseph to them. They admire his handsomeness and the woman publicly reaffirms her intention to seduce him (vv. 22–34).

(4) Joseph is thrown into jail, though no reason for his imprisonment is given. He interprets the dreams of two other prisoners, which clearly resemble the dreams of the Pharaoh's chief butler and chief baker as told in the Bible (Gen. 40). There is a report that does not appear in the Bible about Joseph telling the two Egyptians of the existence of the one and only God, urging them to accept the righteous faith. The dream interpretation serves to prove Joseph's knowledge of things not yet known. It is the miracle that confirms his authority as it were (vv. 35–42).

(5) As in the Bible, Joseph then interprets the dreams of the Pharaoh and is made the overseer of the country's provisions. He does not take on the position until the women who had admired his beauty speaks favorably of him and the wife of his master exonerates him of all guilt (whereby the reason for Joseph's imprisonment is explained in retrospect) (vv. 43–57).

(6) Joseph's brothers come to Egypt, corresponding to the Bible

story. Benjamin (though his name is not mentioned explicitly) is arrested and must stay in Egypt (according to Gen. 42:18–24 it is Simeon) (vv. 58–87).

(7) The brothers come once again to Egypt. Joseph lets his identity be known. Jacob's blindness, suffered from crying over the loss of his two sons, is healed when Joseph's shirt is laid over his face. Joseph calls for the entire family to come to Egypt (vv. 88–101).[179]

The Koranic narrative ends with the meeting between Jacob and his wife and Joseph (vv. 99–100). In the Bible, the narrative is followed by their meeting with the Pharaoh; Joseph's agrarian policy; and Jacob's blessing, death, and burial in Hebron (Machpelah) (Gen. 47–50). The Koran adapted two episodes from these chapters. First, the audience with the Pharaoh was reinterpreted to be an audience with Joseph: "And he [i.e., Joseph] lifted his father and mother upon the throne; and the others fell down prostrate before him." (v. 100).[180] We will return to Joseph's parents in a moment. Second, the brothers attempted to remember the father's recommendation after Jacob's death, since they feared reprisal. Jacob had told them: "So shall ye say unto Joseph, Forgive, I pray thee now, the trespass of thy brethren, and their sin" (Gen. 50:17). In the Koran, it was converted to a prayer of Jacob that the sins of his sons be forgiven: "They [i.e., the sons] said, 'Our father, ask forgiveness of our crimes for us; for certainly we have been sinful.' He said, 'Assuredly I will ask my Lord to forgive you; He is the All-forgiving, the All-compassionate.'" (vv. 97–98).

In the Koran Jacob was transformed into a man of God who, like a prophet (and priests), prayed on behalf of his community. Certain aspects of the suffering of Job have been manifested in Jacob. He is a perfect example of the virtue of patience. He accepted the will of God and showed patience upon hearing that Joseph was swallowed by a wolf (v. 18) and when he received news that another son (Simeon or Benjamin) did not return from Egypt (v. 83). Like Job, Jacob lost his family, at least his two favorite sons, the children of Rachel. The reward for his patience was to be reunited with his children. He also had access to knowledge that was denied ordinary people. As early as in the description of Joseph's dream he predicted that Joseph would receive from God the gift of interpreting stories (v. 6). He also possessed revealed knowledge about the fate of his two lost sons: "'I know from God that you know not. Depart, my sons, and search out tidings of Joseph and his brother.'" (vv. 86–87).

Joseph's role as a prophet has been examined in even greater detail. He suffered injustice and persecution, and proclaimed God's word even under adverse circumstances; in the end he was triumphant. He had access to supernatural knowledge since his childhood. While lying in the cistern, he already knew what would happen in the future in Egypt (v. 15). As an adult he received the power of judgment and knowledge given to prophets, since he was pious (v. 22). God taught him how to interpret dreams (vv. 37 and 101), an ability never given to the Pharaoh's nobility (v. 44). He also possessed the healing powers of a prophet. By laying his shirt over Jacob's eyes, Jacob was cured of his blindness (v. 93). As a prophet, he was protected from sin by God: When the wife of his master wanted to seduce him, "he would have taken her" and given in to temptation, "but that he saw the proof of his Lord." God intervened so that he "might turn away from him evil and abomination" (v. 24). It is also necessary that the individual participate in resisting sin. Thus, Joseph prayed: "'My Lord, prison is dearer to me than that they [i.e., the women] call me to.'" In the end, however, God is forced to intervene to protect people from sin. Joseph's prayer closed with the verse: "'yet if Thou turnest not from me their guile, then I shall yearn towards them, and so become one of the ignorant [i.e., a sinner].'" (v. 33). This is a lesson in dealing with the issues of mercy, predestination, and free will!

Joseph showed his parents respect and obedience. He was the first son of Rachel (Gen. 30:22–24). She later gave birth to another son, Benjamin, and died in childbirth (Gen 35:16–20). When Jacob set out to Egypt, she had already been deceased for a long time. It is stated in the Koran, however, that Joseph lifted "his father and mother" to him on the throne (v. 100). Love of parents is an important aspect of Koranic ethics. Muhammad dedicated a lengthy chapter in sura 46:15–18 to the subject. Parental love was practiced in an examplary manner by the prophets. Noah prayed: "My Lord, forgive me and my parents and whosoever enters my house as a believer" (71:28). Abraham recited a similar prayer (14:41). Solomon thanked God for the mercy shown him and his parents (27:19). Joseph honored his parents by raising them up to him. The fact that Muhammad spoke of "father and mother" although only Jacob or Jacob and Joseph's brothers were meant shows that parental love (at this point at least) was dealt with as a topos. Whenever the virtues of the prophets and other men of God were spoken of, love of parents was a necessary component.

Christian sources presented Joseph as the savior of the Israelites, similar to Christ the Savior.[181] Herein perhaps lies the key why Muhammad interpreted him to be a prophet. His preaching was directed not to his brothers or the Israelites, but to the Egyptians. He had very little success, as is known. When a new king took over who did not know Joseph (Exod. 1:8), the oppression of the Israelites began and Moses appeared as a new savior. A pious Egyptian came to Moses' aid, as shall be discussed later. He was a member of the community founded by Joseph in Egypt (40:34).

The biblical story of Joseph fluctuates between two poles: Jacob and Joseph. The notion has been expressed that it is actually only one story centered around Jacob's fate.[182] According to A. H. Johns, the narrative conveys the idea of reconciliation, and Muhammad viewed Jacob and Joseph as role models for himself.[183] As our discussion has shown, it is primarily the story of a prophet who escaped the persecution of his adversaries and triumphed in the end. The story climaxes in Joseph's prayer of thanks: "O my Lord, Thou hast [in Egypt] given me to rule" (v. 101). In the closing, Muhammad spoke of the plan agreed upon by Joseph's brothers (v. 102). Muhammad himself was in this situation at the time he told this story, probably shortly before the Hidjra, according to Richard Bell.[184] The narrative thus testifies to the hopes of the Prophet for himself and his actions. Later, after Mecca was conquered, Muhammad treated his enemies with as much generosity as Joseph had showed his brothers when they needed his help.

Moses (Mūsā) and the Israelites

The Focus of the Narrative

The story of Moses belongs to the core of the biblical narratives in the Koran. Moses is mentioned in at least forty suras. Most often it is in connection with his meetings with the Pharaoh (referred to by name in the Koran: Firʿaun), the deliverance of the Israelites, and the death of the Egyptians, usually treated within a continuous narrative. Second in terms of quantity is the story of Moses receiving his calling at the burning bush. Others narratives, such as that of his birth and the desert wanderings of the Israelites, play only a subordinate role.

Moses, a Prophet who is Oppressed and then Saved along with the Believers

Sura 28 includes a continuous narrative from the birth of Moses to the exodus of the Israelites from Egypt, closely following the story as it appears in the Bible (Exod. 1–15). The Israelites were oppressed by the Egyptians and the Pharaoh ordered their sons to be murdered. Only the women (i.e., the new-born daughters) were to be spared (vv. 1–6). Moses was set out in a basket and found by the Pharaoh's family and taken in. The Pharaoh's wife (his daughter, according to Exod. 2:5) arranged that Moses' mother was allowed into the court to nurse him, though the Egyptians were not aware of her true identity (vv. 7–13). Moses grew up and was forced into exile after having killed an Egyptian (vv. 14–21). He was accepted in Midian (Madyan) and worked as a servant in order to marry one of the two daughters (of Shuʿayb/Jethro) (this is confused with the story of Jacob and the two daughters of Laban, Gen. 29) (vv. 22–28). Moses saw a vision at the burning bush and received the calling to prophethood to lead the Israelites out of slavery in Egypt. His brother Aaron (Hārūn) assisted him (vv. 29–35). The rest of the story is told very briefly: The Pharaoh refused to listen to Moses (vv. 36–39) and the Egyptians were drowned in the sea (vv. 40–42).

The story of Moses' childhood and adolescence appears again in sura 20, in which the story of his receiving his calling at the burning bush is retold (vv. 9–23). Moses was overwhelmed by the task of confronting the Pharaoh and asked for help (vv. 24–36). In order to encourage Moses and assure him of assistance, God reminded him of his being saved after having been set out in a basket on the Nile (vv. 37–40) and his successful flight after having killed an Egyptian (v. 40). There is another retrospective view in sura 26, though this time it is with respect to Moses' appearance before the Pharaoh. The ruler reminded Moses of the favor he showed him by raising him in his family and confronted Moses with his murder of the Egyptian (vv. 18–20). The Pharaoh made use of a psychological weapon in countering Moses' demand for a good deed, i.e., the release of the Israelites, with a demand for gratitude, reminding Moses that he was not in a position to demand anything; rather, he had to account for the murder he committed.

The story of Moses receiving his calling at the burning bush is dealt with in sura 20 in the greatest detail, corresponding to the story as told in the Bible (Exod. 3:1–4, 17). Moses saw a fire, but there is no mention in the sura of a bush that burns but is not consumed by the flames. Thus, Moses did not approach the fire to view the miracle, as is stated in the Bible, but to take some burning embers, or to receive "guidance." This could refer to "divine instruction," or it can be understood in a very mundane sense, namely, that he hoped to find people around the fire who could give him directions where to go (v. 10). God presented himself to Moses. "Moses, I am thy Lord; put off thy shoes; thou art in the holy valley, Towa [Ṭuwā]" (vv. 11–12).[185] God revealed to Moses the most important aspects of his profession of faith and his obligations: monotheism, performing the liturgical prayer *(ṣalāt)*, faith in divine judgment and recompense (vv. 13–16). God performed two miracles as signs: Moses' staff turned into a serpent and his hand was turned leprous and then healed (vv. 17–23). The content of his task was only outlined: "'Go to Pharaoh; he has waxed insolent.'" (v. 24). Moses asked for eloquence in approaching the Pharaoh and for his brother Aaron to be assigned to assist him (vv. 24–36). After the retrospective look at his childhood, which we have already discussed (vv. 37–40), his task is described in greater detail: Moses was supposed to approach the Pharaoh and present himself as having been sent by God. He was then to demand that the Israelites be set free and announce the prophecy that divine punishment would ensue should God's demands not be satisfied (vv. 42/44–48/50).

Concise versions of the story of Moses receiving his calling can also be found in four other passages in the Koran (19:51–53; 26:10/9–17; 27:7–12; 28:29–35), though nothing of significance is added to what appears in sura 20 (except for a reference to the "nine signs," which shall be discussed shortly). These short versions appear within the scope of other episodes in the story of Moses. The only exception is the narrative in sura 19 about Moses receiving his calling to prophethood, since it appears within the framework of stories about other prophets. It is very short: "And mention in the Book Moses; he was devoted, and he was a Messenger, a Prophet. We called to him from the right side of the Mount,[186] and We brought him near in communion. And We gave him his brother Aaron, of Our mercy, a Prophet." (vv. 51–53).

Moses' (and his brother Aaron's) audiences with the Pharaoh are illustrated in greatest detail in sura 26, once again corresponding closely to the Bible. It starts with the task of demanding that the Pharaoh free the Israelites, which is part of the section on Moses' calling at the burning bush (vv. 16–17). Then Pharaoh reminded Moses, as previously mentioned, of the favors he already received (vv. 18–21); Moses announced that God called upon him to be his messenger, giving him the task of demanding the release of the Israelites (vv. 21–22); Moses told the Pharaoh about the "Lord of all Being," which caused the Pharaoh to respond that Moses was possessed *(madjnūn)* and he threatenned to have him imprisoned (vv. 23–29). Moses demonstrated the two signs that God gave him as divine manifestations: His staff became a snake and his hand turned pale and leprous (vv. 30–33). Moses won the competition that the Pharaoh set up between Moses and the Egyptian sorcerers (vv. 34–45). The sorcerers converted and professed their faith, "'We believe in the Lord of all Being, the Lord of Moses and Aaron,'" which caused the Pharaoh to threaten cutting off their hands and feet, and crucifixion (vv. 46–51).

The story of Moses appearing before the Pharaoh is told in a similar fashion in sura 7:104/102–126/123, except that Moses' telling of the existence of a "Lord of all Being" is omitted. Shorter versions also appear elsewhere (10:75–82; 17:101/103–102/104; 20:49/51–56/58). Sura 11 summarizes the story into a few key words (vv. 96/99–97). An interesting addition was made in sura 28, which provides an explanation for the building of the pyramids. This calls the Tower of Babel to mind, which is not otherwise mentioned in the Koran (Gen. 11:1–9). The Pharaoh commanded his vizier Hāmān,[187] the following: "'Kindle me, Haman, a fire upon the clay [and make it into bricks], and make me a [tall] tower [out of them], that I may mount up to Moses' god; for I think that he is one of the liars.'" (v. 38). This represents the peak of the Egyptian ruler's hubris. He had the pyramids built in an attempt to eliminate mediation by the Prophet and be able to communicate directly with God.

The Pharaoh's exaggerated pride is shown even more clearly in sura 40. Moses was declared a sorcerer and liar (v. 24). The killing of Israelite sons, as commanded in the Bible, in order to keep their numbers in check and prevent them from gaining too much power (Exod. 1:8–22), was misunderstood and reinterpreted by Muhammad. "Slay the sons of those who believe with him," which was evidently seen as a means of weakening Moses' following (v. 25). The Pharaoh then resolved to kill Moses himself, uttering the cynical comment: "Let me slay Moses, and let him call to his Lord" (v. 26). Then "a certain man, a believer of Pharaoh's folk that kept hidden his belief" appeared and gave the "advice of Gamaliel," urging the Egyptians to accept the message of Moses: "If he is a liar, his lying is upon his own head; but if he is truthful, somewhat of that he promises you will smite you."[188] He recalled earlier judgments, the Flood and the decline of ʿĀd and Thamūd, and what Joseph had said (vv. 28–35/37). This is a link to the biblical statement "Now there arose up a new king over Egypt, which knew not Joseph" (Exod. 1:8). The Pharaoh then commanded Hāmān to erect a tower (vv. 36/38–37/39), as has already been mentioned. The pious Egyptian continued his speech, but to no avail (vv. 38/41–46). The hubris of the Pharaoh grew in three stages: First he wanted to kill the children of the believers, then he wanted to kill the Prophet himself, and when this failed, he wanted to eliminate the

Prophet as mediator between God and humankind.

Another example of the Pharaoh's megalomania can be found in sura 79: In response to Moses and the miracles that God offered as a sign, the Pharaoh gathered the Egyptians together and he called out to them: "'I am your Lord, the Most High!'" (v. 24). This was blasphemous, since his intention was not only to eliminate the Prophet as a mediator, but to make himself God.

Among the details of the narrative about Moses' meetings with the Pharaoh, the miracles to prove God's existence—i.e., the rod that turns into a snake and the leprous hand that is healed—played a significant role, especially since they led to the defeat of the Pharaoh's sorcerers. The miracles are almost always mentioned where Moses' appearance before the Pharaoh is described in detail, whereby Muhammad followed the biblical account of Moses' calling to prophethood (Exod. 4:1–9) and his appearance before the Pharaoh (Exod. 7:8–13). The miracles served to provide a reliable distinction between pagan magic and a miracle performed by God.

The ten plagues of the Bible (Exod. 7–12) are alluded to in sura 7:130/127–135/131, although only seven are listed in the Koran, and even these deviate to some extent from the Bible: the dearth and scarcity of fruits (v. 130/127), the flood, locusts, lice, frogs, and blood (v. 133/130), and a seventh "judgment" (v. 134/131) that is not described more specifically. Nine signs are spoken of in sura 17:101/103 without any further description, possibly referring to the seven plagues listed above along with the rod and hand miracles serving as manifestations from God to convince the Pharaoh (cf. also 27:12). The institution of the Passover, the sacrifice of the firstborn, and other details are not dealt with in the Koran, evidently because Muhammad did not feel they were important. In another passage the Koran says that the Israelites were supposed to make of their houses a *qibla,* signifying in the terminology of the Muslims the direction of prayer (10:87). This might be a misunderstanding of Moses' command that the Israelites mark the doorposts and frames with blood of the paschal lamb (Exod. 12:12–28). One might also think of a mezuzah, a box with a parchment scroll affixed to the doorpost in a Jewish home (cf. Deut. 6:9).

In comparison with the detailed description of the earlier history, the demise of the Egyptians by drowning in the sea is presented rather briefly, corresponding to the rules of dramatic narration. The Israelites departed, Moses parted the sea with his staff, the Pharaoh and his soldiers chased after the Israelites and were drowned. Sura 10 tells the story in a slightly different manner than it appears in the Bible insofar as the Pharaoh converted right before drowning: "when the drowning overtook him, he said, 'I believe that there is no god but He in whom the Children of Israel believe; I am of those that surrender.'" (v. 90). But it was too late. God did not accept his repentence; he only wanted to save the Pharaoh's body "that thou mayest be a sign to those after thee." (v. 92).[189] This is perhaps an allusion to the custom of mummification of the corpse and the elaborate burial procedure of the Pharaoh. In the eyes of Jews and Christians, tombs of Egyptian royalty were monuments ("signs") of an abominable demonic cult.

The portion of the story of Moses describing his birth, his audience before the Pharaoh, and the death of the Egyptians represents a type of narrative that we have already encountered elsewhere. A prophet receives a calling and a mission, becomes distressed, and is delivered through the destruction of the enemies. In this sense, the story of Moses and the death of the Egyptians belongs to the category of narratives about judgments. It is told with this emphasis several times in the Koran, as shown in the following table (the verses are listed in parentheses when the order deviates from the usual).

Sura	7	10	11	51	54
1. The Flood	59/57–64/62	71–73	25/27–48/50	(46)	9–17
2. Judgment of the ʿĀd	65/63–72/70		50/52–60/63	41–42	18–22
3. Judgment of the Thamūd	73/71–79/77		61/64–68/71	43–45	23–32
4. Judgment of Sodom	80/78–84/82		69/72–83	(31–37)	33–40
5. Judgment of Midian	85/83–93/91		84–95/98		
6. Summary	94/92–102	74			
7. Moses and the Egyptians	103/101–137/133	75–93	96/99–99/101	(38–40)	41–42

The Wanderings in the Desert and the Sins of the Israelites

Up to now we have considered only the first half of the Koranic story of Moses, i.e., the part dealing with the appearance of the Prophet who prevailed over danger, proclaimed God's word, confronted the mightiest rulers of the world and emerged triumphant. The second half has a very different focus. It is the story of the Israelites who responded to God's gifts with ingratitude. The lists of examples of God's favors and Israel's ingratitude in sura 2:49/46-61/58 and 4:153–162/160 have already been discussed above.[190] The events that took place after the Israelites passed through the parted waters of the sea are told quite thoroughly only in sura 7. Here, too, examples of God's good deeds are alternated with examples of the people's ingratitude. Right after passing through the parted waters, the Israelites demanded that Moses make idols for them (vv. 138/134–140/136).[191] While Moses was on Mount Sinai and received the Tablets of the Law (vv. 142/138–147/145), the Israelites made the Golden Calf and prayed to it (vv. 148/146–153). Moses interceded on behalf of the people (cf. Exod. 32:30–35) and the covenant was renewed (Exod. 34). Moses performed the miracle of getting water from a rock, the cloud offered shade, and the people were fed with manna and quails (vv. 154–160; on their food, see also 20:80/82–82/84). When the Israelites were supposed to conquer the land, "the evildoers of them substituted a saying other than that which had been said to them" and so they suffered God's wrath (vv. 161–162).[192] The story of sending out scouts and the revolt of the people (cf. Num. 13–14) is told more clearly in sura 5:20/23–26/29, where the punishment of wandering through the desert for forty years for refusing to fight for possession of the land (cf. Num. 14:33) is mentioned.

There are two versions of the story of the Golden Calf. In sura 7, it largely corresponds to the biblical account (Exod. 32). While Moses was on Mount Sinai, the Israelites melted their golden jewelry into a calf, which they worshiped as an idol (v. 148/146). In contrast to the Bible story, however, in the Koranic version they acknowledged that they had sinned even before Moses returned (v. 149). When Moses returned and learned of what they had done, he threw the Tablets of the

Law to the ground and demanded an explanation from Aaron (whom Moses had assigned as his representative before ascending the mount, cf. v. 142/138). Aaron excused himself by saying that the people had forced him (to make the idol) (v. 150). Moses asked God for forgiveness for himself and his brother (v. 151). The account ends with a reflection about the punishment of the sinners and the mercy God shows those who repent for their sins (vv. 152–153).

The story is told in greater detail and with deviations from the biblical account in sura 20:83/85–98. God informed Moses of the transgressions of the Israelites under the leadership of the Sāmirī. Moses descended from the mountain and returnd to the camp (vv. 83/85–89/91). Aaron is introduced here as the person who tried to keep the Israelites from worshipping the Golden Calf (vv. 90/92–91/93). He justified his actions to Moses by saying he did not want to use force to keep the people from worshipping the idol, in order to avoid discord (vv. 92/94–94). The Sāmirī was afflicted with leprosy as punishment (and thus banished from the community); the idol was supposed to be burned and the ashes scattered in the sea (vv. 95–97). The section ends with the profession of faith in monotheism (v. 98). There has been much speculation about the Sāmirī.[193] His role here was designed to exonerate Aaron. The name suggests a man from Samaria, i.e., a member of the Samaritans, a Jewish sect that had splintered off from the Jerusalem Temple cult very early. The New Testament describes it as a sect ostracized by the Jews. This suggests that the narrative came from a Jewish source. A narrative with such anti-Samaritan sentiments would have unlikely come from traditional Christian sources.

The slaughter of the golden cow is one of the episodes of the wanderings in the desert. The story is told in sura 2:67/63–71/66, lending the sura its name "The Cow." It clearly corresponds to the biblical story of the "flawless red cow/heifer that had no blemishes." It is the cow that was burned to win the ashes necessary for certain purification rituals (Num. 19:1–10). It is irrevelant that the Koran refers to a golden cow rather than a red one.

Immediately following is another story about a cow (2:72/67–73/68), introduced as the first one by the elliptical temporal clause "And when."[194] There is also a change in narration form, signifying the beginning of a new story. The first part (vv. 67/63–71/66) has the form of a report. The second part (vv. 72/67–73/68) is written in direct speech, with God speaking to the Israelites. It is modelled after the biblical story of the heifer (Deut. 21:1–9) "which hath not been wrought with, *and* which hath not drawn in the yoke." This is the cow that according to biblical law was supposed to be slaughtered in the case of an unsolved murder, serving to exonerate the guilt of innocent blood being shed. Both stories were merged into one in the Koran, which explains why the cow is hinted at in the second story by the personal pronoun "it." Apart from that, the second story became evidence of the resurrection of the dead. The person who was murdered was brought back to life by coming into contact with a piece of the meat of the cow and is able to name the murderer. The narrative ends with the following verse: "even so God brings to life the dead, and he shows you His signs, that haply you may have understanding."

The Decalogue

Whereas the story of the exodus from Egypt and the wanderings in the desert is told in great detail, the Decalogue as the outcome of God's appearance on Mount Sinai is not explicitly named in the Koran. The Tablets with the divine Law that Moses received on the mountain are mentioned (7:145/142), and elsewhere it is said that Moses and Aaron received the "Manifesting Book" (37:117). The contents of the Decalogue are only mentioned briefly in this context in sura 2:83/77–85/79 within the scope of the great conflict with the Jews (2:47/44–110/104). This does not mean that Muhammad did not know its contents. The Koran breathes the spirit of the Decalogue in its divine doctrine and its ethics. Commandments or clusters of commandments appear in isolated passages, resembling the Ten Commandments in content and partly in form.

The list of commandments in Exodus 20 corresponds most closely to the list in sura 17, albeit in a different order and with gaps. Sura 17 states that it is forbidden to honor other gods besides the one God (v. 22); it includes the commandment to obey one's parents (vv. 23–25), together with the obligation to support one's relatives, the needy, and strangers (vv. 26–30); the commandment against killing a child: "And slay not your children for fear of poverty" (v. 31/33); against fornication (v. 32/34); the general law against killing (v. 33/35); and the prohibition of stealing the property of orphans or using dishonest weights and measures (comparable to the seventh commandment) (vv. 34/36–35/37). That is all that is mentioned in sura 17.[195] The law against bearing false witness is mentioned in sura 6. The Decalogue here begins with the characteristic command: "'Come, I will recite what your Lord has forbidden you'" (v. 151). The list is similar to the one in sura 17 (vv. 151ff). It closes with the verse: "And when you speak, be just, even if it should be to a near kinsman [that you are to testify against]" (v. 152). A parallel presentation can be found in sura 25:63–72 (and in shorter form in sura 16:90/92–94/96; 23:2–8; and 60:12).

In surveying all passages containing allusions to the Ten Commandments it is evident that the fourth commandment, to honor one's parents, appears most frequently. In sura 4, similar to sura 17, it also includes mention of orphans, etc. There is also the commandment here to treat slaves justly (4:36/40). In other passages, parental obedience is urged, in sura 46:15–18 in detail, though not in cases where parents use their authority to force the children to hold on to polytheism (29:8–9; also 31:14–15). We already confronted this issue in treating the story of Abraham. This was a central theme in the thinking of Muhammad. Even Jesus called for dissociation from the parents for the sake of faith (Matt. 10:37; Luke 14:26).

It is conspicuous that the third commandment, to honor the Sabbath, is missing. It is treated in the Bible more thoroughly than the other commandments, based on God's resting on the seventh day (Exod. 20:8–11). The punishments mentioned in the Koran for violating the Sabbath have already been discussed. In sura 16 the Sabbath commandment is formally abrogated: "The Sabbath was only appointed for those who were at variance thereon; surely thy Lord will decide between them on the Day of Resurrection, touching their differences" (v. 124). This might call to mind Exodus 16:27, which tells of a division among the Israelites when Moses forbade the gathering of manna on the Sabbath. However, when Muhammad spoke of the Sabbath commandment it clearly had the character of a punishment, similar to other Jewish regulatory laws that were enacted: "Then your hearts became hardened thereafter and are like stones, or even yet harder" (2:74/69). It is reasonable to assume that Muhammad was thinking of Jesus' sermon when referring to the abrogation of the Sabbath commandment. Jesus had often discussed the Sabbath with the Pharisees and scribes (cf. Matt. 12:1–4; Mark 3:1–6, etc.). In Islamic practice, all business is stopped on Friday when Muslims are called to prayer.[196] This represents a middle course between the Jewish Sabbath and the Christian observance of Sunday as a day of rest.

The Company of Korah (Ḳārūn)

The story of the company of Korah and its being punished is also a part of the story of Moses. As is told in the Bible, it deals with the breaking away of a group from the people of Moses. Korah rebelled against Moses and Aaron and demanded a position as priest and a leader of the people. He and his followers "and their houses, and all the men that *appertained* to them, went down alive into the pit, and the earth closed upon them" or they were consumed by a fire from the Lord (Num. 16:32–35). In the Koran, the story is told in sura 28: Korah belonged to the people of Moses. He was so rich that "the very keys of them [i.e., his treasures] were too heavy a burden for a company of men endowed with strength" (v. 76). He rejected the warnings of his contemporaries to trust more in God than in his wealth (vv. 77–78). He was envied for his wealth by those who were concerned with their lives in the here and now (v. 79). Those who were reasonable, however, expected God's reward for faith and righteous deeds, and not for possessions (v. 80). "So We made the earth to swallow him and his dwelling and there was no host to help him, apart from God." His demise serves as a lesson to survivors to rely not on worldly goods but on God's mercy (vv. 81–82).

This narrative was part of the polemics against the unbelieving Meccans. They were afraid of losing control of the city if they converted to Islam (28:57). Muhammad made reference to earlier judgments of cities without explicitly mentioning any particular city (vv.

58-59). Along the lines of 1 John 2:15–17, the passing nature of worldly goods is contrasted with rewards in the hereafter (vv. 60–61). This is followed by considerations about the Last Judgment and the goodness of God as creator of humankind (vv. 62–75). Then the story is told of the wealthy Korah and his demise. There are obvious parallels to the Meccans, with their insistence on maintaining their possessions and their refusal to recognize Muhammad as the Prophet and leader sent by God.

Sura 29:39 mentions Korah in the same breath as the Pharaoh and his vizier Hāmān within the context of a listing of judgments: "And Korah, and Pharaoh, and Haman; Moses came to them with the clear signs, but they waxed proud in the earth, yet they outstripped Us not." When Korah appears along with the Pharaoh and Hāmān, he is understood to be an Egyptian. This is even more obvious in sura 40:24,[197] where the three names are included in the heading of an extensive description of Moses' audience with the Pharaoh (vv. 25–46). This is followed by Hāmān's appearance as the person who built the pyramids on the Pharaoh's orders (vv. 36/38–37/39). The story of Korah could be expected to appear here since he is mentioned in the heading, but it does not.

The Kings of the Israelites

Saul (Ṭalūt) becomes King; David (Dāwūd) slays Goliath (Djālūt)

Virtually nothing is said in the Koran about the Israelite acquisition of land and the period of the judges. The next major event after the deliverance from Egypt and the wanderings in the desert is the installation of Saul as king. Sura 2:246–251 tells the story loosely following the account in the Bible (1 Sam. 8–15). The Israelites demanded that "a Prophet of theirs," namely Samuel (though the name is not mentioned in the Koran), install a king so they could wage war against their enemies. These enemies (in the Bible it is the Philistines) had driven the Israelites from their habitations and tore apart families (v. 246).

The Prophet warned the Israelites, corresponding to the depiction in the Bible, of the burdens associated with having a king, and he installed Saul (Ṭālūt). Samuel rejected the objections of the people that Saul was impoverished, saying that he was chosen by God and that God granted him excessive knowledge and size ["increased him broadly in knowledge and body" (2:248)] (cf. 1 Sam. 10:23). Samuel's statement, that "God gives the kingship to whom He will" (v. 247) has become a standard quotation in Islamic political doctrine, since legitimism in a western sense never existed in Islam. The sign (i.e., the proof) of Saul's being chosen was supposedly the return of the Ark of the Covenant *(tābūt),* according to Samuel's statement. This corresponds to the biblical account, since the Ark was returned by the Philistines even before Saul became king (1 Sam. 5–6). Then the Israelites moved out to battle. They were put to a test (i.e., they were commanded not to drink water from a river) and to take on the struggle with the troops of Goliath (Djālūt). "And they routed them, by the leave of God, and David slew Goliath" (vv. 249–251). It is not mentioned that David was a young boy who vanquished the mighty and heavily armed Goliath with the simplest of weapons (1 Sam. 17). Whereas in the Bible Goliath is a Philistine warrior who challenged the Israelites to single combat, in the Koran he is a king. The Israelites were greatly outnumbered by their enemies. The similarity between the names of the two leaders, Ṭālūt and Djālūt, was intentional, designed to depict the two kings as a opposing poles of a unit.[198] On the one hand was Saul, chosen by God to be king of the Chosen People; on the other, Goliath, the sinful king of a sinful people who had driven God's Chosen People out of their homes and away from their children (cf. v. 246). The third in the unit was David, linked through the name Dāwūd to his adversary Djālūt: The opposition exists in the youthfulness (not mentioned in the Koran) of David and his simple weaponry as compared to the brute strength and heavy arms of Goliath. Dāwūd fought in the name of God; Djālūt in the name of idols, as stated in the Bible (1 Sam. 17:43).

David's reward was to become king: "and God gave him the kingship, and Wisdom, and He taught him such as He willed" (v. 251). The narrative was clearly conceived in Medina. The situation of the Muslims there was the same as that of the Israelites under Saul. They were driven from their homes and their children. Elsewhere Muhammad justified war with Mecca by saying that the Muslims "were expelled from their habitations without right" (22:39–40). Here he used a historical event to show how an outnumbered people could be victorious with the help of God.

The narrative might have been taken from a Christian source. The Israelites initially rejected Saul, according to the Koran, since he did not enjoy good standing. He was from the tribe of Benjamin, the smallest of the Israelite tribes (1 Sam. 10:20–24). Speyer indicated that that is why Ephrem the Syrian saw Saul as an antecedent of Christ. According to Aphrahat, the trial at the river was "symbolic of the baptism and the struggle that the Jews would wage, the struggle for their beliefs."[199] This is a good example of the Christian use of biblical material in a typological interpretation and its implementation with a changed goal in Koranic teaching.

David (Dāwūd) and Solomon (Sulaymān)

As we have seen, David stands in opposition to Goliath, which is expressed through their names as well. On the other hand, David and Solomon—father and son—form a unit in the Koran; they are linked through positive characteristics. This was expressed more strongly here than in the Bible, wherein David was not permitted to build the Temple because of his sins. Gods assigned this task to Solomon.

The Temple is not discussed directly in the Koran. As we have already discussed, Abraham recited the prayer to consecrate the Kaaba after it was completed. In sura 17, David is introduced as the author of the Book of Psalms: "and We have preferred some Prophets over others; and We gave to David Psalms *(zabūr)*" (v. 55/57). Koranic statements such as "And with David We subjected the mountains to give glory, and the birds, and We were doers." (21:79; also 34:10; 38:18–19) bring to mind passages in the Psalter, where all of nature is called upon to join in praising God (e.g., Psalm 98:8). David is presented in the Koran as the producer of coats of chain mail (21:80; 34:11), corresponding to legends of David told in biblical literature.

Solomon and David were both considered wise judges (21:78; 27:15). This is expressed mostly in short comments. The most extensive narrative about David is the one about the sin he committed with Bathsheba, wife of Uriah, including Nathan's parable, and the king's repentance. It appears in sura 38:21–25 and is so condensed in comparison to the biblical narrative (2 Sam. 11–12) that it is difficult to understand if the story is not already known. The introductory comment served to reinterpret it into a clear demonstration of David's wisdom as a judge: "We strengthened his kingdom, and gave him wisdom and speech decisive" (v. 20). This is followed by the story of two opponents in a trial who appeared before David to present their case. One of them was the owner of a single sheep and he accused the other, the owner of ninety-nine sheep, of stealing his only sheep (vv. 21–23). This clearly resembles the story of Nathan, with slight deviations; Nathan confronted the king with his sins in the form of a parable (2 Sam. 12:1–12). Of course David acknowledged the wrongdoing, but he recognized as well that the story was directed at him: "And David thought that We had only tried him; therefore he sought forgiveness of his Lord, and he fell down, bowing, and he repented" (v. 24). The Koran prescribes prostrating oneself *(sadjda)* when this passage is recited, in emulation of David's repentance.

Rabbinical literature presents David as the great penitent. There have also been many attempts to exonerate him totally of guilt.[200] His repentance is reflected in the penitential psalms that have also been adopted by Christianity. The site of David's sin and repentance must have been assumed, even in early Jewish tradition, to be his palace in western Jerusalem, near the present-day Citadel of David. Christianity later assumed this tradition. The "Pilgrim of Piacenza," who visited Jerusalem in the sixth century, reported of monks who resided in "David's Tower." The tower was considered the place where David wrote the Psalter *("ubi Psalterium decantavit").*[201] A repenting David evidently did not fit into the picture desired of a king once Christianity became the state religion and the emperor, also an emulation of David, was seen as the divinely chosen king and representative of Christ. Jewish tradition was less burdened by such concerns, maintaining the image of a repenting David and elaborating upon it. Muhammad encountered both images of David. His indecision in choosing one or the other is reflected in the Koranic narrative that starts with the glorification of David and then switches to the image of the repenting king.

The story of Solomon, even more than that of David, is shrouded in legend in post-biblical literature. This is echoed in the Koranic representation of Solomon as well. Solomon was characterized as a universal ruler. He ruled over the powers of nature and the world of the spirits (21:81–82; 34:12; 38:36–39); he knew the language of the animals (27:16), and the animals thus knew of his decisions. The ants, for example, learned that Solomon's army was setting out and they could get to safety (27:17–19); the hoopoe *(hudhud)* was his messenger to the Queen of Sheba (27:20). The biblical description of the construction of the Temple and the Temple equipment (2 Chron. 1–9) marks the beginning of the legendary portrayal of Solomon as a great builder. This is true of the account in the Koran as well. He controlled the "Fount of Molten Brass"; the jinn, whose assistence he took advantage of, were "fashioning for him whatsoever he would—places of worship, statues, porringers like water-troughs, and anchored cooking-pots" (34:13). His castle floor was covered with glass plates, so that the Queen of Sheba mistook the floor for a "spreading water," when she came to visit him (27:44).

As lord over nature, some parallels can be made between Solomon and David. And as we have already seen, they appear together as wise judges. They also complement each other with respect to their sins. David coveted his neighbor's wife and had her husband killed, whereby he violated the fifth and tenth commandments. Solomon is seduced by worldly goods, i.e., fast-running steed. Here, the horses might have been confused with those that the kings of Judah installed at the entrance to the Temple in honor of the sun. Josiah had the statues removed in the course of consecrating the Temple (2 Kings 23:11). Nevertheless, the Koran states that through the horses, Solomon neglected his obligations to God (38:30–33). This was a violation of the first three commandments dealing with the human being's obligations to God, whereas David violated commandments dealing with human beings' obligations to each other. David's repentance is considered in the Koran, but not his punishment. According to the biblical account, he was forbidden to build the Temple since he has bloody hands; the task was passed on to Solomon (1 Chron. 28:3). Solomon's punishment was also commensurate to the sin. In the Koran it is stated, "Certainly We tried Solomon, and We cast upon his throne a mere body; then he repented" (38:34–35). Because Solomon did not acknowledge God as the highest lord, he temporarily lost his position as ruler. He emulated his father in his repentance. In this narrative, father and son are portrayed as complementing each other on the basis of their sins. Solomon was repentant because his father was repentant.

The longest narrative on Solomon is about his relationship to the Queen of Sheba (27:17–44). It has many fairytale aspects. Solomon set out with his army of jinn, humans, and birds (vv. 17–19). When the birds in his army were reviewed, the king noticed that the hoopoe was missing (vv. 20–21). The bird brought tidings about the Sabaeans: they are ruled by a queen and worshiped the sun (vv. 22–26). Solomon sent the hoopoe to bring a message to the queen, demanding that she accept Islam. The queen spoke with her council and resolved to appease Solomon with a present (vv. 27–35). Solomon threatened a military attack (vv. 36–37) and instructed one of the spirits in his service to capture the throne of the queen (vv. 38–41). She was thus stripped of her power and submitted to Solomon (this is not stated explicitly in the Koran, however). She visited Solomon, viewed the palace, and converted to Islam by declaring: "'My Lord, indeed I have wronged myself [by not having faith], and I surrender with Solomon to God, the Lord of all Being'" (vv. 42–44).

In the Bible, the Queen of Sheba is a witness to Solomon's wisdom and wealth. He solved the riddle that she posed to him; while viewing his palace she was impressed by his wealth. They gave generous gifts to each other, as is befitting of royalty (1 Kings 10:1–13, etc.). The story in the Koran appears as part of a series of stories about prophets and their mission: Moses and the Pharaoh (vv. 7–14); Solomon and the Queen of Sheba (this story) (vv. 17–44); Ṣāliḥ and the Thamūd (vv. 45–53); Lot and the destruction of Sodom (vv. 54–58). The story of Solomon and the Queen of Sheba stands in opposition to that of Moses and the Pharaoh; whereas the Pharaoh refused to accept what Moses said and suffered his ruin, the Queen of Sheba accepted the faith and receives the greatest of honors. The two subsequent narratives deal with the message of the prophets and the resulting punishment. Perhaps they were added here because of their related subject matter.

The story of the measures taken by Solomon against the Sabaeans is a prime example of the war against the pagans that Muhammad waged against the Meccans from his residence in Medina. It contains at its core a significant rule of holy war *(djihād),* the battle against the unbelievers, namely that enemies must be told to accept Islam before the war against them is begun. Only if they do not respond immediately can war be waged. Legends have reduced the relationship between Solomon and the Queen of Sheba to a love story. Goethe used it in *West-Eastern Divan* and he mentioned the hoopoe in his poem "Gruss" [Salutation] as the matchmaker bringing the two lovers together.

The End of the Israelites

A concise version of the story of Israel from Moses to the destruction of the Second Temple can be found in sura 17:2–8. The section can be divided into two parts: (1) the appearance and prophecy of Moses (vv. 2–3), and (2) the threat of the two-time destruction of the Temple (vv. 3–8). Moses spoke of faith in the one God *(tauḥīd)* and recalled the Flood. This recollection contains a prophecy of an impending judgment: Just as the people died in the Flood because they practiced idolatry, Israel would be punished for abandoning God. The punishment would be that enemies enter the city and the place of worship, i.e., the Temple *(masdjid),* (v. 7) and destroy them both. The Israelites would then be granted a period of repose: "Then We gave back to you the turn to prevail over them, and We succoured you with wealth and children, and We made you a greater host" (v. 6). Then, however, the second part of the prophecy was carried out: The Israelites sinned once again and the city and Temple were entered and destroyed, "as they entered it the first time" (v. 7).

The prophecy of a double judgment in part two refers without a doubt to the destruction of Jerusalem by Nebuchadnezzar, the Babylonian captivity, the return, and the destruction of Herod's

Temple by the Romans. Muslim Koran commentators also interpret the passage in this way. Here, however, this is all yet to come and is prophesied as a punishment. It can be seen as the continuation of Moses' prophecy. One naturally thinks of Moses' prophecy in Deuteronomy when at the end, war and banishment (Deut. 28:47–68), return, and conversion (Deut. 29:28–30:14) were prophesied. Muhammad went yet a step further, following the first judgment with the last and final worldly judgment. The Israelites could still have hope in the mercy of God: "Perchance your Lord will have mercy upon you" (v. 8). Insofar, this narrative is revealed to be Muhammad's warning to the Jews to accept Islam. Eternal punishment was threatened should they remain impenitent. The section closes with the following verse: "and We have made Gehenna [i.e., hell] a prison for the unbelievers." The expression "prison" *(ḥaṣīr,* in this form a hapax legomenon in the Koran) might be an allusion to the Babylonian captivity of the Israelites: Hell is even harsher than that prison, with no hope of liberation or return.

Narratives from the New Testament

An Overview

In terms of number, there are far fewer narratives in the Koran from the New Testament than from the Old Testament. Except for isolated passages, these are limited to three major complexes, i.e., sura 3:33/30–57/50, sura 5:110–120, and sura 19:1–33. Sura 4:157–158 should also be listed, wherein the Crucifixion of Jesus is mentioned and then denied. As has been said in previous chapters, Muhammad was familiar with the Gospel *(indjīl)* and combined all sacred Christian Scriptures under this heading. He evidently did not know to distinguish between the four Gospels, the Acts of the Apostles, the Apostolic Epistles, and the Revelation. Although he did not mention them explicitly, these Scriptures are nevertheless suggested or quoted in the Koran, either directly or through another source. Speyer compiled a list of such passages at the end of his book on biblical narratives in the Koran. The only figures from the New Testament that were known to Muhammad were Zachariah (Zakaryāʾ), John the Baptist (Yaḥyā), Mary (Maryam), and Jesus (ʿĪsā). The Apostles and other disciples are mentioned collectively, but not individually by name.[202]

Sura 3 includes stories about Jesus covering the entire period from Adam, which marked the beginning of the genealogy, to the Last Judgment. The focus here is the announcement of Jesus' birth. The miracles that Jesus performed are listed briefly, and his selection of disciples is suggested; there is also mention of the persecution by the Jews and Jesus being saved by rising up to heaven. According to Muhammad, the Jews will finally acknowledge Jesus as a true prophet at the Last Judgment. Suras 19 and 3 have some aspects in common, but the story of Jesus' birth is more extensive in the former. Sura 5 includes narratives that are reminiscent of Jesus' miracle of the loaves, the Last Supper, and Jesus' mortal fear in the garden of Gethsemane. These are fragments of the Passion of Jesus, which is the only part of Jesus' life told as a unified block in the Gospels. The Crucifixion was reduced to a vague hint in the Koran, in sura 4:157. Jesus' rising up to heaven, on the other hand, is mentioned twice (3:55/48; 4:158). Jesus, like Muhammad and other prophets, appears at the Last Judgment as a witness for his community, which clearly rejects the Christian notion that he will return "to judge the living and the dead," as stated in the *Apostles' Creed.* Muhammad was also unfamiliar with the idea of the preexistence of Jesus; any similarities to the Logos doctrine are thus purely superficial.

The characterization of Jesus is more elaborate in the Koran than that of the other prophets. Upon closer examination, however, his function was reduced to activities similar to theirs: He preached the word of God, confirmed his prophetic predecessors, and prophesied his successor, namely, Muhammad; he also performed miracles that attested to his mission, found followers as well as opponents, was persecuted, faced a dangerous situation, and was finally saved by God.

The picture of Mary painted in the Koran corresponds more closely to Christian teachings than does the Koranic image of Jesus. Mary is portrayed in the Koran as an innocent virgin who gave birth to Jesus without having had relations with any man. There are also hints in the Koran of the *Mater dolorosa* that resemble the portrayal in the Gospel According to John. In the Koran, however, Mary did not suffer at the cross, but as a mother who was slandered by the Jews because of her child.

Jesus (ᶜĪsā) in the Salvation History

The story of Jesus, his mother Mary, Zachariah, and John the Baptist is told in detail in sura 3:33/30–57/50. The narrative can be divided into two parts, the first of which extending up to the announcement of the birth of Jesus (vv. 33/30–44/39) and the second from then up to his rising up to heaven (vv. 45/40–57/50). They are separated by an elliptical temporal clause in verse 45/40.[203]

The first part begins with a genealogy, similar to the Gospel According to Matthew (Matt. 1:1–17). Whereas the Gospel genealogy includes Joseph's line (as does the one in Luke 3:23–38), in the Koran it is Mary's genealogy. Jesus is referred to almost stereotypically in the Koran as "son of Mary." The Koran does not mention Joseph at all. It is not of significance here that the Koranic geneaology goes back to Adam, whereas the St. Matthew Gospel starts with Abraham; in Luke 3, the genealogy is traced all the way back to Adam (Luke 3:23-end). Only the most important characters are mentioned in the Koran: "God chose Adam and Noah and the House of Abraham and the House of Imran above all beings, the seed of one another" (vv. 33/30–34). ᶜImrān is the biblical Amram, father of Moses. Adam and Noah appear only as individuals; Abraham and Amram, on the other hand, as progenitors of large families ("houses"), in which faith and virtues were inherited from one generation to the next.[204] The biblical Amram had two sons and a daughter: Moses, Aaron, and Miriam (1 Chron. 6:3). In Arabic, the name Miriam and the name Mary are both rendered as Maryam. In the Koran, Miriam/Maryam has been merged into one person with Mary/Maryam, mother of Jesus. This "mistake" might be based on a typological interpretation that Muhammad was somehow exposed to. Theologians of the early church saw the stories of Moses, the exodus of the Israelites from Egypt, and the wanderings through the desert as physical antecedents as it were for the mysteries of Christian faith. The bush that burned but was not consumed, where Moses received his prophetic calling, was understood as the archetype of Mary's perpetual virginity. And Moses, who saved his people, was an archetype of Jesus, who redeemed humanity; safe passage through the parted sea of reeds was seen as the archetype of baptism; and the manna in the desert was the typological image of the Eucharist.[205]

The narrative following the genealogy is strongly reminiscent of the apocryphal Protevangelium of James.[206] According to this narrative, largely a legend about the mother of Jesus, Mary was brought to the Temple as a child and raised there by the priests. This Gospel had a great impact on the portrayal of Jesus' childhood within the Eastern Rite churches. In the Koran, however, much is omitted. Amram's wife (no name is mentioned) was pregnant and promised to dedicate the child to the service of God should it be a son (v. 35/31). The child, a daughter, was then born. The mother named the child Mary and placed her and her descendants—Jesus is intended here—under the protection of God "from the accursed Satan" (v. 36/31). Mary's childhood and her becoming a Temple virgin are summarized in one verse: "Her Lord received the child with gracious favour, and by His goodness she grew up comely, Zachariah taking charge of her. Whenever Zachariah went in to her in the Sanctuary, he found her provisioned. 'Mary,' he said, 'how comes this to thee?' 'From God,' she said. Truly God provisions whomsoever He will without reckoning." (v. 37/32). As a small child, Mary was already treated in a special way, as described in the Protevangelium of James: "And her parents made her chamber a sanctuary. And they did not allow anything dirty or impure to come near it" (ch. 6.1). Zachariah does not appear in the Protevangelium until Mary is twelve years old and plans have already been made for her marriage (ch. 8ff.). When the Koran speaks of Mary being fed by God in the Temple, this is also an element taken from the Protevangelium of James: "She was in the temple of the Lord like a dove that is fed; and she took her nourishment from the hand of an angel" (ch. 8.1). In chapter 13.2, when Joseph noticed that Mary was pregnant, he said to her, "Why has thou altogether humbled thyself, thou who wast reared in the Holy of Holies, and hast received food from the hand of an angel?"[207]

After the story of the birth of Mary, and her childhood and entrustment to Zachariah, the Koran reports how Zachariah prayed in the Temple for offspring, received the announcement of the birth of John the Baptist, and could not speak for three days (vv. 38/33–41/36). This story is based on the Gospel According to Luke (Luke 1:5–25), except that in the Gospel Zachariah remained without speech until John was born.

The elliptical temporal clause in verse 42/37 marks a break, where the narrative turns from the St. Luke Gospel back to the Protevangelium of James: "And [at that time] when the angels said, 'Mary, God has chosen thee, and purified thee; He has chosen thee above all women.'" In the Protevangelium, the Angelical Salutation is a combination of Luke 1:28 and 42: "And lo! a voice was heard which said to her: 'Hail, to thee O favored one! the Lord is with thee: blessed art thou among women'" (ch. 11.1). In the Koran, the angels continue: "'Mary, be obedient to thy Lord, prostrating and bowing before Him.'" (v. 43/38). This wording parallels the announcement of the birth of Jesus with the preceding announcement of the birth of John the Baptist, where at the end Zachariah was commanded: "And mention thy Lord oft, and give glory at evening and dawn." (v. 41/36 end). The first part of the story of Jesus ends with a few dramaturgic comments in which Muhammad referred to the revelatory character of the narrative (v. 44/39). At the end of this verse, there is a somewhat puzzling mention of quills that are cast in order to decide who should care for Mary. This is an allusion to the Protevangelium of James (ch. 8–9), where lots were cast to determine a spouse for Mary. It fell to Joseph's lot.

The second part of the story of Jesus also begins with the elliptical temporal clause "When the angels said" (v. 45/40), though the preposed conjunction "and" is missing, since this part was originally an independent piece. The announcement that closes the first part is taken up again, this time with a clear allusion to Luke 1:31-35. "Mary, God gives thee good tidings of a Word[208] from Him whose name is Messiah, Jesus, son of Mary; high honoured shall he be in this world and the next, near stationed to God. He shall speak to men in the cradle, and of age, and righteous he shall be." (vv. 45/40–46/41). Mary's objection was rejected by the angel (this time in singular as in the Gospel!) with the following argument: "'Even so,' God said, 'God creates what He will. When He decrees a thing He does but say to it 'Be' and it is'" (v. 47/42). As suggested above, this is a harsh rejection of the Logos theology that seems to be insinuated in the salutation of the angel, when it brought Mary "a Word from Him," i.e., from God. It is clearly stated here that Jesus was created in Mary's womb by the creative word of God, and thus has nothing to do with the preexistent logos from the

Gospel of John. The Logos is not that which was begotten by God, but the instrument he used in creating. Muhammad's statement is an acknowledgment of the human nature of Jesus, and a refutation of the doctrine of his divine nature. This is also evident in the name the angel gave to Jesus. "Son of Mary" is actually inappropriate in speaking directly to Mary. The name "Jesus Christ, Son of Mary" had already become so idiomatic in Muhammad's speech (or that of his sources), that he used it even where the context would have demanded another wording.[209]

That Jesus would be respected in this world and the next, and that he would be among those near to God, are references to his prophethood. Reference to his talking to the people as an infant was taken from the Infancy Gospels of the Apocrypha.[210] As the angel continued, God would teach Jesus "the Book, the Wisdom, the Torah, the Gospel" (v. 48/43). Torah and Gospel refer to the complete Jewish and Christian revealed Scriptures, respectively. This implies that Jesus would learn the Torah, which already existed at the time, not through his own human efforts, but that he would receive it again as a revelation. Muhammad found himself in exactly the same situation. He received the Koran as a new "Arabic" revelation. In the same way, as he repeatedly emphasized, he was revealed the stories from the Bible and did not hear them from other sources.

Following the announcement of Jesus, without any transition, is a list of the miracles he performed as signs of his authorization. He proclaimed them personally (v. 49/43). This appearsto be the speech in the cradle that the angel had prophesied. The first of these miracles he performed as a child; he formed sparrows out of clay and, as God created Adam, he breathed life into them. This story is told in the Apocryphal Gospels.[211] The other miracles are those of the canonical Gospels, i.e., healing of the blind and the leper, and raising of the dead. The miracle prophesied last in this list is more difficult to interpret. The end of verse 49/43 was translated by Arberry as follows: "I will inform you too of what things you eat, and what you treasure up in your houses [without having seen]. Surely in that is a sign for you, if you are believers." The addition included in brackets corresponds to Paret's translation, reflecting the traditional Muslim interpretation.

Henninger's translation is approximately "And I will tell you what you should eat and store in your houses."[212] Whereas Paret's comments give more the impression of Jesus having prophetic abilities, Henninger offers a normative statement within the scope of the Jewish dietary laws. However, this cannot be derived from the text itself; there is obvious reference to a miracle. In his commentary to 3:49, Paret leaves open the possibility that "in your houses" refers only to "store/treasure up," such that it would mean "And I will tell you what you eat and what you store in your houses." According to this interpretation, Jesus was a clairvoyant, which is the conclusion Paret draws. This does not lead to a satisfactory understanding, however. It is also possible that this is an allusion to the miracle of the loaves. The Gospels speak of one (Matt. 14:13–21, etc.) or two (Matt. 15:32–39; Mark 8:1–10) miracles of the loaves performed by Jesus. After the first time, twelve baskets of bread remained filled after everyone had eaten and after the second, seven baskets remained [for another meal]. The miracle of the loaves is closely connected typologically to the manna in the desert (and the institution of the Eucharist). The Israelites gathered a double ration on the sixth day, as commanded by Moses, and saved it for the Sabbath, since the Sabbath is a day of rest, on which they were not allowed to gather manna (Exod. 16:22–31). Muhammad might have had a source that interpreted Jesus' miracle of the loaves—in a typological sense—as the fulfillment of the meal in the desert through the manna from heaven. A portion of the manna was eaten immediately and a portion was saved; the people did the same thing as commanded by Jesus: A portion was eaten immediately (they were hungry, as is explicitly stated), and a portion was carried home and saved for another meal.

The prophecy of the miracles precedes the list of subjects Jesus spoke of in his sermon (vv. 50/44–51), i.e., confirming the Torah and mitigating the Jewish ritual laws. This alludes to the subjects treated in the Sermon on the Mount and the debate on the validity and binding nature of the law. This discussion took place between Jesus and the Jewish scholars, and among the Apostles; it was reflected in New Testament Scripture. At the end of verse 50/44, Jesus refers to his authorization, namely the "sign from your Lord" that he brought with him. It is perhaps a reference to the Gospels as revealed Scripture, just as Muhammad spoke of the Koran as a "sign." The Arabic word *āya* has two meanings: "miracle" and "Koranic verse."[213] Since Jesus possessed the "sign," he commanded obedience: "so fear you God, and obey you me." At the very end, the content of divine doctrine is outlined again and the human nature of Jesus is emphasized, excluding reference to Jesus' being the son of God, as is claimed by Christians: "God is my Lord and your Lord; so serve Him. This is a straight path." (v. 51/44 end). We shall return to this point later.

Jesus, like all prophets, found unbelievers and sought helpers, i.e., believers and followers (vv. 52/45–53/46). This is a reference to the selection of the Apostles (Matt. 10:1–4, etc.) or the sending out of the seventy-two disciples (Luke 10:1–12). The disciples declared themselves to be God's helpers and they professed their faith in him. Jesus commanded them to prove they were "Muslims." This command carries over into a prayer, wherein they professed their faith and prayed to be rewarded at the Last Judgment: "Lord, we believe in that Thou hast sent down [as a revelation], and we follow the Messenger [i.e., Jesus]. Inscribe us therefore with those who bear witness [to the truth]!"

The following section deals with the persecution by the Jews (v. 54/47) and God's announcement of the assumption, i.e., Jesus being raised up into heaven: "Jesus, I will take thee to Me and will raise thee to Me, and I will purify thee of those who believe not." (v. 55/48). Jesus' life is put into the framework of a biography of a prophet, since Muhammad accepted that as a given. The Prophet spreads the word of God; he is given miracles to confirm his authority; he finds supporters and helpers, but even more adversaries who threaten his life. In the end, he is saved by God's intervention. Whereas Noah was saved when his enemies were drowned in the Flood, Abraham was saved through God's intervention at the pyre, and Moses and the Israelites were saved by the drowning of the Egyptians, Jesus was saved by being raised up into heaven. According to Koranic teachings regarding Jesus' nature, it can only be an "assumption" and not an "ascension." This is made clear in the Koran by using the verb *rafaʿa* ("taking up"). God said to Jesus: "'I will take thee to Me and will raise thee to Me'" (v. 55/48).[214]

Jesus' supporters on earth are also taken care of. God said to Jesus:

"I will set thy followers above the unbelievers till the Resurrection Day." (v. 55 center/48). The followers are the Christians; the unbelievers the Jews, who rejected Jesus' teachings and wanted his death. They were afflicted with "a terrible chastisement," or "abasement and poverty," as we have already seen in 2:61/58.[215] The Temple was destroyed and they were dispersed throughout the world, having to live under Christian rule. These conditions were to remain unchanged until the end of the world. At the Last Judgment, the conflict between the two religions will be resolved; the unbelievers will be punished and the believers rewarded (vv. 56/49–57/50).

Jesus Saves His Mother (sura 19:1–33)

Jesus' birth and childhood are also told in sura 19:1–33. The sura bears the heading "Mary" (Maryam); the section under discussion consists of two parts: Zachariah and John the Baptist (vv. 1–15) and Mary and Jesus (vv. 16–33).

The first part begins with Zachariah's prayer for a son, the announcement of the birth of John and Zachariah's three days of silence (vv. 1–11). The text is very similar to the corresponding section in sura 3:38/33-41/36. What is missing in sura 3, however—the birth of John—appears in sura 19 in fragments. The birth itself is definitely not mentioned. The story begins after the birth of John. He was commanded "O John, take the Book forcefully [into your possession]" (v. 12). Since Zachariah was a priest (Luke 1:5) and according to Deuteronomy 17:18 the Torah was entrusted to the priests' care, the order that John received could be interpreted such that he was admonished to take good care of the Scripture. According to Islamic tradition, which was certainly based on earlier models, the priests in the Temple prepared copies of the Torah.[216] As son of a priest, John was thus told to follow in the footsteps of his father. It is further stated that John had already been given "judgment" as a child, which is a parallel to the narrative about Jesus as a twelve-year-old in the Temple, "sitting in the midst of the doctors, both hearing them, and asking them questions" (Luke 2:41–50). Just as Jesus was "subject" unto his parents in

Nazareth (Luke 2:51), John "was godfearing, and cherishing his parents" (vv. 13–14). The short section ends with the blessing: "Peace *(salām)* be upon him, the day he was born, and the day he dies, and the day he is raised up alive!" (v. 15).

As a parallel to the announcement of John received by Zachariah, this is followed by Mary's being told of Jesus (vv. 16–19), using similar wording as in sura 3. The setting and the circumstances are different, however. Whereas the account in sura 3 gives the impression that the announcement was received by Mary in the Temple, where she was living a secluded life in the care of Zachariah, it is stated in this passage that Mary withdrew herself from her people to an "eastern place." (v. 16). It was here where she received the announcement of the birth of Jesus. There has been much speculation about the "eastern place." Islamic tradition places it east of the Temple *(miḥrāb)*, explaining that Mary had entered child-bearing age and therefore had to leave the Temple.[217] Wilhelm Rudolph refers to M. Dettinger in citing the Christian origin of this narrative: According to Ezekiel 44:1, the eastern gate of the Temple was opened only by God. The early church used this as a typological reference to Mary and the entrance of the divinity into her womb *(solus Christus clausas portas vulvae aperuit)*.[218] In any case, Muhammad used "eastern place" to mean a site outside of the Temple (and perhaps outside of Jerusalem). We shall see that Mary left the "eastern place" to give birth, and withdrew to a "distant place."

"And she took a veil apart from them; then We sent unto her Our Spirit that presented himself to her a man without fault" (v. 17). According to Richard Bell, the veil is a vague recollection of Mary's activities in the Temple, where she participated in the production of the curtain to the inner sanctuary (Holy of Holies), as is told in the Protevangelium of James.[219] Muhammad, on the other hand, believed that she was concerned for her safety, since she was no longer in the Temple. Instead of the angel (or angels) who brought the announcement, the Spirit *(rūḥ)* appeared here. Paret refers to 21:91, where it is said that Mary was chaste; "And she who guarded her virginity, so We breathed into her of Our spirit" (also 66:12). Heikki Räisänen, too, is of the opinion that the spirit served the same function as that of the angels.[220] Since Mary thought it was an evil spirit, she recited an apotropaic phrase (v. 18). After this there is a dialogue between Mary and the spirit (vv. 19–21), similar in many ways to the one between Zachariah and the angel.

This is followed by the account of the birth of Jesus (which is not mentioned in sura 3): "So she conceived him, and withdrew with him to a distant place. And the birthpangs surprised her by the trunk of the palm-tree. She said, 'Would I had died ere this, and become a thing forgotten!' But the one that was below her called to her, 'Nay, do not sorrow; see, thy Lord has set below thee a rivulet. Shake also to thee the palm-trunk, and there shall come tumbling upon thee dates fresh and ripe. Eat therefore, and drink, and be comforted'" (vv. 22–26).

It is easy to recognize elements in this story from that of Hagar's and Ishmael's being cast out. Hagar wandered in the desert, close to starving and dying of thirst. She deposited the child under a bush, and from heaven the angel showed her the well (Gen. 21:8–19). In the Pseudo-Matthew (Infancy Gospel of Matthew), which was known in the West in the eighth and ninth centuries and which might have had an eastern precursor, the same story of Mary and Jesus on their flight to Egypt is told.[221] It is difficult to say whether Muhammad's source was the Pseudo-Matthew or something else that either directly or indirectly traces back to Genesis 21. The fact that Mary and Joseph could not stay at the inn in Bethlehem and had to resort to other quarters (Luke 2:7) could be seen as a parallel to Hagar's being cast out, though Ishmael was already born at that time, whereas Mary arrived at the palm when she was entering labor. The "distant place" mentioned in 19:22 might be the same place as the "height *(rabwa),* where was a [fertile?] hollow and a spring" in 23:50/52. This description, too, corresponds more to Egypt than to Bethlehem (which is never referred to by name in the Koran).

Jesus pointed out the palm tree and the water to his mother and, as the text continues, gave her instructions for her conduct upon her return: "and if thou shouldst see any mortal, say, 'I have vowed to the All-merciful a fast, and today I will not speak to any man.'" (v. 26). Mary's life was threatened since she—a virgin—returned from the desert with a child. People calumniated against her: "'Mary, thou hast surely committed a monstrous thing! Sister of Aaron, thy father was not a wicked man, nor was thy mother a woman unchaste'" (vv. 27–28). She was called "Sister of Aaron," following from the statement in sura 3:35 that her mother is the spouse of Amram.[222] Under Jewish law the penalty for an unmarried woman being unchaste was death by stoning (Deut. 22:20–21) or burning (Gen. 38:24). Jesus spoke out for his mother in this threatening situation. Much to the amazement of all, he spoke as a child from his cradle (v. 29): "He said, 'Lo, I am God's servant; God has given me the Book, and made me a Prophet'" (v. 30). With the expression "God's servant," Jesus spoke of himself as a mortal human being. When the title "God's servant" is associated with prophethood and receiving of the Scriptures, Moses is brought to mind, who was also referred to as the "servant of the Lord" or "servant of God" (Deut. 34:5; Neh. 10:29; Rev. 15:3). Peter called Jesus the "servant of God" in his speech on Pentecost (Acts 3:13 JB).[223]

In contrast to Muhammad, who according to tradition first received his calling to prophethood at the age of forty, Jesus was a prophet from birth. If Mary was the mother of such a child, then the origins of the child cannot be questioned, but rather Mary must be blessed. As is stated in the Gospel, "Blessed *is* the womb that bare thee, and the paps which thou hast sucked," to which Jesus responded "Yea, rather, blessed *are* they that hear the word of God, and keep it" (Luke 11:27–28). This is apparently what Muhammad was thinking of when he subsequently spoke of Jesus being blessed, and when listing the most important commandments: prayer *(ṣalāt)*, giving alms *(zakāt)*, cherishing the parents, and avoidance of arrogance (perhaps the commandment against killing was meant here, which follows the commandment to parental obedience in the Decalogue) (vv. 31–32). At the end, Jesus blessed himself: "Peace *(salām)* be upon me, the day I was born, and the day I die, and the day I am raised up alive!" (v. 33).

A parallel can clearly be drawn between this closing blessing and the preceding narrative about Zachariah and John the Baptist, which ends with the same blessing (even if there it was pronounced by a third party). Jesus, too, spoke not only of his birth, but of his death and resurrection. His Crucifixion was denied by Muhammad. Islamic tradition has resolved the obvious difficulties by suggesting that the death of Jesus is a reference to the end of the world. It accepts Christian eschatological opinions that Jesus will come down from heaven, vanquish the Antichrist (Dadjdjāl), and then die. Then the Last Judgment will come and Jesus will be raised with the dead.[224]

The Rejection of Jesus and the Falsification of God's Word; Gethsemane and the Last Supper

Important episodes from the life and works of Jesus are told in sura 5:110–120. There are four parts of varying lengths, each of which beginning with an elliptical temporal clause. The context is the Last Judgment, when God asked the prophets about the reception their prophecies enjoyed among the people to whom they were sent (v. 109). The development of the entire piece is very complex, raising many questions deserving of special treatment that goes beyond the scope of this book.

The first part (all of verse 110) reports how God told Jesus to remember the grace that was shown him (and his mother) on numerous occasions. Four instances are mentioned, each one marked by an introductory elliptical temporal clause:

(1) strengthening by the Holy Spirit, so that he could already speak in the cradle (and was thus in a position to save his mother from certain death); as an adult he spread the word of God, having received God's grace;

(2) God taught Jesus Wisdom, the Torah, and the Gospel;

(3) Jesus was given the power of performing miracles; this manifested itself in his ability to form birds out of clay and breathe life into them, healing the ill, and raising the dead;

(4) Jesus was saved from danger by God: "and [at that time] when I restrained from thee the Children of Israel [so they could bring you no harm] when thou camest unto them with the clear signs, and the unbelievers among them said, 'This is nothing but sorcery manifest.'"

The individual examples of God's grace were already mentioned in sura 3:46/41–49, 3:54/47, and 19:29–30, but in a different context. Strengthening by the Holy Spirit (1) and being saved (4) resemble Luke 4:16–30, where it is told how Jesus entered the synagogue in

Nazareth, stood up to read, was given the book of the Prophet Isaiah, and read "The Spirit of the Lord GOD *is* upon me; because the Lord hath anointed me. . . ." (Isa. 61:1). Jesus incurred the anger of the congregation because he implied that God condemned Israel and chose the pagans. The Jews were inexplicably prevented from killing him by pushing him over the edge of the mountain their city was built upon.

This raises the question as to the situation facing Jesus when he was reminded of the four instances in which God showed his mercy. An answer can best be found by examining the Koran for analogous situations experienced by other prophets. One example is the narrative about Moses receiving his calling at the burning bush. When he was told to confront the Pharaoh, Moses asked for "strength"; God gave him Aaron to assist him and reminded him of his being saved from the Nile and the distress he had suffered after killing the Egyptian. Having been strengthened and encouraged in this way, he was told to go to the Pharaoh and demand the release of the Israelites (20:9–48/50). The feelings of Moses at the burning bush were the same as those experienced by Jesus on the evening before his agony at Gethsemane (Matt. 26:36-46). He knew what he was about to face and was afraid. "And there appeared an angel unto him from heaven, strengthening him. And being in an agony he prayed more earnestly: and his sweat was as it were great drops of blood falling down to the ground" (Luke 22:43–44). Even though the Crucifixion of Jesus is denied in the Koran, 5:110 might contain one aspect of Jesus' Passion. In Gethsemane, Jesus was reminded of earlier occasions of having been supported and saved. From this experience, Jesus should trust that God would save him yet another time.

Now to the second of the four parts mentioned above: It begins (v. 111) with an elliptical temporal clause and consists of only one verse. This second part deals with the selection of the disciples and their profession of faith. The wording is reminiscent of sura 3:52/45, which was discussed earlier.

The third part (vv. 112–115) is linked to the second via an elliptical temporal clause without conjunction, giving the impression that the subsequent narrative is part of the profession of faith of the disciples. The story is about the table and food that Jesus prayed God would send down from heaven. This serves a multiple purpose, as can be understood from the request of the disciples: "They said, 'We desire that we should eat of it and our hearts be at rest; and that we may know that thou hast spoken true to us, and that we may be among its witnesses.'" (v. 113). The disciples wanted to eat of the food on the table, obviously in its literal meaning. In addition, they wanted Jesus to perform a miracle proving his authorization from God and they offered to bear witness to the miracle. Jesus asked God to "send down upon us a Table out of heaven, that [with its meal] shall be for us a festival *(ʿīd),* the first and last of us, and a sign from Thee. And provide for us; Thou art the best of providers." (v. 114). God granted the request: "Verily I do send it down on you; whoso of you hereafter disbelieves, verily I shall chastise him with a chastisement wherewith I chastise no other being." (v. 115).

The narrative is based on events that are typologically interpreted in the theology of the early church, i.e., giving manna to the Israelites in the desert, the miracle of the loaves, and the institution of the Eucharist.[225] The manna was a real meal, as was the meal offered with the miracle of the loaves. The Eucharist is a tangible meal with supernatural aspects. The Gospel According to John explicitly refers to the miracle of the loaves as miraculous proof of Jesus' prophethood: "Then those men, when they had seen the miracle that Jesus did, said, This is of a truth that Prophet that should come into the world." (John 6:14). Jesus' request that the table be a festival and a sign (v. 114) is a reference to the institution of the Eucharist and an allusion to the Passover meal and the commemorative aspect of the Last Supper (cf. Luke 22:19, etc.). A more specific indication of the Eucharist is God's threat that anyone doubting the divine source of the table would be punished as no one in the world had been punished (v. 115). This calls to mind Paul's account of the Last Supper, with the warning: "But let a man examine himself, and so let him eat of *that* bread, and drink of *that* cup. For he that eateth and drinketh unworthily, eateth and drinketh damnation to himself, not discerning the Lord's body [from ordinary bread]" (1 Cor. 11:28–29).

The fourth part (vv. 116–120) also begins with an elliptical temporal clause and reports, as Paret writes in his commentary to 5:116, "of a dialogue between God and Jesus that had not yet taken place, but would instead take place according to verse 119 [and 109] at the Last Judgment, i.e., in the future." In these verses God sits in judgment and hears a curious profession of faith from the Christians. This is why he turns to Jesus, who, as their prophet, must bear witness for his followers. God asks, "O Jesus son of Mary, didst thou say unto men, 'Take me and my mother as gods, apart from God?'" (v. 116). The fact that Muhammad referred to such a concept of Trinity is certainly based not on an error on his part, but on conclusions he drew from his encounters with Christians in the Ḥidjāz.[226]

Jesus rejected the accusation that he preached a divinity comprised of father, son, and mother. "I only said to them what Thou didst command me: 'Serve God, my Lord and your Lord.'" (v. 117, 1st half). The next statement clarifies the fact that the scene described here, as already mentioned, is a dialogue between God and Jesus at the Last Judgment. Looking back on his earthly life, Jesus says, "And I was a witness over them, while I remained among them; but when Thou didst take me to Thyself, Thou wast Thyself the watcher over them; Thou Thyself art witness of everything" (v. 117, 2nd half). This is intended to mean that Jesus was accountable for the faith of his followers only until he was taken up to heaven (i.e., departure from his earthly life). God assumed the responsibility for the period from Jesus' being raised up to the Last Judgment. He can admit people to preach false doctrine and then be subject to punishment (vv. 118–120).

Jesus' Sermon

It is helpful to sum up by examining the contents of Jesus' sermon, starting with his statements about himself. In sura 19, he spoke as a child in his mother's arm and introduced himself as "Lo, I am God's servant; God has given me the Book, and made me a Prophet." (v. 30). This clearly rejects the Christian doctrine of Jesus' divine nature. This viewpoint is expressed just as clearly when he repeatedly stressed his purely human nature: "'God is my Lord and your Lord; so serve Him. This is a straight path'" (3:51/44; cf. also 5:72/76; 5:117; 19:36;

43:64).

Jesus demanded obedience of the people because he was a prophet: "I have come to you with a sign [i.e., with the Scripture or a miracle] from your Lord; so fear you God, and obey you me" (3:50/44). Obedience shown the prophets resulted from fear of God; the prophet demanded obedience in the name of and by order of God. As a prophet, Jesus received the Scriptures, i.e., the Gospels (57:27). They contain "guidance and light, . . . confirming the Torah before it, as a guidance and an admonition unto the godfearing" (5:46/50). In the scene where Mary was told she would bear a son, the angel said to her, "And He [i.e., God] will teach him the Book, the Wisdom, the Torah, the Gospel" (3:48/43).

In describing his teaching, it is repeatedly stated that Jesus confirmed the Torah (3:50/44; 5:46/50; 61:6). However, he also permitted some things that had previously been forbidden (3:50/44). This conveys generally what is said in New Testament Scripture about the validity of Jewish laws and their relevance for Christians. This subject certainly played a major role in discussion between Jews and Christians in Muhammad's environment. It had to be clear to objective observers that Christians lived according to different, less stringent laws than the Jews did, especially regarding ritual purity and diet. As far as the Decalogue is concerned, it was claimed that Jesus made allusions to the individual commandments, e.g., obedience to his mother (19:32). This also includes God's command in Jesus' sermon: "and I am your Lord; so serve Me" (21:92; 23:52/54), which alludes to the first verse of the Decalogue, "I *am* the LORD thy God" and the two succeeding commandments, dealing with the obligations of the people to God (Exod. 20:2–23).

Jesus approved of some aspects of Judaism and its laws and disapproved of others, which of course simply intended to mean that he, as all prophets before him, preached Islam, the unchanging religion of humanity since the beginning of time. The disciples professed their faith in Islam, under his authority and testimony (5:111), and, at the same place where Jesus recalled the Decalogue (or at least parts of it), he proclaimed two of the five "pillars of Islam" that were later designated, namely, the obligation to participate in liturgical prayer *(ṣalāt)* and to pay alms *(zakāt)*. At their core, these two obligations contain all the other commandments. When asked "Master, which *is* the great commandment in the law?" (Matt. 22:36), Jesus referred to love of God and love of one's neighbors; "On these two commandments hang all the law and the prophets" (Matt. 22:40). Summarizing the Ten Commandments into two main categories is also taught in the Talmud,[227] so it is impossible to determine definitively whether Muhammad was drawing upon Jewish or Christian sources.

Among the tasks of the prophets was to confirm the prophecies of the predecessors and prophesy the coming of a future prophet. Even Adam was promised righteous guidance in the future, as we have seen earlier. After the Kaaba was completed, Abraham prayed for the coming of a prophet from the ranks of the Arabs, his descendants through Ishmael, which is basically the same as prophesying a future prophet. Jesus did the same thing: "'Children of Israel, I am indeed the Messenger of God to you, confirming the Torah that is [or: was there] before me, and giving good tidings of a Messenger who shall come after me, whose name shall be Aḥmad'" (61:6). Islamic Koran exegesis has always assumed this to be a reference to Muhammad, thus concluding that Aḥmad is another name for Muhammad. This is based on the fact that both names have the same root *(ḥ-m-d)*. Muslims later assumed Aḥmad to be the "Comforter" *(parákletos)* in John 14:26, possibly as a result of Christian influence. And the prophecy of the sending of the Holy Ghost, as this passage is interpreted in Christian theology, was seen as a reference to Muhammad.[228]

According to the Koran, an important matter of concern in Jesus' sermon is the unity of the community. Preserving the unity is a commandment that God imposed upon all prophets. "Perform the religion, and scatter not [into different groups] regarding it" (42:13/11). Jesus observed this commandment and said in the name of God: "surely this community of yours is one community, and I am your Lord; so serve Me" (21:92; cf. also 23:52/54). But his sermon fell on deaf ears: "but they fell into variance, and some of them believed, and some disbelieved; and had God willed they would not have fought one against the other; but God does whatsoever He desires" (2:253). When this is said in direct connection with Jesus, it is clear that the unbelievers were the

Jews and the believers, Jesus' followers, i.e., the Christians. Jesus' sermon on the unity of the community is reminiscent of the high-priestly prayer (John 17), wherein Jesus spoke of the unity of the community: "keep through thine own name those whom thou hast given me, that they may be one, as we *are*" (v. 11); and "Neither pray I for these alone, but for them also which shall believe on me through their word; That they all may be one" (vv. 20–21). There is yet another indication that Muhammad was acquainted with this or a related text. After verse 11, Jesus said, "While I was with them in the world, I kept them in thy name: those that thou gavest me I have kept. . . . I pray . . . that thou shouldest keep them from the evil" (vv. 12–15). The last sentence must be understood as referring to the time after his death, since it is a farewell prayer that he recited right before he was arrested. Sura 5:117 contains a similar statement by Jesus. Here he accounted for himself to God, described the contents of his sermon, and then said to God, "And I was a witness over them, while I remained among them; but when Thou didst take me to Thyself, Thou wast Thyself the watcher over them; Thou Thyself art witness of everything."

Jesus' parables are very important in the Gospels. The Koran, too, includes a number of them, though here none of the parables was told by Jesus. The Koranic parable of the grains of corn (2:261/263–265/267) deals with paying alms and most closely resembles the Gospel parable of the sower told by Jesus (Matt. 13:1–9, etc.)[229] This is also true of the parable of the rich and the poor (18:32–44), an elaborate story—unlike most Koranic parables—about a poor believer and a wealthy unbeliever. It echoes the parable of the rich spendthrift and the poor Lazarus (Luke 16:19–31). Paret finds similarities between sura 57:12–13 and the parable of the wise and the foolish virgins (Matt. 25:1–13), though the Koran passage is not part of a parabolic story. Instead, the details of the parable were transferred directly to the actors, i.e., the believers and the hypocritical men and women that face the Last Judgment.[230]

The Crucifixion (Sura 4:156–157)

Whereas the raising up of Jesus is described several times in the Koran as a story of salvation from the enemies, there is only one account of the Crucifixion. It appears in sura 4 within the framework of a long list (vv. 153–160) of wrongdoings of the Israelites, or Jews, which was already treated above, under the heading, "The Transgressions of the Jews." As was said earlier, the Jews were not accused of having killed Jesus, but of claiming to have done so. The charge appears in the text within the context of slander of the mother of Jesus. In order to understand the passage it is important to take into consideration the additions that Paret placed in parentheses, which express the interpretation according to Islamic tradition: "and for their [the Jews'] unbelief, and their uttering against Mary a mighty calumny, and for their saying, 'We slew the Messiah, Jesus son of Mary, the Messenger of God'—yet they did not slay him, neither crucified him, only a likeness of that was shown to them [*walākin shubbiha lahum*], [so that they mistook that other man for Jesus and killed him]" (vv. 156–157).

Mary and Jesus do not belong together here as mother and son, but as objects of slander. This is the Koranic version of empathy of the mother with the sufferings of the son, as illustrated by John the Apostle: Mary stood at the cross with other women (John 19:25). Christian piety developed this into the image of the *Mater dolorosa,* the "sorrowful mother." According to John, Jesus cared for his mother even as he was dying by giving her into the care of the beloved disciple, who was there to witness the event (John 19:26). The Koran deals with this as an example of the son's care for his mother, as described above regarding another aspect: When she came out of the desert with the child and her life was threatened because she was suspected of having had illicit sexual relations, she was saved by the words of the child, who presented himself as a prophet. It is apparent how closely related these two episodes are as regards the motif of a son's concern for his mother.

Muhammad decided on a solution that avoided professing faith in the crucified Jesus (according to the traditional Islamic interpretation of the Koran, which Paret also followed): Someone else who was mistaken for Jesus, or who resembled Jesus, was crucified in his place. The verb *shabbaha* means "comparing someone with another; causing something to become doubtful by making things so similar that they are difficult to distinguish from one another," passive: *shubbiha* "vague, unclear, dubious" appears in this form only once in the Koran. Docetic doctrine was popular, especially in Gnosticism, with its strict distinction between the material and the spiritual. It is conceivable that Muhammad was influenced by Gnostic groups in interpreting the Crucifixion of Jesus as an event that never actually took place. It corresponded to his understanding of prophethood and God's justice if Jesus did not suffer death, but was saved, as the other prophets had been saved.

The fact that the Jews were doubtful regarding Jesus and the Crucifixion can be derived from the following comment, which is difficult to understand due to the unclear antecedent of the personal pronouns in the original: "Those who are at variance concerning him [or: it] surely are in doubt regarding him [or: it]; they have no knowledge of him [or: it], except the following of surmise; and they slew him not of a certainty" (v. 157 end/156). According to Paret's commentary, "They cannot say with certainty if they killed him."

But what happened to Jesus if someone else was crucified in his place? The following verse offers relevant information: "no indeed; God raised him up to Him; God is All-mighty, All-wise" (v. 158/156). This gives the impression that the raising up of Jesus into heaven was directly connected to the attempted Crucifixion with respect to time. The Jews could have recognized their error and continued their search for the real Jesus, but he had escaped the reach of his enemies. His story was not over yet, however, as can be derived from the next verse: "There is not one of the People of the Book but will assuredly believe in him before his death, and on the Resurrection Day he will be a witness against them" (v. 159/157). "Before his death" is unclear: It could refer to the People of the Book who convert prior to their respective deaths. It is more likely, however, that the possessive pronoun refers to Jesus: "Before Jesus' death all the People of the Book will believe in him." "People of the Book" refers to all Jews who did not believe in him and wanted to crucify him. When Jesus returns "with glory" and sits in judgment, as the Christian faith states, then they will have to believe in him. On the other hand, that cannot be the intended meaning if it is Jesus' death that was spoken of. Jesus' death must take place before the general resurrection, because he was taken up into heaven, but has remained a mortal, subject to death as all other mortal beings are. It might be possible that Jesus will come down from heaven, vanquish the Antichrist, and then die and be buried. It is stated elsewhere that Jesus is "knowledge of the Hour [of the Last Judgment]" (43:61), which must be interpreted to mean that his coming down from heaven will signal the Judgment. After he has satisfied his earthly task, the world will come to an end and the dead will be resurrected and gathered for the Last Judgment. Jesus will not be a judge, however, as Christians believe, but a witness for the Christians when they face the judgment.

The Crucifixion of Jesus represents a difficult problem in the Koran. At the same time it represents the core of Christian soteriology. Thus an additional viewpoint seems necessary. Räisänen examined the complex of Jesus' Crucifixion, death, and rising to heaven.[231] After carefully comparing all relevant passages, he concluded that Muhammad must have assumed that Jesus died a natural—i.e., not a violent—death and did not die on the cross. According to Räisänen, Muhammad polemicized against the notion of Jesus' death by crucifixion in his debate with Jews, and for a natural death in his debate with Christians. Consequently, Räisänen does not relate the death that Jesus spoke of in his blessing in 19:33 to the eschatological events, but to Jesus' natural death. He also does not relate 43:61 ("And it [the Koran?] is the knowledge of the hour") to Jesus and his return, which signals the Last Judgment, but instead says, "the natural interpretation is likely that the Koran contains information saying *that* [Räisänen's emphasis] the hour of Judgment is coming." We had concluded that the list of examples proving God's mercy shown to Jesus in 5:110 referred to Jesus' situation in Gethsemane; Räisänen denies any connection between Jesus' being saved as mentioned at the end of 5:110 and Luke 4:28–30, doubting "that Muhammad knew such details of Gospel tradition." He also presents the passage as evidence of the fact that Muhammad believed a crucifixion did not take place.

Perhaps a look at Islamic tradition can help us better understand verse 4:157. To start with, we can assume that not everything that was known on the Arabian peninsula in Muhammad's time in the way of stories about Jesus (or other subjects) made its way into the Koran. It is also true that not everything about Koranic statements in Islamic tradition is to be considered secondary, as it could include parallels or additions to what is told in the Koran. Ṭabarī (tenth century) cited a number of sources written by older authorities in his commentary to 4:157.[232] They all explained the Crucifixion of Jesus in a docetic sense (which Räisänen expressly rejects, albeit without any explanation). One particularly interesting account included in Ṭabarī's work was traced to Wahb ibn Munabbih, a Persian of southern Arabian descent who lived in the seventh century and was supposedly familiar with Jewish and Christian traditions. The account ascribed to Wahb follows the Passion of Jesus as it appears in the Gospels: the Last Supper, the fear of Jesus in Gethsemane, the sleeping of the disciples despite Jesus' warning, the prophecy of Peter's denial before the rooster crows three times (which is part of the Last Supper); Judas' betrayal and Jesus' arrest; the chastisement and crown of thorns. The Crucifixion, however, did not take place according toWahb's account. "And finally they brought him to the wood on which they wished to crucify him. But Allāh raised him to Himself, and they crucified the resemblance which was made for them." Jesus later appeared to the women who wept for the man who was crucified and comforted them, saying: "naught but good has come to me. This [i.e., the Crucifixion] is something which has been made a resemblance for them."

According to other sources, God took Jesus up to him on the same day or even the same moment, since his likeness *(shibh)* or form *(ṣūra)* was "taken on" by another. In one traditional source, the one who was given the form of Jesus actually took his place (at the Last Supper?) and was arrested by the Jews pushing their way in, while Jesus had been raised up to heaven. A number of sources agree that Jesus asked the disciples present which one of them wanted to take on his likeness and be killed in his place. He promised a place in Paradise to whomever was prepared to do that. A disciple or a man named Sardjis (Sergius) declared himself willing and Judas Iscariot kissed him, thinking the man was Jesus. It seems to be just punishment when these sources report that God gave the form of Jesus to the traitor Judas or to a Jew named Titanus, who wanted to arrest Jesus but could not find him, and that this man was then seized by the Jews and crucified.[233]

A story attributed to Wahb is then told in which not only the Jews but the Christians, too, are deceived. In the story, the disciples who were with Jesus in the house (of the Last Supper?) left and went their separate ways, only one remaining in the house with Jesus. This one was given Jesus' form, while Jesus rose up to heaven. The disciple was seized and crucified instead of Jesus. Both the Jews and the disciples—since they had not witnessed the transfiguration and his assumption—believed it was Jesus who was crucified. The disciples felt justified in their belief, since they had indeed witnessed Jesus' mortal fear in Gethsemane.

These narratives have an obvious docetic character. They are evidence of how sophistocated Gnostic doctrine could be put in concrete terms and trivialized in popular tradition. Their naïveté and realism are reminiscent of the Pistis Sophia, a Gnostic gospel showing how the spirit, which was identical to the child Jesus, embraced and kissed Jesus and became one with him (the spirit separated from Jesus before the Passion).[234] Muhammad might have learned the story of the salvation and rising up of Jesus as passed down by Ṭabarī or in a similar form. The narrators might have been Christians with Gnostic leanings. The problem was first and foremost in the union of the human and divine nature in Jesus.

It can be summarized that only three episodes from the Passion of Jesus are included in the Koran: the Last Supper (5:112–115), his mortal fear in Gethsemane (in fragments) (5:110), and the salvation of Jesus on the cross, together with his rising up to heaven (4:157–158).

Jesus' death is also discussed in 3:55/48, albeit with less clarity: "When God said: 'Jesus, I will take thee to Me (*innī mutawaffīka*) and raise thee to Me.'" The phrase *innī mutawaffīka* is based on the verb root *tawaffā*, the basic meaning of which is "to die." The verse would then be: "Jesus, I will let you die and raise thee to Me." That would be in contradiction to 4:157, where Jesus was saved from the cross and raised up to heaven. Koran commentators found ways of resolving the contradiction by declaring that the two verbs "to let die" and "to raise up" must be interchanged, a practice that can also be found elsewhere in the Koran. The passage must be interpreted as follows: "Jesus, I will raise thee to me and will let you die." Jesus would be taken up from the earth, would return at the end of the world, vanquish the Dadjdjāl, and then die and be buried. At the Last Judgment he would be resurrected from the dead with all of humanity and would be a witness for his community at the Judgment. Other commentators avoid the word "to die," interpreting *innī mutawaffīka* to mean that Jesus earthly existence has come to an end, without affecting Jesus' role at the end of the world.[235]

The Present-Day Situation and Its Foundation in History

Introductory Comments

As a revealed religion, Islam—like Judaism and Christianity—is strongly focussed on and definitively grounded in history. Recollections from the life and work of the Prophet Muhammad are a guiding force behind both doctrine and practice. According to Muslim faith, the Koran in its entirety is a divine revelation, announced to the Prophet by the angel Gabriel sentence for sentence, word for word, syllable for syllable, and letter for letter, for him to pass on to his community. As the bearer of divine knowledge, Muhammad is considered a model concerning all matters of the community and the individual; his emulation is a high priority in the lives of the believers. Just as Jesus was surrounded by his Apostles and other disciples, "helpers" *(anṣār)* in the terminology of the Koran (3:52/45), Muhammad had his "companions" *(ṣaḥāba)*. As the Apostles transcribed the Gospels, the Companions carefully recorded not only the words of the revelation, but everything the Prophet did or said, down to the most trivial of actions and utterances, passing it down to posterity as "rules, or mode and manner of conduct" *(sunna)*. This tradition has been assigned nearly equal authority as the Koran itself; it was documented, at first orally and then in writing, in comprehensive collections, much of which was certainly ascribed to the Prophet after the event. These traditions, handed down in the literary genre of the Ḥadīth ("narration"), are regarded as authentic by pious Muslims and, together with the Koran, are used as sources even today in making binding decisions in questions of faith.

The "apostolic" period in Islam is the time of the first four of Muhammad's successors—Abū Bakr, ʿUmar, ʿUthmān, and ʿAlī—who ruled from 632 to 661 and took on a special position of trust within the close circle of "companions." Plaques with their names hang in Sunni mosques. These serve the same function in Islam as the diptych tablets on the altar did for the early church, with the names of the Apostles, the first popes, and the saints commemorated in the religious services; the Missale Romanum has a prayer specifically for this purpose, to be recited in the canon of the Mass, beginning with the words "Communicantes, et memoriam venerantes" (communicating with and honoring) and followed by the names of Mary, the Apostels and other saints, the popes, etc. And just as the church took shape during the time of the Apostles and the first popes and started to spread throughout the world, the major Muslim conquests took place during the reigns of the first four caliphs; rules for coexistence with Jews and Christians were laid down at this time as well. These rules have retained their validity to the present day and can be called back into the consciousness of Muslims whenever they are "forgotten." The four caliphs carry the title, "the Rightly Guided," since they were close confidants of Muhammad and knew his intentions better than anyone else. This quality became all the more illuminating, since their successors, the Umayyads, were no longer recognized by pious Muslims as legitimate leaders of the Islamic community. Muslims tend to look to the magnificence of early Islam and view all that came later as a decline. To them, history is a teacher and not an object of academic curiosity. This is essentially an ahistoric viewpoint, but that need not concern us here. The subject forces us to look at the origins in order to understand the present.

In Shiʿite Islam, the tradition, or *sunna,* is also recognized, but the bearers are not the "companions" and Muslims of later generations in general, but only the relatives and direct descendants of Muhammad. Of the four "rightly guided" caliphs, Shiᶜites acknowledge only ᶜAlī, the fourth, who was a cousin of Muhammad. The imams (literally: leader), descendants from the marriage of ᶜAlī and Muhammad's daughter Fatima, are considered by all Shiᶜite groups to be the legitimate leaders of the community and the state. Concerning the doctrine of Holy War *(djihād),* which shall be discussed below, Shiᶜite belief differs from that of the Sunnis insofar as the Shiᶜites regard it as permitted and to some extent an obligation even against opponents within Islam, i.e., primarily the Sunnis. As far as our specific subject is concerned, with respect to Jews and Christians the attitudes of the Shiᶜites do not differ significantly from those of the Sunnis.[236] Since they, too, are a minority, they have historically been willing to make concessions for pragmatic reasons. The Fatimids, for example, who were Shiᶜites, favored the Christians and consequently did not interfere with Christian pilgrimages, so that the Crusades did not start until the Fatimids lost Jerusalem to the Seljuks, who were Sunnis.

The Conquests; Muslims and Non-Muslims

Militance and peaceableness exist side by side in Islam,[237] and Muhammad practiced both of them. After settling in Medina, he took up the struggle against Mecca and later extended it to other adversaries. Pagans were forced to accept Islam and agreements were made with the People of the Book, i.e., primarily Jews and Christians, provided they were willing to live under Muslim rule. They enjoyed a certain degree of religious freedom, but were obliged to pay special taxes. The basis for this can be found in sura 9:29, which states that war against those who have received Scriptures must be waged "until they pay the tribute out of hand and have been humbled."[238]

The triumphant advance of Islam began shortly after Muhammad's death, when the foundations were laid for the system of Islamic states as it exists today. Initially, the conquests did not serve primarily the spread of Islam, but the establishment of Islamic state rule in the conquered regions. The Islamic state was identical to the Islamic community (Arabic: *umma).* It was an association based on persons, not primarily on a territory, similar to the Christian state in the Middle Ages. The state ruled over a territory, but did not occupy the entire area. Other communities also resided within the same territory, in this case the Jewish, Christian, Zoroastrian *(madjūs),* and other communities.

In the eleventh century, the Sunni scholar al-Māwardī composed a systemic description of Islamic government on the basis of traditions passed down from the Prophet, taking into consideration the practice that had developed over four centuries.[239] It is still considered generally valid in conservative and fundamentalist circles today. The system divides the world into two parts, the "House of Islam" *(dār al-islām),* under Islamic jurisdiction, and the "House of War" *(dār al-ḥarb),* that which is not yet under Islamic jurisdiction. The Islamic community is theoretically in a state of ongoing war with this part of the world. Following the example of Muhammad, who agreed to a cease-fire *(hudna,* literally: windless calm) with Mecca in the treaty of al-Ḥudaybiya,[240] the war can be temporarily interrupted if, for example, the enemy is strong and one's own strength is insufficient, but Muslims are obligated to resume the struggle as soon as circumstances allow. Before a military clash can be initiated against unbelievers, they must be called upon to accept Islam *(daᶜwā).* Al-Māwardī assumed that Islam was sufficiently known throughout the world at that time to eliminate the need for *daᶜwā,* and he stressed that Muslims could and must take up the struggle against unbelievers everywhere and at any time, without having formally issued an appeal for the unbelievers to accept either Islam or subjection.

This theory of war *(djihād)* has a lot in common with *bellum iustum* as it was defined by St. Augustine. Similar to the Roman state since Theodosius the Great, the Islamic state no longer tolerated any pagan cults on its territory. Pagans, as has already been mentioned, had no choice but to accept Islam or death. The People of the Book, on the other hand, were free to practice their religions, though their situation was essentially dependent on whether they had willingly surrendered or were vanquished in war. Islamic law distinguished between cities or regions that came under Islamic rule as a result of peace treaties *(ṣulḥan)* or those where aggression had been necessary *(ʿanwatan).* The former were allowed to retain their religious institutions and secular property. They became *ahl al-dhimma,* or "protected persons," under certain conditions (which will be explained below) and were required to pay poll *(djizya)* and land *(kharādj)* taxes. The poll tax was required according to the Koran (9:29) and, as maintained by al-Māwardī, the land tax was dictated by oral tradition *(ḥadīth).* If they broke the contract of protection, they had to be given a certain period of time to leave Islamic territory, according to more tolerant jurists. Stricter legal interpretations declared them outlaws, giving Muslims the right to kill or enslave anyone who broke the contract. Their property was confiscated and distributed among the Muslims.

At first the conquests involved Christian or Zoroastrian territories, but the goal was not missionary in nature. Islam had emerged among Arabs and maintained an exclusively Arabic character for a long time. When the Umayyads seized power in 661, they built up an essentially Arab empire, as Julius Wellhausen illustrated in his renowned history of the Umayyads, with its characteristic title *Das arabische Reich und sein Sturz* [The Arab Empire and its Fall] (Berlin, 1902). The empire was ruled by a small class of Arab Muslims, an elite military caste who subsisted on war spoils and taxes collected from the subjugated People of the Book and devoted their lives exclusively to waging war. They were virtually prohibited from engaging in trade and agricultural activities and lived in isolation from the native population in garrison cities set up near the older centers, such as Kufa (near Nadjaf), Basra, and al-Fusṭāṭ ("the tent").[241] Islam was tied to Arabic culture so that converting to the religion of the conquerers was a prerequisite to being adopted by an Arab tribe as a client *(maulā,* plural *mawālī).* The conquerers could not remain that exclusive for long. Once the clients grew in number they were in a position to push through demands for full civil rights. Under the Abbasids (750–1258), which moved the center of the empire from Syria to Mesopotamia, setting up Baghdad as the new capital, Islam developed into a world religion in the true sense of the term, penetrating the conquered territories and extending beyond them.

The Situation of Jews and Christians in the Islamic State

The legal framework that was just outlined could give the impression that the People of the Book were able to live relatively uncontrolled under the protection of Islam. In practice, however, the picture was very different. It is true that the situation improved initially. This was the case for Jews in Iran and the Byzantine Empire, where Zoroastrianism and Christianity, respectively, had been the state religions before Islam. Neither the Zoroastrian nor the Christian state had guaranteed constitutional rights of religious minorities as was the case in Islam, where these rights were laid down in the Koran, i.e., in divine law. The situation of the Jews in these two states could do nothing but improve after the Arab conquest. The same was true in Spain. The Visigoths had severely limited the rights of the Jews; not a single synod convened that did not demand measures to force their conversion. Here, too, the Arabs were truly liberators and, in a certain respect, a flourishing culture developed in the interaction between Arabs and Jews.[242]

The situation of the Christians varied from denomination to denomination. Greek Orthodox Christians were considered suspect by the Muslims, since their ecumenical patriarch resided in Constantinople, the capital of the enemy, at least until the Turks conquered the city in 1453. This is why they were referred to as Melchites, subjects of the emperor (from the Syrian *malka),* who was considered the true leader of their church. Only members of the ancient Middle Eastern churches seemed to have a better position. The Copts, Syrians, and Armenians were Monophysites who had split off from the Greek Orthodox Church in terms of dogma and jurisdiction. Before the Arab conquest, they had been subjected to various forms of oppression by the Byzantine authorities. The Nestorians experienced a similar situation. They had suffered a long period of persecution under the Sassanids and were not able to become unified internally and externally until the sixth century. They, too, received the Arabs as liberators and experienced an apogee at the time Mesopotamia, under Abbasid rule, was the center of Islam.[243]

The North African church was colonial. Unable to win over the Berber population, it disappeared when the Arabs conquered the region and Roman culture declined. Judaism, on the other hand, found acceptance among the Berbers. Led by a *kāhina* as their "high priestess," the Judeo-Berber tribe of the Jawara resisted the Arabs until the late seventh century. The resistance collapsed with the death of the priestess, and her followers either converted to Islam or dispersed throughout the area of present-day Algeria.[244] Later, Jews also came to North Africa from the East, and, during and after the Reconquest, from Spain as well.

In signing treaties with the conquerers, the bishops and heads of communities served as representatives for their respective groups. This might have been beneficial for the Christians since they were stronger and greater in number than the Jews, and had wider, well-run, and better organization. In agreements extant from the early period, Christians are usually named as the contractual partner. As we have already seen regarding the Koran, Jews and Christians were not always clearly distinguished from each other. The agreements have been attributed to ʿUmar b. al-Khaṭṭāb, second successor to Muhammad and reigning caliph when the major Muslim conquests took place from 634–644. In principle the agreements are still valid today. Their original purpose, as demonstrated recently by Albrecht Noth, was to make it possible for Muslims to preserve their identity and to distinguish the People of the Book from the conquerers, who were at first only a small minority. They were later misinterpreted and used as an instrument of restriction and oppression.[245]

The conditions placed upon the People of the Book were partly religious and partly political and social in nature. Whatever Muslims rejected on religious grounds had to be hidden from public view and remain inconspicuous: The loud striking of the wooden clapper *(nāḳūs)* as a call to prayer instead of bells was banned; the cross, representing the greatest scandal to Muslims, was not allowed to be displayed in public; whatever was considered unclean in Islam had to be kept away from Muslims; in order to assure the separation of the two communities in public, all People of the Book had to wear identifying clothing or a belt *(zunnār);* Jews, specifically, had to sew a patch of cloth of a conspicuous color onto their clothing. Jewish and Christian men were not permitted to marry Muslim women (though the reverse was allowed); if the slave of a Jew or Christian converted to Islam, he or she had to be sold to a Muslim. Even in the case of death, separation was guaranteed. Jews and Christians were not permitted to have cemeteries near a Muslim cemetery.

Other restrictions resulted from their not belonging to the Islamic community. Protected people were excluded from military service since only Muslims were allowed to participate in the *djihād,* a religious event. Consequently, they were not allowed to carry weapons or wear military dress. Nevertheless, they were required to contribute to the waging of war. They had to take in Muslim travelers (i.e., soldiers on a military campaign) for a certain number of days, and had to keep up roads and bridges (that could be used for military purposes). They were not entitled to any war spoils of the Muslims, nor did they participate in any way in decisions regarding the spoils. They were not permitted to buy prisoners of war (as slaves). Some theologians even felt that the income from the poll tax had to be used exclusively for the *djihād*, which meant that Jews and Christians living under Muslim rule were made to finance the war against their coreligionists beyond the border.

Some stipulations were intended to humiliate the People of the Book and demonstrate the superiority of the Muslims. Thus the former were allowed to ride only donkeys or mules, they were not allowed to use a saddle, and they had to sit side-saddle. It was considered a matter of course that Jews and Christians had to offer their seats in public to a Muslim. People of the Book who dared to physically assault a Muslim lost their protected status and were declared outlaws.

Since the People of the Book were only tolerated, they had no chances to better their status; the status quo at the time the contract was signed was maintained. Of course they were permitted and even encouraged to convert to Islam, but the reverse was not allowed. Renegades were subject to death. Even converting from one of the religions of the *ahl al-dhimma* to another was not permitted. The churches and synagogues remained in the possession of the respective communities, insofar as they peaceably entered into contracts with the conquerers; otherwise they could be confiscated and converted into mosques. New churches or synagogues were not allowed to be built, though it was permitted to renovate existing buildings. As far as is known, the poll tax that was paid to the Muslims had to be gathered by the community as a whole. The heads of the respective communities were responsible to the Muslims to see that the terms of the contract were satisfied. Thus they gained power and consequently, the ethnarch [from *ethnos* (nation) and *-archos* (ruler)] emerged, a typical figure in the Islamic countries. He led the community in all secular and religious matters, exercised a high level of authority, and at times could even accumulate wealth. The ethnarch was chosen by the respective community, though approval of the Islamic authorities was required; this cleared the way for simony, i.e., the buying of offices.

In general, the situation of the *ahl al-dhimma* was mixed. Up to the tenth or eleventh century, the conditions they lived under were generally calm. They played an important role in intellectual and financial matters as scholars, physicians, merchants, and bankers, and some even climbed to high positions in the state, although this has been disputed by Muslim theorists. Nevertheless, the protected communities were all decimated by a steady stream of converts to Islam. This was less the case among Jews, who had suffered persecution even before the Arab conquest and were experienced in resistance. It is still disputed whether the treatment they received was worse than that of the Christians. It seems that Christians were less resistant to the lure of Islam. Islam was the religion of the victors and that alone made it attractive. Having enjoyed a brief revival in the Mongolian period, eastern Christianity suffered most severely from the military campaigns of Timur (1370–1405), which depopulated vast regions. Around this time at the latest, Christianity became a minority religion in areas where it had once been practiced exclusively.

In the Ottoman Empire, the status of Jews and Christians was regulated by the millet system (from Arabic *milla:* religion or religious community) and geared to conventional standards. Many Jews who were expelled from Spain in 1492 settled in areas under Ottoman rule. Since they retained their Romance language, Ladino, they formed a self-contained ethnic-religious group. However, the Jews never comprised more than a relatively small minority in the Ottoman Empire. Christians were much greater in number as a result of the Ottoman conquests in Anatolia and the Balkans, which were thoroughly Christian. As the power of the Ottoman Turks declined, the European states showed more and more interest in the Christians. A mission formed by American Protestants developed in the nineteenth century along the eastern Mediterranean. It first targeted primarily the Muslims, but due to the inherent hopelessness of the situation it soon turned its attention to the eastern Christians.[246] Protestant communities thus emerged, at first within the confines of the Western consulates and legations that enjoyed special status as of 1535 as a result of the capitulation agreements, and then as a result of missionary activities among the eastern Christians.

The situation of the *ahl al-dhimma* in the Ottoman Empire improved noticeably with the stepwise introduction of a modern constitution starting in 1839, which served to abolish essential elements of the traditional millet system. In the course of these reforms, the difference in citizen rights between Muslims and others that had determined Islamic life for more than a millenium was lifted. Now there were Ottoman citizens of the Islamic, Jewish, and Christian faiths, comparable to the situation in Europe, where the emancipation of the Jews took place at about the same time. All restrictions that had applied to Jews and Christians were removed; they were eligible for military service and, in theory, could participate fully in affairs of the state.

The Ottoman reforms were designed, among other reasons, to provide Jews and Christians with rights equal to those of the Muslims in an effort to counter the intervention of Christian powers in the internal affairs of the empire. The vast majority of Muslims did not approve of the reforms. The regulations pertaining to the *ahl al-dhimma,* which according to tradition were decreed by Caliph ᶜUmar, were not seen merely as a human act; pious Muslims believed they came from divine revelation that had been laid down in the Koran and through oral tradition. Muslims were traditionally permitted and even obliged to act in lieu of the government if it failed to satisfy its obligations. This paved the way for serious rioting against Christians in Lebanon and Syria, and led in the end to the Turkish massacres of Armenians in Anatolia toward the end of the century. This nationalistic development was brought to an inglorious end in World War I by the Young Turks.

Franz Werfel accurately illustrated the situation in his well-known novel *The Forty Days of Musa Dagh,* including a report of efforts by conservative Muslims to resist the nationalistic politics of Enver Pasha and save the Armenians through reference to Islamic laws.[247]

The persecution of Christians by no means came to an end with Atatürk's founding of the modern Republic of Turkey as a nation-state, the elimination of the sultanate and caliphate, and the absolute separation of state and Islamic tradition. The ecumenical patriarch in Constantinople had already come under attack when Greece liberated itself from Ottoman rule in 1830 in the war of independence;[248] then, the nationalistically fomented hatred toward Greeks was vented in bloody persecution. Most of the Greek population left the country at that time and the Turks that remained in Greece were sent to Turkey. The animosity still exists today. Things were not as difficult for Jews. Turkey is the only country in the Middle East that recognized the State of Israel and established diplomatic relations as soon as it was founded.

After the reforms in Turkey, the decline of the Ottoman Empire after World War I, and the achievement of national independence after World War II, most Islamic countries adopted constitutions based on Western models, but in contrast to Turkey, the others are attempting to preserve Islamic traditions. Islam has generally been declared the state religion, though at the same time freedom of religion is proclaimed, albeit with the restriction—reminiscent of former regulations—that the public order not be disturbed. The conventional special taxes and other conditions that protected people had been subject to are no longer mentioned.[249] They can also participate in the government. In a country with a large Christian minority such as Egypt, many Christians have held seats in the government in the last few decades. Heads of state normally must be Muslim, however. In Lebanon, where a majority of the population is Christian and coexistence among the different religious groups is anchored in the constitution, the president is required to be Christian and the prime minister Muslim.

Religious holidays of non-Islamic religious communities are officially recognized by the state in Iraq. Jordan has recently approved the building of four new churches for the Greek-Orthodox Palestinians. Even Saudi Arabia, which according to ᶜUmar's decree has been considered free of Christians since the seventh century, has become more open to liberal politics and in 1975 a Greek Orthodox bishop was allowed to establish a seat at al-Hasa for the Orthodox foreign laborers of Greek and Arab (Palestinian) descent. This complies with former regulations to the extent that native eastern Christians are tolerated, whereas clerics of Western denominations are generally still denied entry to the country, and it is even illegal to import Bibles. Saudi authorities seem particularly intent on keeping Muslims from having contact with Christians though participation in religious services, etc.[250] In contrast, countries with a large degree of tourism have permitted the building of churches for the spiritual welfare of visitors.

Greek and eastern Christians have always played a significant part in spreading western thought within the Islamic world. They were generally more willing than Muslims to open themselves to the West, both spiritually and economically. In the Middle Ages, this was expressed though the union with Rome, which a segment of the Eastern Rite Christian population supported. This resulted in a westernization of the church, especially in modern times, and threatened isolation from the surroundings. On the other hand, Christians long established in Arab countries greatly contributed to developments in national thought. This movement proved successful whenever it was combined with Arab nationalism. Christians initiated the renaissance of the Arabic language and literature in the nineteenth century. Many significant theorists of Arab nationalism were Christians. Parallel to this, Christian Arabs tried to present themselves as part of the Arab national culture. Scholars such as Louis Cheikho (1859–1927) have examined the Christian contribution to Arab science and culture in the Middle Ages.[251]

However, the development of a modern nation-state with a population of homogeneous citizenship is being hindered by counter forces of various kinds, above all Islamic fundamentalism, which has been represented since the 1930s in the eastern Mediterranean Arab states by the Muslim Brotherhood *(ikhwān al-muslimūn).* After the Six-Day War in 1967 and Nasser's death in 1970, conservative forces started gaining new steam in Egypt. Christians were subjected anew to restrictions: the construction of new churches was obstructed; a quota system was instituted regarding university admissions; Christians were barred from high government positions; polemics started appearing with attacks on the Christian faith; Christians were accused of complicity to Zionism as a result of the Second Vatican Council's declaration on Judaism.[252] In Pakistan, which was the first modern state established that was essentially Muslim (Pakistan means "land of the pure," i.e., of the Muslims), fundamentalism gained ground through the activities of spiritual leaders such as Abūʾl-Aʿlā al-Mawdūdī (1903–1979), who supported efforts for the creation of an Islamic state in which Jews, Christians, and other minorities would be treated as *ahl al-dhimma*, as was common in the beginnings of Islam, allowing only minor concessions to recent developments.[253] Mawdūdī was a prolific writer and his influence far-reaching.[254] Many of his ideas have already been implemented in the constitution of the Islamic Republic of Iran. Religious minorities are represented in the parliament, but members of these groups are more or less treated as in earlier times, which implies that only those religious communities are recognized that were already present when Islam was brought to Persia. The Bahāʾī are regarded as renegades, since this religion did not emerge in Persia until the nineteenth century and its members were, in its early stage, ex-Muslims. They are considered to have basically forfeited their lives, as demonstrated by trials and the resulting death penalties Bahāʾī have received.[255] In Turkey, too, fundamentalism—having been previously defrocked by Atatürk—has been on the rise since the 1980 military coup, with all the related negative consequences for the religious minorities. Since then, the situation has undergone several changes. Concessions have been made to the Roman Catholic Christians; this suggests that attitudes toward the Greeks is determined in part by the conflict on Cyprus, which has been ongoing since 1974. Other Christian denominations also suffered greatly, especially the Christians of Tur Abdin ["mountain of the servants (of God)"] in the highlands southeast of Diyarbakir. The Christians there were Monophysites and spoke (Turoyo) Aramaic. They had been settled there since early Christian times, and churches and monasteries covered the area. For reasons nonreligious in nature, which must be sought in Turkish policies against other national minorities as well, such as the Kurds, the Christian population had to leave their homeland, most of them resettling in Germany.

In principle Jews and Christians faced the same legal situation. Muhammad's attitude toward the Jews was stricter than it was toward the Christians, though according to recent research he worked closely with the Jews in Medina. His secretary, who also helped prepare the Koran, was a Jew who had converted to Islam.[256] The Jews had more in common with Islam than the Christians did, as regards uncompromised monotheism for example, which is a point of contention between Muslims and Christians, but which Jews and Muslims share. Jews were also constantly oppressed under Christian rule and could welcome the Muslims to some extent as liberators. This was the case especially in Spain, where, after being a persecuted minority under the Visigoths, they became a community under Islamic rule that contributed considerably to cultural developments. This was also true in other parts of the Islamic world. Bernard Lewis has even spoken of a "Jewish-Islamic symbiosis." There were certainly also times and regions where the situation of the Jews was less favorable, but it would be somewhat rash to speak of a fundamentally hostile attitude of Muslims toward Jews. In any case, ethnically and racially grounded antisemitism did not exist.[257] As a prominent Muslim scholar noted, "Of the three great Semitic religions, Islam is the least conscious of race and ethnicity."[258] This should by no means conceal the fact that although the Jews, like the Christians, were tolerated, they were denied full civil rights and were subject to numerous other prejudices. Their situation improved considerably in the nineteenth century in areas that were directly influenced by Europe, such as Algeria as of 1830, and in areas that came under European control, such as Egypt in 1882. On the fringes, such as in Yemen and Morocco, Jews lived under medieval conditions and could hardly reckon with external protection. Especially in Morocco, they suffered oppression and degradation by the Muslims. They were forced to live in ghettos, had to walk barefoot in the cities, and had to be recognizable as Jews through their dress. They had to endure maltreatment, even by adolescents, and were not allowed to have public synagogues, which were allowed in other Islamic countries. Even foreign Jews who visited the country on business had to conform to the same regulations regarding dress and conduct that applied to their Moroccan coreligionists. The easing of restrictions that the well-known Jewish philanthropist Sir Moses Montefiore succeeded in getting the sultan to approve applied only in the port cities.[259] Jews were faced with other hardships in Palestine. At Easter time they had to be protected by Ottoman authorities from the fanaticism of Greek Orthodox pilgrims.[260] On the other hand, they remained almost entirely untouched by the Christian massacre in Damascus in 1860. Consequently, they were accused by eastern Christians of having participated in the unrest.[261] The situation of the Jews in Islamic countries improved when the Alliance Israélite (est. 1860) and the Anglo-Jewish Association (est. 1871) started taking up their concerns. The significance of these organizations for Jews was similar to that of the union with Rome and the mission for the Christians.

Islam in Europe; Islamic Missionization

Islam and Christianity remained two separate worlds well into modern times. Whereas Christian traders and diplomats had little difficulty visiting Islamic countries and possibly even settling there, Muslims always had strong reservations against traveling in Christian regions, not to mention settling there. It was only possible to live according to the laws and regulations of Islam, without being forced to make compromises, in an Islamic country and under the protection of the Islamic community. This pertained to, for example, maintaining ritual purity, observing dietary laws, fulfilling legal transactions, and many other spheres. Hardly a human activity exists that is not somehow subjected to religious laws and regulations. Under the given circumstances it is not surprising that up to the eighteenth century, most Muslims that went to Europe, aside from the few legates and other diplomats, were prisoners of war; a religious Muslim would not dream of voluntarily entering the "house of war" for peaceful purposes. The captivity usually led to conversion, whether forced or of free will, though this was often merely feigned. The situation did not change until the era of the

Enlightenment, when Frederick the Great, for example, said "if Turks and heathens come and want to populate the country, then we shall wish to build mosques and churches for them."[262] The king did in fact accept Muslims into his services who came to Germany as scattered soldiers during the Russo-Turkish Wars and granted them freedom of religious expression.

Though Muslims were merely tolerated during the Enlightenment, they were guaranteed full freedom of movement in the Christian world following the Revolution of 1789 in France, and following the introduction of modern constitutions in the nineteenth century in most European countries (in Spain not until 1968). In the course of political developments, the number of Muslims immigrating to European countries has grown in inconceivable proportions since the mid-nineteenth century. In Europe and overseas, Muslims have formed local communities and regional associations, mostly on a private basis.[263] Centralized organizations in the Islamic world have started dealing with their concerns and the idea of spreading Islam through planned missionary activities has entered their field of vision. The oldest organization of this kind, the Islamic World Congress (Muʾtamar al-ʿālam al-islāmī) was founded in 1949 in Karachi. The Muslim World League (Rābiṭat al-ʿālam al-islāmī) followed in Mecca in 1962. Both of these have a more or less informal character. A central body, the Organization of the Islamic Conference (Munaẓẓamat al-muʾtamar al-islāmī), was founded at a government level in the early 1970s with its headquarters in Jidda.[264] The Congress and the League have divided their services such that the former is responsible for affairs within the Islamic world and the latter deals with the Muslim diaspora. The League has been publishing a magazine since 1974, which also appears in English as the *Journal of the Muslim World League.*

Despite all these endeavors to establish a centralized organization, implementing and preserving unity in Islam is becoming more and more difficult, as it is for Judaism and Christianity as well. Khomeini's rise to power divided the Islamic world. Iran and Libya founded the International Islamic Council and the Islamic World Organization in opposition to the existing Congress and League. It seemed natural that Islam, weakened by internal strife and the predominance of the West, would look to Rome for practical solutions, taking the papacy and the Catholic Church, with its internal unity and missionary strength, as a model. A high-ranking Kuwaiti official stated in 1968 that a "Vatican-type" organization should be created by the Islamic states to supervise the affairs of the Islamic world.[265] In 1984, it was publicized in the media that a convention of Muslim scholars in Cairo called for centralized leadership and suggested Azhar University as a suitable site to be declared extraterritorial like Vatican City.

As regards organized missionary activities, it must be noted that these had been foreign to Islam. Its appeal was seen in its mere existence, and it had more converts than most other religions. Even the Muslims who brought Islam to southern Asia and sub-Saharan Africa were not primarily missionaries. They came for business purposes and through their economic predominance they had an impact economically and culturally. It is certainly no coincidence that the notion of organized Islamic missionary work developed first in India, where the relevant activities of the Anglican church and other Christian communities among Hindus and Muslims had served as a model.[266] And it is not surprising that a group within Islam that is considered sectarian by the orthodox was the first to plan and carry out missionary activities. This was the Ahmadiyya, founded in northern India in the late nineteenth century; its more radical wing viewed their founder, Mirza Ghulam Ahmad, as the new prophet, thus placing themselves outside traditional Islam.[267] The founder combined eschatological ideas from both Islam and Christianity, which certainly added to the attraction of this movement, bringing success in Africa and Europe. Their missionary methods were based on a Christian model. Thus their preaching was done in the native language, the Koran was translated, adaptations were made to correspond to the culture and mentality of the target group, and schools, day care facilities, and hospitals were established. Their success is impressive, though greater in Africa than in Europe and North America. The number of members is estimated by the Ahmadiyya to be several million. Their activities have been considerably hindered, however, since this wing of the Ahmadiyya was declared an anti-Islamic sect in 1974 and expelled from the world Islamic community. In Rabwa,[268] near Lahore (Lāhaur) in Pakistan, where their center is located, they suffered bloody persecution.[269] The other wing of the Ahmadiyya, the Ahmadiyya Society for the Spread of Islam (Ahmadiyya andjuman-i ishāᶜat-i islām), views the founder not as a prophet but a reformer *(mudjaddid),* thus remaining within the sphere of orthodox Islam. They do missionary work for Islam using Koran translations and a wealth of modern writings, particularly in the English-speaking realm. Their European center is in Woking, near London.

The Ahmadiyya represent only one of many efforts of Islam and Islamic groups to gain followers in the West. The widespread search for a new religious orientation has led throughout the Western world to an increasing number of converts. This is at least in part due to efforts undertaken by the central Islamic organizations. In addition to addressing the concerns of immigrant Muslim communities, they have taken up missionary activities among the native populations; even Iranian Islam was (and is) participating. In view of the greater task of winning over the world of unbelievers for Islam, the Shiᶜites were (and are) willing to put aside denominational differences between them and the Sunnis. There seemed to be fertile ground after World War II; and after the failures of communism and materialism, Islam was seen as in a position to give life new meaning, to end exploitation and oppression, and to challenge the decline in moral standards. Islam aimed to harmonize the spiritual and material aspects of being, bringing faith, justice, and freedom.[270] The Muslim World League included spreading the message of Islam *(daᶜwa)* as a goal in their rules when it was founded in 1962. Later on, it developed a program for missionary activities that, like the Ahmadiyya, was modelled in many details on Christian missionary efforts. It called for missionary schools in all theology departments at Islamic universities; a standing conference of Muslim theologians to advise on the worldwide preaching of Islam; an Islamic solidarity fund to promote the *daᶜwa;* a major broadcasting center "Voice of Islam" in Jidda; a modern Koran printing works, including an office for the express purpose of circulating the Koran in Europe, Asia, and Africa; and a health and social service center operated within the scope of missionary activities.[271]

In recent years, initiatives have been started at denominational and national levels regarding the issue of missionization. Not related to the Congress, the Society for the Islamic World Mission was founded in 1983 in Karachi. Muslims in Bengal founded an Islamic Mission in the United Kingdom, which targets Germany and Spain in addition to England. Egypt has also been active. Azhar University changed its curriculum in 1973–74 to focus on Koran study instead of law and the study of traditional writings. This was intended to give members of other faiths the chance to judge Islam based on its core and thus form a more sound opinion. Missionaries are supposed to take intensive English classes in order to be prepared for activities in western Europe and North America. *Mimbar al-islām* (Pulpit of Islam), with the subtitle "Journal for Islamic Culture," is the official publication of the High Council for Islamic Affairs; founded in 1960, it planned to publish editions in European languages for missionary purposes, in addition to the Arabic edition.[272]

Of the many activities that have been carried out, those with regard to Japan deserve special mention. The country holds a special position in the Islamic mission movement. It is considered promising for missionary efforts because of its resistance to Christianity. There is an Islam Congress of Japan, which places copies of the Koran in all hotel rooms, similar to the Gideon Bible Society. In addition, it aims to present every Japanese household with a copy of the Holy Book of Islam. The Islamic World Congress is also active in Japan; at its 1981 meeting in Tokyo, it started a worldwide movement for a comprehensive and just peace.

Dialogue instead of Missionization

As Muslims started developing missionary activities, Christians were shifting their focus from missionization to dialogue. This represented a development that has long since been completed with respect to international law, i.e., that sovereign states recognize each other as legitimate and equal partners. Efforts to engage in dialogue had been made by individuals and private groups before churches and religious institutions started taking up the cause. The Muslim-Christian dialogue started in France, since North Africa was an obvious place to initiate activities. Charles Lavigerie (1825–1892), who became the archbishop of Algiers in 1867, founded the Order of Our Dear Lady of Africa, with the White Fathers and White Sisters, to organize activities among the Muslims.At the time of its founding, the goals were still those of a traditional mission. Charles de Foucauld (1858–1916) initiated a transitional stage: He settled as a hermit among the Tuareg in the Ahaggar and wanted to set an example through his actions. He has been emulated by members of the religious order of the Petits Frères and Petites Soeurs de Jésus since 1930. Also following this tradition was the Benedictine Abbey founded after the Second World War in Tilimsān (Algeria) by Raphael Walzer, former abbot primate of Beuron. It aimed to further understanding between Muslims and Christians, but had to be abandoned because of the opposition it met from the indigenous population. Louis Massignon (1883–1962), theologian and Middle Eastern scholar, went yet a step further. He showed considerable sensitivity in his in-depth involvement with Islamic mysticism and attempted in this way to draw connections to Islam. Through his efforts, the Dar el-salam ("House of Peace") institute was set up in 1940 in Cairo. It is a meeting place for Christians and Muslims to participate in joint religious events and lectures on a wide variety of subjects concerning religion and culture in Islam and Christianity. Since 1951 lectures by Christians and Muslims have been held every Tuesday, and they are published in the *Mardis de Dar el-salam* journal.[273]

Louis Massignon was the person who finally succeeded in taking the step from mission to dialogue. Numerous Catholic and Protestant institutions have since taken on the task of dialogue. With respect to the Protestants, the impetus came from the United States, where a strong missionary movement in the Middle East had emerged in the nineteenth century. It was believed that converting Muslims to Christianity would hasten the Second Coming of Christ, which is being awaited as a herald of the Last Judgment. Missionary efforts aimed at Muslims proved unsuccessful, as had been expected, though continued interest in Islam was expressed in the United States. A decisive event was a discussion between Muslims and Christians held in 1954 in

Bhamdoun, organized by the American Friends of the Middle East association. One resolution that came out of that meeting was to establish the World Fellowship of Muslims and Christians. Subsequently, a series of meetings on the Islamic-Christian dialogue have taken place among various groups and organizations in Lebanon. In 1965 in Beirut, a lecture series on Christianity and Islam took place in Coenaculum, a cultural center opened in 1946. The response was so positive that it was resolved to set up an Institute for Comparative Religion. At the time, there was considerable optimism regarding the domestic situation and future of the country. The manifesto published after the event characterized Lebanon as an "especially appropriate site for a coming together of Christianity and Islam."[274]

The goals of a dialogue received a decisive impetus on October 28, 1965 at the Second Vatican Council through the "Declaration on the Relationship of the Church to non-Christian Religions," called the Nostra Aetate. It consists of five chapters: Chapter 1 refers to the one and only community of all nations, as willed by God, and to the fact that God's "providence, the proof of his goodness, and his advice for salvation" refer to all of humanity. Chapter 2 deals with the relationship of Catholicism to Hinduism, Buddhism, and the "other religions throughout the world." Chapter 3 is dedicated to Islam; chapter 4 to the Jews, the "house of Abraham," to which the Christians are related in faith. In chapter 5, Catholics are urged to display brotherly attitudes toward non-Christian religions. Any discrimination of a person "on the basis of race or skin color, status or religion" is rejected "since this is in contradiction with the spirit of Christ."[275]

Jews and Muslims are also referred to in the "Dogmatic Constitution of the Church," called the Lumen Gentium, the former because "from their flesh and blood came Christ" (Rom. 9:5 JB); the latter because they believe in the God of Abraham (chap. 2, no. 16).[276] The Palestinian issue, the most crucial topic in the envisaged dialogue, is reflected in the fact that all of chapter 3 of the Nostra Aetate is devoted to Islam. Originally, the declaration was supposed to be limited to the relationship of the church to Judaism. After Arab protests against the initial version, which treated Judaism as well as other non-Christian religions, but failed to grant Islam individual consideration, amendments were made and the current version was passed in November 1964. Common ground was emphasized, including monotheistic faith in God the Creator and in divine revelation; obedience to God's instruction; veneration of Jesus as a prophet; veneration of Mary; belief in the resurrection of the dead and the Last Judgment; common aspects in terms of ethics and piety. Muhammad was not mentioned, since it would then have been necessary to make a statement on his prophethood. The declaration did, however, include a statement that Muslims do not recognize Jesus as God, to insure that they could identify with the explanation as pertaining to their faith. Catholics (and Muslims: "all") were asked "to strive for mutual understanding and work together for the protection and promotion of social justice, the moral good, and especially peace and freedom for all of humanity."

This declaration represents the fruits of efforts by Louis Massignon and other pioneers of Christian-Islamic understanding. It has had both organizational and practical consequences. The newly formed Secretariat for Non-Christian Affairs in the Vatican established a division for Muslim relations. This division publishes three bulletins annually and has also published a handbook for the dialogue.[277] To support the dialogue in academic circles, the Pontificio Istituto di Studi Arabi e d'Islamistica was founded in Rome. It is run by members of the Order of the White Fathers and holds colloquiums and publishes relevant literature including, since 1975, the journal *Islamochristiana* (with an extensive bibliography of literature related to the dialogue).

After the Catholic church expressed support for a dialogue through Vatican II, and Protestant churches showed similar interest, international bodies of Protestantism, the Oriental Churches and the Greek Orthodox Church passed corresponding resolutions. At the 1969 meeting of the World Mission and Evangelism Division of the World Council of Churches in Canterbury, a subdivision was set up called Dialogue with Peoples of Living Faiths and Ideologies (DFI). The first major meeting took place in 1972 in Broummana, Lebanon, after the World Council of Churches discussed the issue of dialogue at their 1971 meeting in Addis Ababa and defined the following goals of a dialogue: Joint actions in the service of people in pluralistic societies;

improved mutual understanding; embedding Christianity in different cultures.[278] There was consensus at the meeting in Broummana to refer to Islam and Christianity not as two religions, but as two "traditions."[279]

There has been varied response to the Western willingness to dialogue by Christians living in Islamic countries, since they are directly impacted by such dialogue and are forced to confront the current problems of coexistence. The Vatican declaration on the issue of Judaism, chapter 4 of the Nostra Aetate, brought outrage from Christians living "on the front," since it could be interpreted as a statement in favor of Zionism. After Vatican II initially accepted the statement in November 1964, the head of the Jacobite Church, patriarch of Antioch Mar Ignatius Yaᶜqūb, issued his own statement on the issue of Judaism, from his residence in Damascus. Based on a large selection of quotes from the New Testament, he strove to prove the responsibility of the Jews for the death of Jesus and the resulting consequences for Judaism.[280]

It is doubtful whether the statement of the Jacobite patriarch helped to win the favor of the Muslims. As I shall explain below, the Muslims had not objected to the Vatican statement on Judaism. In any case, the Greek Orthodox church refrained from trying to win over Arabs, i.e., Muslims, by condemning the Jews, and, at the plenary session of the World Council of Churches in Addis Ababa, it demanded that missionary activities be abandoned, instead calling for the initiation of a dialogue. The generally positive atmosphere proved able to assert itself.[281] On neutral territory, in Boston, there was a first meeting between Orthodox and Muslim theologians in 1985. The synodal commission of the ecumentical patriarch organized the meeting, where questions of spirituality, the relationship of Islam to Judaism and Christianity in the Koran, religious policy in the Ottoman Empire, etc. were discussed.[282]

Aside from the abovementioned Catholic institutions, many institutions were established at denominational, ecumenical, national, or international levels, and meetings, colloquiums, and conferences of different kinds have taken place. Numerous study centers, some of which have adapted their programs in view of the dialogue, deal with relevant questions. One of the most significant is the Hartford

Seminary Foundation in Hartford, Connecticut; it publishes a journal called *The Muslim World.* From 1911 to 1947 it was subtitled "A quarterly review of current events . . . and the progress of Christian missions in Moslem lands"; since 1948 it reads: "A quarterly journal of Islamic study and of Christian interpretation among Muslims." Islamic activities in the dialogue include the Islamic Foundation, founded in 1966 in Leicester, England. The foundation publishes *Study Papers, Situation Reports, Documents,* and *Christianity, a Series of Bibliographies.* The Centre for the Study of Islam and Christian-Muslim Relations, affiliated with Selly Oaks College in Birmingham, publishes *Research Papers, Muslims in Europe, News of Muslims in Europe, Bimurca, Bulletin on Islam and Christian-Muslim Relations in Africa, Newsletters,* and the journal *Islam and Christian-Muslim Relations* (since 1990). The Henry Martyn Institute in Hyderabad, which had been founded in the nineteenth century for missionary activities among the Muslims in India,[283] has also changed its program; since 1972 it has been publishing the *Bulletin of the Christian Institutes of Islamic Studies.*

Muslims have not only participated in events initiated by Christians, but have also developed their own activities and have supported the dialogue, as is stated in the Koran: "Dispute not with the People of the Book save in the fairer manner" (29:46). There has, however, been some resistance from the conservative camp. In his reply to the 1968 New Year's address of Pope Paul VI to the heads of all religions of the world, Pakistani theologian Abūᵓl-Aᶜlā al-Mawdūdī, known for his fundamentalist theories, protested Christian missionary work, especially in southern Sudan, and the attacks of Christian scholars against Islam. In the political sphere, he demanded that the church desist from all support of Israel (the Six-Day War was still fresh in his mind). He also rejected the suggestion to internationalize Jerusalem, which was supposedly made by the Vatican.[284]

The Muslim world, represented by its central organizations, accepted in principle the offer of a dialogue with Christians, albeit with restrictions that develop due to current events, as we shall see. The Islamic World Congress dealt with the issue of a dialogue for the first time at a meeting in Beirut in 1973. Two years later the Congress had defined its relationship to the Catholic church and called upon the Protestant church to enter the dialogue as well. A key conference on the Christian-Islamic dialogue with fifteen representatives from each side and 300 observers took place in Tripoli, Libya, in 1976. We shall return to this later.

Due to the improved climate, Muslims are beginning to learn about Christian theology and philosophy, thus creating the complement to Western study of Islam. To name only a few examples, the University of Tehran held a two-day colloquium in 1974 in commemoration of the 700th anniversary of the death of St. Thomas Aquinas. The subject of the opening lecture was "The Ecumenical Ideas of St. Thomas Aquinas."[285] A King Faisal chair was created at the University of California for the study of the religion and culture of Islam. This is designed to provide non-Muslims with a chance to study the science of Islam at Saudi Arabian universities.[286]

Muslims have also opened up to discourse with Jews. Of course, the actual impact of the dialogue in this direction is still minimal. The Vatican II declaration on Judaism enraged eastern Christians because they feared its being used by Arabs to question the solidarity with Arabs that Christians have shown. The declaration was generally accepted by Muslims, after initial objections were resolved. Local Christians took exception to the exoneration of the Jews regarding the death of Jesus, since they felt this was contradicted by testimony in their Scriptures. A rumor evidently circulated in Nazareth that the Council intended to "correct" the New Testament and remove entire sections. Maronite archbishop Khoury also had to devote a sermon to dismissing the same rumor.[287] Muslims did not feel affected by the statement of the Vatican since they view this text from the New Testament to be not authentic. In other words, since Jesus was not killed, the question of Jewish guilt is moot.

The real acid test, however, is the dialogue between Jews and Muslims in the State of Israel, where the Muslim population is largely identical with the Arab population. Here, dialogue has a dual function; it is religious as well as political, and it is often difficult to say which of the two sides of the same coin is more important. It was already acknowledged in the 1920s that understanding must be sought with the

Arabs. Organizations and associations have varied considerably, using different methods and programs in pursuing the single goal of mutual understanding: first the Peace Association (Berit Shalom), then the League for Jewish-Arab Understanding, and finally Unity (Ihud). The last named is the only one of the three that survived for a few years beyond the founding of the State of Israel. These efforts were aimed primarily toward political and cultural spheres. It is much more difficult to implement peaceful coexistence in everyday life. The recent founding of the Neveh Shalom settlement (Settlement of Peace) near Latroun by Bruno Hussar, a Dominican friar, was an attempt to bring together Jews and Arabs (Muslims) in a village community. A "peace school" allows visitors from Israel and abroad to experience for themselves and study the problems of diverse ethnic and religious groups living together.

Dialogues between Christians and Jews, Jews and Muslims, Muslims and Christians invariably lead to the desire for a trialogue. Shortly after the Vatican II declaration in 1965, a standing conference of Jews, Christians, and Muslims in Europe was formed. For several years it has been conducting international study seminars in the Hedwig Dransfeld House in Bendorf.[288] The Paris organization Fraternité d'Abraham, founded in 1967, also serves understanding between Jews, Christians, and Muslims. It holds monthly meetings, chooses different subjects for discussion, and has been publishing a quarterly newspaper since 1975.[289] Since 1974, the "Rencontres de Sénanque entre Juifs, Chrétiens et Musulmans" has been taking place in the Provençal Sénanque Abbey, the mother house of the Cistercians of the Immaculate Conception.[290] Efforts for a trialogue are being undertaken in the United States as well. The Interreligious Peace Colloquium in Washington, D.C. organized a conference in Lisbon, Portugal in 1977 called "The Muslim-Jewish-Christian Conference on the Changing World Order: Challenge to our Faiths."[291] The Kennedy Institute of Ethics at Georgetown University in Washington, D.C. is an interreligious research center. In 1978 a "Jewish-Christian-Muslim Ongoing Trialogue Group" was formed there and several colloquiums are held each year on different subjects.[292] In Egypt, too, after the peace treaty was signed with Israel, bringing together the three religions was at least the subject of discussion. Sadat had planned to set up a shrine dedicated to the three religions on Djebel Musa, Sinai, where Moses received the Tablets according to the Christian and Muslim traditions. Sadat also wanted to be buried there. The abbot of the St. Catherine monastery and archbishop of Sinai suggested instead to declare the mountain exempt, as the holy shrine of Judaism, Christianity, and Islam.[293]

The notion of trialogue also became popular in South America, where there are large Jewish and Muslim populations. One relevant event was the dedication of the Plaza Maimonides in Buenos Aires in autumn 1986. Representatives of the Jewish, Christian, and Muslim communities were present. Maimonides was called the "father of the dialogue between the great monotheistic religions." At about the same time, the International Council of Christians and Jews convened in Salamanca, and Muslims also participated in the sessions.[294]

Conditions for a Dialogue and Its Subject Matter

Dialogue has been defined as "the serious address and response between two or more persons, in which the being and truth of each is confronted by the being and truth of the other."[295] It presupposes that the partners have a certain level of awareness of each other and it aims to further this awareness. Muslims can look back on a long tradition of interaction with Jews and Christians, since they came into contact with each other from the very beginnings of Islam. Jews and Christians that converted to Islam brought information with them that could be exploited for apologetics and polemics. An early example of this is ʿAlī b. Rabbān al-Ṭabarī, a Jew who converted to Islam. He wrote a book under Caliph al-Mutawakkil in the mid-3rd/9th century, in which he used numerous Bible quotations in an effort to prove that Muhammad was the Messiah prophesied in the Bible.[296]

But the Muslims did not have to rely on converts in order to become familiar with the Bible and the New Testament. In monasteries in Palestine, the Bible had already been translated into Arabic at a very early stage, so Muslims had access to it if they so desired.[297] The

Spanish Muslim Ibn Ḥazm, who lived in the 4th/11th century, had exceptional knowledge of the Bible. He prepared a monumental work on the history of religion using numerous Bible quotations to prove that the Scriptures of the People of the Book *(ahl al-kitāb)* were falsifications. In doing this, he was taking up and intensifying an accusation that Muhammad had made against the Jews because of how they dealt with the Bible.[298] In order to refute the Christian claim that Jesus was crucified, Ibrāhīm b. ʿUmar al-Biḳāʿī, who lived in the 9th/15th century in Damascus, quoted extensively and verbatim from the Passion of Jesus as it is told in the Gospels, in his Koran commentary to sura 4:157, where Jesus' death on the cross is denied.[299] This is only a brief sampling from the long list of Muslims who were extremely well-versed in the Bible.

In contrast to this, the Koran did not become available in the West until about 500 years after Muhammad's time, via the Latin translation that Peter the Venerable of Cluny had commissioned in Spain. Since the early nineteenth century, Muslims were becoming increasingly proficient in Western languages; at the same time they became familiar with the results of historical, critical Bible exegesis, thereby acquiring new material for the thesis that Christians do not possess the complete and unadulterated teachings of Jesus. Rahmatullah of Delhi dedicated several hundred pages of his work opposing the Christian mission in India, *Iẓhār al-ḥaḳḳ* (Manifestation of the Truth), to this topic. He cited extensively from Christian exegetic literature that he had access to in English.[300]

Muslims welcomed converts to impart knowledge of Jewish or Christian teachings, because they had little trust in followers of Moses or Jesus. That was the case in the early period and it remains just as valid today. A former priest of the Chaldeans, an Eastern Rite church in union with Rome, wrote a treatment after converting to Islam using scholarly theological literature of Western provenance to prove that the biblical prophecy of the Messiah was referring to Muhammad. The author was a follower of the Ahmadiyya, but that does not impact the fundamental arguments used.[301] Muslims could make use of two—i.e., the Jewish and the Christian—interpretations regarding questions of Muhammad's being prophesied in Jewish and Christian Scripture. Old

Testament passages that Jews applied to the Messiah were interpreted by Christians as referring to Jesus. These passages were interpreted by Muslims as referring not to Jesus, but to Muhammad. Passages in the New Testament where Jesus speaks of the "Comforter" (Paraclete, John 14:26, 15:26) or the coming of the kingdom of God were applied to Muhammad and Islam.

The confrontation of Muslims with the Bible is a major subject in Muslim polemical, apologetic literature. On the one hand, the Bible serves to provide evidence of the falsification of the Scripture *(taḥrīf* and *tabdīl);* on the other hand, it is used to attest to Muhammad's prophetic mission and present Islam as being founded by God's will. This argumentation becomes untenable if a radical falsification of Scripture is assumed, as some Muslim polemicists have done, such as Ibn Ḥazm, who was mentioned above. Others critics do not go quite that far and assume that the Bible of the Jews and Christians offers by and large the unabridged and unadulterated text; the charge of *tabdīl* and *taḥrīf* applies solely to the interpretation. Ibn Taymiyya (died 728/1328), an archconservative theologian from Damascus who influenced Sa'udi Wahhabism and is still highly esteemed today, represented both positions. Depending on his needs, he regarded the Bible either as fundamentally falsified or he rejected merely the Jewish or Christian exegesis.[302]

Debate about the Bible is a central aspect of polemics against the Jews. Muslim theologians generally accuse them of misinterpreting the contents of the Bible. Another issue in discourse with Jews is the question of Judaism being abrogated, i.e., replaced, by Islam, which is seen as the complete and final revelation. A third point involves the evidence for Muhammad's prophethood.[303]

Polemics and apologetics against Christians span a wider spectrum than those against the Jews. This developed out of the mere fact that, in terms of number, Christians were far more powerful than the Jews and the foreign policies of Islamic states were greatly influenced by their contact with Christian Europe. Debate about the nature of the Scripture and its interpretation also played a role in anti-Christian polemics. Muslims renounce the Christian doctrine of Jesus having both a divine and a human nature, rejecting it as incompatible with the oneness of God. That also encompasses opposition to the Trinity doctrine, which Muhammad had clearly spoken out against. Muslim denial of Jesus' Crucifixion necessitates a rejection of the Christian dogma of redemption, which focusses on Jesus dying as a sacrifice offered for the sins of humanity. According to Muslim interpretation, Jesus' teachings coincided exactly with Islam, but they were distorted by Paul the Apostle and assumed their present form as accepted by Christians. Other polemicists held Constantine the Great responsible for falsifying Jesus' teachings, incorrectly assuming he declared Jesus' teachings to be the state religion of the Holy Roman Empire.

According to Muslim belief, Jesus will not be a judge at the Last Judgment, corresponding to Christian doctrine, but a witness for the true faith of his followers, who did not go astray by following Paul. Other points of contention involve daily practices, i.e., the lacking ritual purity of the Christians, dietary laws, marriage law, etc.

In the course of its history, Islam produced a wealth of apologetic, polemical literature directed against Jews and Christians.[304] Great theologians such as al-Ghazālī (died 505/111), who became known for his work *Iḥyāʾ ʿulūm al-dīn* (Renewal of the Religious Sciences), have dealt with this subject,[305] as have poets, especially the Egyptian Muhammad b. Saʿīd al-Būṣīrī (7th/13th century), famous for his panegyrics to Muhammad.[306] The controversy is still very much alive and the subjects have not changed, even if contemporary Muslim theologians know Christianity, its emotionality and forms of organization, much better than their counterparts in the Middle Ages and early Modern Age did.[307] A serious impediment to fruitful discussion is the unwillingness and, for reasons that must be sought in the intellectual history of the Middle East, the incapability of Muslims to turn to methods of historical criticism when dealing with theological matters. Furthermore, most Christian teachings dealt with and attacked in the Koran have been supported by only a minority of Eastern or Western Christians, both in the past and at present.[308]

That which has been presented here is certainly adequate to show that dialogue among the three religions faces great obstacles since it requires that all three accept each other as equals and realize that allowing controversial points to exist side by side does not mean abandoning one's own position. It is all the more remarkable that there has been a virtually unfathomable number of conferences, seminars, and other events on the topic since the mid-1960s. Only two of the most important events shall be described here. The First International Muslim-Christian Congress was held in 1974 in Cordova. Delegations from more than twenty Islamic countries participated in the meeting, which according to organizer Mikel de Epalza was eminently practice-oriented. As de Epalza reported, main topics of discussion were:

(1) The presentation of Islam by and for Christians in such a manner that the Muslims would recognize their faith and would feel that justice was done to it.

(2) The presentation of Christianity by and for Muslims in such a manner that the Christians would recognize their faith and would feel that justice was done to it.

(3) The relationship between political and religious expansion.

(4) Contemporary forms for religious education in Islam and Christianity.

(5) Concrete fields for joint action and cooperation between Muslims and Christians.

Controversial questions of dogma were excluded totally. A highlight of the event was the Islamic Friday prayer *(ṣalāt al-djumᶜa).* It was held in the cathedral of Cordova, the former Great Mosque that had been converted to a church by Ferdinand III of Castile after the Reconquest in 1236. The essential architectural structures were preserved and not until later was a Gothic building erected within the mosque. We shall return to this issue below.

Political controversy could not be totally avoided in Cordova. A series of resolutions were passed with a clear political message: The PLO should be recognized as the only legitimate representative for the Palestinians. The Arab character of Jerusalem should be maintained. Israeli aggression in the Aqsa Mosque should be condemned (this refers to the arson attack by a mentally deranged person in 1969). Actions should be undertaken to liberate the territories occupied by Israel.[309]

It also proved inevitable that current political affairs be incorporated into the discourse at the seminar on the Islamic-Christian dialogue in 1976 in Tripoli (the second event to be described here), organized by the Libyan head of state. The concluding resolution consisted of twenty-four points.[310] It is a good example through which to illustrate the chances and limitations of the dialogue. Points 1 and 2 were worded such that they resembled the two parts of the Islamic profession of faith: the one and only God and the divine mission of Muhammad. Mention of monotheistic faith common to both religions was followed by a sentence in which the prophets in general were honored. This was designed to appease the Christians who could not accept reference to Muhammad's prophethood. The prophets were called the "prophets of the revealed religion." This corresponds to referring to the Holy Scriptures of the two religions jointly in point 12 as "revealed Books." The wording seems to have escaped the attention of the Christian participants, who apparently had difficulty understanding the Arabic text. Unwittingly, they acknowledged the Koran as a revealed book. After the profession of faith came a survey of the significance of religion in ethics and the organization of state and society (points 3–7). The next section dealt with freedom of religion, world peace and arms limitations, harmony of science and religion, and the religious education of the younger generation (points 8–11). Issues were then raised that had led to controversy in the past, i.e., the assessment of each religion's Holy Scriptures by the other religion, and the seizure of places of worship. In order to avoid misunderstandings, it was resolved that the "revealed Books" be translated (point 12). The Christians hoped Muslims would engage in "historical research" and studies of the Holy Scripture (Old and New Testaments) in order to better understand and accurately judge them (point 13). Muslims were urged to abandon the old accusation made against Christians (and Jews) that they falsified Scripture. Points 15–17 form a block; they dealt with revising school textbooks, exchanging university lecturers, and refraining from exerting pressure on adherents of the other faith to convert. As far as school textbooks are concerned, Christians were interested in consulting Muslim theologians regarding everything that had to do with the presentation of Islam, and refusing to accept anything they did not approve. The civil war in Lebanon was criticized in point 18. It was stated that it was not a war of religion; and a division of the country was rejected. Scientific and technical developments in the Third World and a just distribution of goods among industrialized and developing countries were the subject of point 19. The situation of Muslims in the Philippines was briefly mentioned and a resolution of the conflict was urged (point 22). Finally, the institution of a mixed commission for the implementation of the resolutions was considered.

Points 14, 20, and 21 were skipped over here, since they require special treatment. Point 14 was worded as follows: "The Muslims request the Christians to do everything in their power to separate the church from the mosque in Cordova. This should be implemented as soon as possible." In order to understand what this means, some elaboration of the comments made above about the Cordova mosque are necessary. The cathedral of Cordova was built as a mosque by Muslims in the eighth to tenth centuries. When Christians reconquered the city, they converted it into a church. This explains the name "la Mezquita" (Spanish for mosque), which is unusual for a church. Since the mosque was built so that the direction of prayer was south, facing Mecca, and the orientation of the church had to be east, the church was erected crosswise inside the mosque. Style elements in the church also contribute to its awkwardness in the building that was obviously constructed in an Islamic tradition. For this reason, monument curators and art historians have been demanding for a long time that the church be removed from the mosque and rebuilt elsewhere. Such demands took on a religious quality in Tripoli. Restoring the mosque would not be difficult since the prayer niche *(miḥrāb)* in the oldest part of the complex was maintained intact and could resume its former function immediately. On the occasion of the regular Christian-Islamic meetings in Cordova, Islamic services *(ṣalāt)* are held in the cathedral, as has already been mentioned. This recently stirred up bad feelings in the population, though this might have been caused in part by the demands from Tripoli. It is perhaps difficult to understand why the building should be returned to its original state, which would comply with aesthetic and art historical criteria, but would not take into account the fact that the edifice has been used for Christian purposes for 750 years and an autochthonous Muslim community comparable to the Christian one does not exist in Cordova. The word "separation" *(faṣl)* in point 14 allows for the interpretation that the building should merely be divided into a Christian and an Islamic part. This would be technically feasible without requiring any major reconstruction. This idea, too, was met with resistance from the Christian side, which is understandable, and it remains doubtful whether the Muslims would be able to come to terms with it.

Points 20 and 21 of the concluding resolution in Tripoli were of a purely political nature, demonstrating more than the others the difficulty in communication with Muslims as long as the Palestinian question is not resolved. Zionism was condemned as an aggressive, racist movement, and the right of the Palestinians to return to their homeland was postulated. The Arab character of Jerusalem was stressed and internationalization rejected. Finally, the release of all prisoners "in occupied Palestine," above all the *ʿulamāʾ* and the Christian clergy, was demanded, as well as the liberation of all occupied territories. A standing commission was called for to anticipate any attempts to change the Islamic and Christian character of holy sites. Representatives from the Vatican declared that these last two points had been inserted later and they refused to accept them.

In contrast to the political demands made in Tripoli, it cannot be ignored that Muslims have come far in approaching Christians in other matters. Christians, too, have made concessions, whereby it is irrelevant whether they took the demands regarding the cathedral in Cordova seriously or not. The Tripoli seminar was just one of many similar events. On the one hand, the dialogue movement has spread out geographically, reaching as far as central Asia.[311] On the other hand, after events in Iran and because of the growing tendency toward fundamentalism throughout the Islamic world, the willingness to dialogue has diminished in the West. The Christian side is starting to again doubt the justification for religious pluralism. Certainly some things have also been taken to an extreme in implementing the dialogue, and practices of the ecumenical movement have been transferred to the dialogue without any critical reflection. The president of the Vatican Secretariat for Non-Christians spoke in this context at an Islamic-Christian consultation in November 1984 in Windsor Castle, listing the areas in which the dialogue could be implemented. He spoke pragmatically of a dialogue on coexistence in daily life and at the workplace, in the social services, the defense of human rights, promotion of religious life, and the acknowledgement of God. He also said that there is a great willingness for reconciliation. The last thing he mentioned is perhaps what has mistakenly been regarded alone as dialogue, namely, the discussion of faith and its contents, the rituals and rules of conduct, and regulations valid in the respective religious communities.[312]

Rising fundamentalism, the Iranian Revolution of 1979, the war in Bosnia, and events in Algeria have seriously impaired the confidence that accompanied the interfaith dialogue when it was started in the 1960s. Nevertheless, religious fanaticism and the violation of human rights as took place in Bosnia have been denounced, and the international community has been called upon "to end this tragedy through dialogue."[313] The expectations of a dialogue have been dampened, as illustrated by a speech given by Pope John Paul II on October 24, 1994 at a meeting in Rome of bishops in Pakistan. He criticized the situation of Christians in Pakistan and their status as second-class citizens; he denounced the injustice and intolerance and demanded religious freedom as "the cornerstone of the entire structure of human rights." But he did not abandon the thought of a dialogue with Islam: "Even when such dialogue is difficult or even unwelcome, the Catholic Church cannot forsake it." Discourse about faith and dogma is no longer the main focus, however. The Pope sees "the Church's social doctrine" as "a bridge linking Christians and Muslims in a shared commitment."[314]

Notes

1. A thorough study of the subject is provided in W. Atallah, "Les survivances préislamiques chez le prophète et ses compagnons," *Arabica* 24 (1977), 299–310. The topics covered include, among others, oaths, superstition, divination, sorcery, and warfare.
2. Cf. Norman Daniel, *Islam and the West: The Making of an Image* (Edinburgh: University Press, 1960; 3rd ed. 1966). For a survey of Islamic studies from the beginnings to the present, see W. Montgomery Watt, Alford T. Welch, *Der Islam* I (Stuttgart and Berlin, etc.: W. Kohlhammer, 1989) *(Die Religionen der Menschheit* 25/1), 17–38.
3. For an analysis of this important document, see Robert B. Serjeant, "The 'Constitution of Medina,'" *The Islamic Quarterly* 8 *(1964), 3–16;* ———, "The Sunna Jami'ah. Pacts with the Yathrib Jews, and the taḥrīm of Yathrib: Analysis and Translation of the Documents Comprised in the So-Called 'Constitution of Medina,'" *Bulletin of the School of Oriental and African Studies* 41 (1978), 1–42.
4. Julius Wellhausen, *Das arabische Reich und sein Sturz* (Berlin: Georg Reimer, 1902).
5. Theodor Nöldeke, *Geschichte des Qorāns* (Göttingen, 1860). The work was reedited and expanded by Friedrich Schwally, a student of Nöldeke, in three parts: *Über den Ursprung des Qorāns* (Leipzig, 1909); *Die Sammlung des Qorāns* (Leipzig, 1919); *Die Geschichte des Korantextes,* with O. Pretzl (Leipzig, 1938. Reprint Hildesheim and New York: George Olms, 1981).
6. Julius Wellhausen, "Zum Koran," *Zeitschrift der Deutschen Morgenländischen Gesellschaft (ZDMG)* 67 (1913), 630–34.
7. Notable here are, e.g.: Abraham Geiger, *Was hat Mohammed aus dem Judentum aufgenommen?* (Leipzig: A Geiger, 1902); and Abraham I. Katsh, *Judaism in Islam. Biblical and Talmudic Backgrounds of the Koran and its Commentaries, Suras II and III* (New York: University Press, 1952), reprinted 1962 as *Judaism and the Koran.* See also Joshua Finkel, "Old Israelitish Tradition in the Koran," *The Moslem World* 22 (1932), 169–183, who supports Geiger's thesis.
8. Adolf von Harnack, *Lehrbuch der Dogmengeschichte,* (Tübingen, 1909, reprinted Darmstadt: Wissenschaftliche Buchgesellschaft, Reprint 1964), II: 529.
9. Wilhelm Rudolph, *Die Abhängigkeit des Qorans von Judentum und Christentum* (Stuttgart: W. Kohlhammer, 1922). Although the title here is deceiving, Rudolph supported the theory of dependence on Christianity.
10. Richard Bell, *The Origin of Islam in its Christian Environment* (London: Frank Cass & Co., 1926; reprinted 1968).
11. Tor Andrae, "Der Ursprung des Islams und das Christentum," *Kyrkohistorisk arsskrift 1923–25* (Uppsala and Stockholm, 1926).
12. Karl Ahrens, "Christliches im Qoran," *ZDMG* 84 (1930): 15–68, 148–190.
13. *Der Islam* 16 (1928), 299.

14. Günter Lüling, *Über den Ur-Qur'ān. Ansätze zur Rekonstruktion vorislamischer christlicher Strophenlieder im Qur'ān* (Erlangen: H. Lüling, 1974).
15. Jacques Jomier, "Le nom divin 'al-Raḥmān' dans le Coran," *Mélanges Louis Massignon* (Damas: Institute Français de Damas, 1957), II: 361–38.
16. Charles Cutler Torrey, *The Jewish Foundation of Islam* (1933; reprinted with an introd. by Franz Rosenthal, New York: KTAV Publ. House, 1967).
17. Joseph Horovitz, *Koranische Untersuchungen* (Berlin and Leipzig: Walter de Gruyter & Co., 1926).
18. Heinrich Speyer, *Die biblischen Erzählungen im Qoran,* Ph.D. dissertation (Frankfurt/M., 1921; 3rd printing: Hildesheim, and New York: Georg Olms, 1971).
19. Frants Buhl, *Das Leben Muhammeds,* German trans. Hans Heinrich Schaeder (Heidelberg: Quelle & Meyer, 1930; reprinted Heidelberg: Quelle & Meyer, 1955).
20. Tor Andrae, *Mohammed, sein Leben und sein Glaube* (Göttingen: Vandenhoeck & Ruprect, 1932).
21. W. Montgomery Watt, *Muhammad at Mecca* (Oxford: University Press, 1953); ———, *Muhammad at Medina* (Oxford: Clarendon Press, 1956), and ———, *Muhammad's Mecca. History in the Qur'ān* (Edinburgh: University Press, 1988).
22. Rudi Paret, *Mohammed und der Koran. Geschichte und Verkündigung des arabischen Propheten,* 5th rev. ed. (Urban-Taschenbücher 32) (Stuttgart: W. Kohlhammer, 1980). A commendable overview of the history of research on the life of Muhammad is offered by Maxime Rodinson, "Bilan des études mohammadiennes," *Revue historique* 229 (1963), 169–220.
23. Theodor Nöldeke, "Hatte Muhammad christliche Lehrer?" *ZDMG* 12 (1858), 699–708. According to Nöldeke, Muhammad met the monk Bāḥīrā in Syria and had a brief discussion with him, but it was not decisive in Muhammad's development.
24. Clement Huart, "Une nouvelle source du Qoran," *Journal Asiatique,* 10th ser., (1904), 4:125–167.
25. For a critical evaluation, see Tilman Seidensticker, "The Authenticity of the Poems ascribed to Umayya Ibn Abī al-Ṣalt," in J. R. Smart, ed., *Tradition and Modernity in Arabic Language and Literature* (Richmond, Surrey: Curzon Press, 1996), 87–101.
26. Hubert Grimme, "Der Logos in Südarabien," *Orientalische Studien,* for Theodor Nöldeke on the Occasion of his 70th Birthday, ed. C. Bezold (Giessen: A. Töpelmann, 1906), I:453–461.
27. Youakim Moubarac, "Les noms, titres et attributs de Dieu dans le Coran et leurs correspondants en épigraphie sud sémitique," *Le Muséon* 68 (1955), 325–368.
28. Johann Fück, "Die Originalität des arabischen Propheten," *ZDMG* 15, n.s. (1936), 510–525.
29. Gustav von Grünebaum, "Von Muhammads Wirkung und Originalität," *Wiener Zeitschrift für die Kunde des Morgenlandes* 44 (1937), 29–50.
30. Joseph Henninger, *Spuren christlicher Glaubenswahrheiten im Koran* (Schöneck and Beckenried: Neue Zeitschrift für Missionswissenschaft [10], 1951).

31. Denise Masson, *Le Coran et la révélation judéo-chrétienne, études comparées,* 2 vols (Paris: Adrien Maissonneuve, 1958).
32. Jacques Jomier, *Bibel und Koran,* (Klosterneuburg, Klosterneuburger Bibelapostolat, 1962).
33. Youakim Moubarac, *Pentalogie islamo-chrétienne,* 5 vols (Beirut: Imprimerie Catholique, 1972–73).
34. Apart from a German translation of the Koran (Gütersloh, 1987), which was harshly criticized by Arne A. Ambros, *Wiener Zeitschrift für die Kunde des Morgenlandes* 79 (1989), 272–274, Khoury has been working on a monumental commentary since 1990: Der Koran, arabisch-deutch. Translation and commentary by Adel Theodor Khoury (Gütersloh: Gütersloher Verlagshaus Gerd Mohn, 1990 ff.). Vol. 7, covering sura 9:1–19, appeared in 1996.
35. Ludwig Hagemann, *Propheten, Zeugen des Glaubens. Koranische und biblische Deutungen* (Graz, Vienna, Cologne: Styria, 1985).
36. Walter Beltz, *Die Mythen des Koran, der Schlüssel zum Islam* (Berlin and Weimar: Claassen, 1979).
37. F. E. Peters, *Children of Abraham: Judaism, Christianity, Islam* (Princeton: University Press, 1982); ———, *Judaism, Christianity, and Islam: The Classical Texts and Their Interpretation* (Princeton: University Press, 1990).
38. Walter Strolz, *Heilswege der Weltreligionen,* vol I: *Christliche Begegnung mit Judentum und Islam* (Freiburg, Basel, Vienna: Herder, 1984).
39. Don Wismer, ed., *The Islamic Jesus. An Annotated Bibliography of Sources in English and French* (New York and London: Garland, 1977). The work exhibits some deficiency with respect to the selection of the titles.
40. For a list of translations in European languages, beginning with the Latin translations in the Middle Ages, see *Le Saint Coran. Traduction Intégrale et Notes de Muhammad Hamidullah,* 12th ed. (Paris: Mu'assat al-Risāla, 1406/1986).
41. Heikki Räisänen, *Das koranische Jesusbild. Ein Beitrag zur Theologie des Korans* (Helsinki: Missiologianja Ekymeniikan Seura [20], 1971); and ———, "The Portrait of Jesus in the Qur'an: Reflections of a Biblical Scholar," *The Muslim World* 70 (1980), 122–133.
42. Patricia Crone and Michael Cook, *Hagarism: The Making of the Islamic World* (Cambridge: University Press, 1977). Their thesis, based upon very scant textual evidence, was generally rejected by Islamicists.
43. John Wansbrough, *Quranic Studies: Sources and Methods of Scriptural Interpretation* (Oxford: University Press, 1977).
44. Leone Caetani, *Annali dell'Islam,* 10 vols (Milan, 1905. Reprinted Hildesheim and New York: Georg Olms, 1972).
45. Ibn Isḥāq, *The Life of Muhammad. A translation of Ibn Ishaq's Sirat Rasul Allah,* with introduction and notes by A. Guillaume (Oxford: University Press, 1955; fifth printing 1978); and F. Buhl and A. T. Welch, "Muhammad," *Encyclopaedia of Islam,* new ed. (1991), VII: 360–376. For an exhaustive analysis of Ibn Ishaq's *Life of Muhammad,* cf. Rudolph Sellheim, "Chalif und Geschichte," *Oriens* 18/19 (1967), 33–91.
46. Uri Rubin, *The Eye of the Beholder—The Life of Muhammad as Viewed by the*

Early Muslims: A Textual Analysis (Princeton: The Darwin Press, 1995) (Studies in Late Antiquity and Early Islam 5).

47. Arthur John Arberry, *The Koran Interpreted,* 2 vols (London and New York: Allen & Unwin and MacMillan, 1955). The numbering of verses corresponds to the official edition of the Koran (Cairo, 1926), followed by those given by Arberry in cases where the numbering differs by more than one cipher. In some cases the translation by Rudi Paret, *Der Koran* (Stuttgart, Berlin, Cologne, and Mainz, W. Kohlhammer, 1962) and Rudi Paret, *Der Koran,* commentary and concordance, 2nd printing (Stuttgart, etc.: W. Kohlhammer, 1977) have been consulted and/or quoted.
48. Torrey, *The Jewish Foundation of Islam,* 1–13. See also Moshe Gil, "The Origin of the Jews of Yathrib," *Jerusalem Studies in Arabic and Islam* 4 (1984), 203–224.
49. Arent Jan Wensinck, *Muhammad and the Jews of Medina,* trans. and ed. Wolfgang H. Behn, 2nd ed. (Berlin: Adıyok, 1982). According to Anton Baumstark, *Oriens Christianus* 37 (1953), 21, there are strong arguments supporting the existence of an Arabic translation of the Pentateuch dating from the pre-Islamic period.
50. Cf. Irfan Shahid, "The Martyrs of Najran. New documents," *Subsidia Hagiographica* 49 (Brussels: Société des Bollandistes, 1971).
51. The cathedral was not torn down until after the middle of the eighth century; cf. Theodor Nöldeke, *Geschichte der Perser und Araber zur Zeit der Sasaniden,* translated from the Arabic chronicle by Tabari, with extensive commentary and supplements (Leiden: E.J. Brill, 1879), 200ff., especially p. 201, n. 1; cf. also Ibn Ishaq/Guillaume, 21; on its architecture, see Barbara Finster and Jürgen Schmidt, "Die Kirche des Abraha in Ṣanᶜāʾ," in *Arabia Felix,* ed. Norbert Nebes (Wiesbaden: Otto Harrasowitz, 1994), 67–85.
52. Cf. Ludwig Brandl, "Sokotra—die ehemals christliche Insel," *Oriens Christianus* 57 (1975), 162–177, and M. C. Simeone-Senelle,"Suḳuṭra," *Enc. of Islam,* new ed., IX:806b–811a.
53. Cf. M. R. Al-Assouad, "Dhū Nuwās," *Encyclopaedia of Islam,* new ed., II: 243b–245a.
54. On the two Eastern Rite churches, see Bertold Spuler, "Die nestorianische Kirche," and ———, "Die westsyrische (monophysitische/jakobitische) Kirche," *Handbuch der Orientalistik,* vol 8: *Die Religionsgeschichte des Orients in der Zeit der Weltreligionen* (Leiden and Cologne: E.J. Brill, 1961), 120–216. Cf. also J. Spencer Trimingham, *Christianity among the Arabs in Pre-Islamic Times* (London and Beirut, Longman Group, 1979).
55. Ibn Ishaq/Giullaume, *The Life of Muhammad,* 653.
56. For example, there is knowledge of Nabataean merchants from Syria who sold groceries in Medina; cf. Ibid., 612.
57. Ibid., 84.
58. Ibid., 193.
59. Because he had such a beautiful voice, he became Muhammad's personal prayer caller *(muezzin);* later he apparently also administered the Prophet's personal

finances; cf. Ibn Ishaq/Guillaume, 236, 446.
60. Watt, *Muhammad at Medina,* 396.
61. Ibn Ishaq/Guillaume, 668.
62. Tor Andrae, *Der Ursprung des Islams und das Christentum,* 201.
63. Ibn Ishaq/Guillaume, 58ff; Ṭabarī I 1162 (cited in Ibn Ishaq/Guillaume, 113).
64. Ibn Ishaq/Guillaume, 136, 162f.
65. Ibid., 79–81. For a variant of this event, see p. 82.
66. Armand Abel, "Baḥīrā," *Encyclopaedia of Islam,* new ed., I: 922f. Both A. Sprenger ("Mohammed's Zusammenkunft mit dem Einsiedler Bahyra," *ZDMG* 12 [1858], 238–249) and T. Nöldeke ("Hatte Muhammad christliche Lehrer?" *ZDMG* 12 [1858], 699–708) considered young Muhammad's trip to Syria to be a historical fact.
67. Ibn Ishaq/Guillaume, 103; V. Vacca, "Zaid b. ᶜAmr," *Enzyklopaedie des Islam* IV:1233a.
68. Ibn Ishaq/Guillaume, 115.
69. Ibid., 659f.
70. Ibid., 21ff.
71. Meir J. Kister, "The Campaign of Ḥulubān. A New Light on the Expedition of Abraha," in: *Le Muséon* 78 (1965), 425–436.
72. Ibn Ishaq/Guillaume, 73.
73. Cf. Theodor Nöldeke, *Die Geschichte des Qorāns,* 2nd ed., ed. Friedrich Schwally; part 1: *Über den Ursprung des Qorāns*, 93.
74. Ibn Ishaq/Guillaume, 146.
75. Ibid., 152, 154f., 527.
76. See my article: Heribert Busse, "Jerusalem in the Story of Muhammad's Night Journey and Ascension," *Jerusalem Studies in Arabic and Islam* 14 (1991), 1–40.
77. Ibn Ishaq/Guillaume, 227.
78. See R. B. Serjeant, "The Sunna Jāmiᶜah, Pacts with the Yathrib Jews, and the taḥrīm of Yathrib: Analysis and Translation of the Documents Comprised in the So-Called 'Constitution of Medina,'" *Bulletin of the School of Oriental and African Studies* 41 (1978), 1–42.
79. Ibn Ishaq/Guillaume, 235f.
80. Ibid., 241, 263.
81. Ibid., 247–70.
82. Ibid., 523, 525. The traditions concerning the expulsion of Jews and Christians vary; there are reports according to which ᶜUmar exiled the Christians from Nadjrān and Fadak (near Khaybar), or he intended to do so; cf. A. J. Wensinck, *A Handbook of Early Muhammadan Tradition* (Leiden: E.J. Brill, 1927), 118.
83. Cf. the detailed explanation of the discussion in R. Paret, "Ibrāhīm," *Encyclopaedia of Islam,* new ed., III:980–81.
84. Ibn Ishaq/Guillaume, 9, 38.
85. This applies, for example, to the essay on the construction of the Ḥaram in Mecca, written by Fauziyya Ḥusain Maṭar and published in 1982 in Jidda.
86. In the following, Bible quotations are generally cited from the Authorized (King James) Version. In some cases, the Jerusalem Bible translation was deemed more

fitting, and these passages are cited appropriately with JB following the verse number.

87. Reinhart Pieter Anne Dozy, *Die Israeliten zu Mekka von Davids Zeit bis ins 5. Jahrhundert unserer Zeitrechnung. Ein Beitrag zur alttestamentlichen Kritik und zur Erforschung des Ursprungs des Islams,* German trans. from Dutch (Leipzig: Engelmann, etc., 1864).
88. Ibn Ishaq/Guillaume, 85f.
89. al-Azraḳī, *Akhbār Makka,* Die Chroniken der Stadt Mekka, ed. Ferdinand Wüstenfeld, F.A. Brockhaus, Leipzig. 1857–1859. Reprinted Hildesheim: Georg Olms, 1981. I:110–113, trans. p. 104f.
90. Gaming arrows were used by pagan priests at the Kaaba to draw lots proclaiming God's will, similar to the Urim and Thummim in the breastplate of the Jewish high priest.
91. Ibn Ishaq/Guillaume, 552.
92. Günter Lüling, *Der christliche Kult an der vorislamischen Kaaba als Problem der Islamwissenschaft und christlichen Theologie* (Erlangen: H. Lüling, 1977). This has since been thoroughly refuted in: Uri Rubin, "The Kaʿba: Aspects of its Ritual Functions and Position in Pre-Islamic and Early Islamic Times," *Jerusalem Studies in Arabic and Islam* 8 (1986), 97–131.
93. On both of these authors, cf. Berthold Altaner and Alfred Stuiber, *Patrologie*, 8th ed. (Freiburg, Basel, Vienna: Herder, 1978), 315–318, 509–511. On the subject, cf. Karl Bihlmeyer, *Kirchengeschichte,* rev. ed. by Hermann Tüchle, part 1 (Paderborn: Ferdinand Schöningh, 1962), 362.
94. al-Azraḳī, I 113. (Trans. p. 106); cf. also Ibn Ishaq/Guillaume, 552.
95. See N. F. Faris and Harold W. Glidden, "The Development of the Meaning of the Koranic Hanif," *The Journal of the Palestine Oriental Society* 19 (1939–40), 1–13; here, they derive the word from the Nabataean, where it referred to a follower of its somewhat Hellenized Syro-Arabic religion. The authors think the word was tranferred to Arabic in the pre-Islamic period. Both the Nabataean and the Koranic *ḥanīfs* do not drink wine, thus distinguishing themselves from Christians and Jews.
96. Ibn Ishaq/Guillaume, 99.
97. Sura 3: 154/148; 5:50/55; 33:33; 48:26.
98. He lived as a monk, *tarahhaba,* which is a verb form derived from Arabic *rāhib,* monk. *Rāhib* is a true Arabic word, according to Sigmund Fraenkel, *Die aramäischen Fremdwörter im Arabischen* (Leiden: E.J. Brill, 1886), 267f.
99. Ibn Ishaq/Guillaume, 236f.
100. Ibid., 105.
101. Most of the time, *taurāt* and *indjīl* appear together, corresponding approximately to the Old Testament and the New Testament, respectively; cf. sura 3:3/2; 3:48/43; 3:65/58; 5:66/70; 7:157; 9:111 *(taurāt, indjīl, qurʾān).* Psalter *(zabūr)* always appears alone: sura 21:105; 4: 163/161; 17:55/57.
102. A comprehensive list of citations ("Zitate und Hinweise auf solche") has been given by Speyer, *Die biblischen Erzählungen im Koran,* 429–461. See also, Edmund Beck, "Eine christliche Parallele zu den Paradiesesjungfrauen des

Korans?" *Orientalia Christiana Periodica* 14 (1948), 398–405; Régis Blachère, "Regards sur un passage parallèle des Évangiles et du Coran," *Mélanges d'Islamologie,* ed. Pierre Salmon (Leiden: E.J. Brill, 1974), I, 69–73; David Brady, "The Book of Revelation and the Qurʾān: Is there a Possible Literary Relationship?" *Journal of Semitic Studies* 23 (1978), 216–225; Arne A. Ambros, "'Höre, ohne zu hören' zu Koran 4:46 (48)," *ZDMG* 136 (1986), 15–22.

103. Cf. Joseph Horovitz, *Koranische Untersuchungen* (Berlin and Leipzig: Walter de Gruyter & Co., 1926), 78ff.
104. Erwin Gräf, "Zu den christlichen Einflüssen im Koran," *ZDMG* 111 (n.s. 37) (1962), 396–398; also in: *Der Koran,* ed. Rudi Paret, (Darmstadt: Wissenschaftliche Buchgesellschaft, 1975), 188–191.
105. A few examples are given by Eric F. Bishop, "Islam in the Psalter," *Muslim World* 55 (1965), 19–27.
106. Anton Baumstark, "Zur Herkunft der monotheistischen Bekenntnisformel im Koran," *Oriens Christianus* 37 (1953), 6–22.
107. Cf., for example, Camille Hechaimé, *Louis Cheikho et son livre 'Le christianisme et la littérature chrétienne en Arabie avant l'Islam'* (Beirut: Imprimerie Catholique, 1967).
108. Clément Huart, "Une nouvelle source du Qoran," *Journal Asiatique,* 10th ser. (1904), 125–167; J. Frank-Kamenetzky, *Untersuchungen über das Verhältnis der dem Umaiya b. Abiʾs-Salt zugeschriebenen Gedichte zum Qoran* (Kirchhain N. L.: Max Schmersow, 1911); Seidensticker (see above, note 25), 96: " . . . a balancing of all arguments about authenticity (of Umayya'a poetry) aginst each other still has to be carried out."
109. The Tablets of the Law that Moses received on Mount Sinai are called *alwāḥ (*sing. *lauḥ)* (7:145/142, 150/149, 154/153). There is no mention in the Koran of the material, according to Exod. 31:18, "tables of stone, written with the finger of God." In the story of Noah, there is mention of the planks *(alwāḥ)* used to build the ark ("well-planked vessel") (54:13). They are of course made of wood (cf. Gen. 6:14). The Hebrew *lu'ah* also has both meanings; cf. Arthur Jeffery, *The Foreign Vocabulary of the Qurʾān* (Baroda: Oriental Institute, 1938), 254. According to Exod. 32:16, "the tables *were* the work of God." The phrase "safely preserved tablet" is also reminiscent of the "testimony" kept in the Ark of the Covenant (cf. Exod. 25:16, etc.) and represents the earthly counterpart as it were of the heavenly tablets.
110. The name *ṣuḥuf,* "scrolls," (sing. *ṣaḥīfa)* also appears, referring both to the proto-Scripture in heaven (80:13; 81:10) and the Scriptures that Abraham (53:37/38; 87:19), Moses (53:36/37; 87:19), and Muhammad (98:2) had held in their hands.
111. Cf. Paret, commentary to 2:62.
112. Speyer, *Die biblischen Erzählungen im Koran,* 450.
113. Cf. Lothar Coenen, et al., ed., "Israel," *Theologisches Begriffslexikon zum Neuen Testament* (Wuppertal: R. Brockjhaus, 1977).
114. According to Jeffery, *The Foreign Vocabulary of the Qurʾān,* 281. However, the origin and etymology of the word are still disputed.
115. The same idea can be found in 3:19/17, 45:17, and 98:3.

116. God's trial or test *(balā᾽* and derived forms) of humanity is mentioned in the Koran approximately thirty times, e.g., Abraham is tested by a promise of progeny (2:124/118) and the commandment to sacrifice his son (37:106); the Israelites by the oppression of the Pharaoh (2:49/46; 7:141/137); the Muslims in Medina by the attacks of the Meccans (2:155/150; 3:154/148; 33:11), etc.
117. Cf. also Watt, *Muhammad at Mecca*, 112ff.
118. The name comes from the fact that the Muslims around Medina dug a trench *(khandaḳ)* to ward off the expected Meccan attack. The word *khandaḳ* has Persian origins, which demonstrates the strength of the Iranian influence at this time in the Ḥidjāz.
119. On this battle, see Meir J. Kister, "The Massacre of the Banu Qurayẓa: a Reexamination of a Tradition," *Jerusalem Studies in Arabic and Islam* 8 (1986), 61–96.
120. On the lot arrows at the Kaaba, see above, note 90.
121. On the chronological order, cf. Paret, commentary to 5:3. Paret cites Erwin Gräf, who also dated the regulations shortly after the Hidjra.
122. On the "scrolls," see above, note 110. This might be reminiscent of writings such as the apocryphal "Apocalypse of Abraham."
123. See René Dagorn, *La Geste d'Ismael d'après l'onomastique et la tradition arabe* (Geneva and Paris: Librairie Champion, 1981).
124. Christiaan Snouck Hurgronje, *Het Mekkaanische Feest* (Leiden, 1880), Verspreide Geschriften I (Bonn and Leipzig: Kurt Schroeder, 1923), 1–124.
125. Youakim Moubarac, *Abraham dans le Coran* (Paris: Librairie Philosophique J. Vrin, 1958).
126. Edmund Beck, "Die Gestalt Abrahams am Wendepunkt der Entwicklung Muhammads," *Le Muséon* 65 (1952), 79–94; also in *Der Koran,* 111–133. For a summarizing discussion, see Rudi Paret, "Ibrāhīm," *Encyclopaedia of Islam,* new ed., III 980–981.
127. Paret evidently interpreted v. 57/54 to mean that the Israelites' ingratitude constituted the wrongful deed, and that they longed for the wealth of food in Egypt. This is taken up again later in 2:61/58. I believe this refers to the dietary laws in general.
128. Cf. Paret, commentary to 2:58f, which discussed the difficulties surrounding this passage and the solutions suggested by Speyer, Jeffery, Hirschfeld, and others.
129. In Lev. 26:41 the "uncircumcised heart" of the Israelites is spoken of, because they broke the covenant. In Rom. 2:29, a circumcision of the heart is mentioned.
130. Cf. Ismar Elbogen, *Der jüdische Gottesdienst in seiner geschichtlichen Entwicklung* (Frankfurt/M., 1931; reprinted Hildesheim: Georg Olms, 1962), 469f.
131. Relevant here is a story passed down by Agapius of Mabbug (first half of the tenth century) that the Jews falsified the Bible chronology in order to veil Daniel's calculation of the coming of the Messiah. Constantine the Great is said to have received a copy of the Septuagint, which was kept in Alexandria, in order to correct it; cf. Agapius Mabbugensis, *Historia universalis,* ed. L. Cheikho (Louvain: Secrét du Corpus scriptorum Christianorum Orientalium [65], 1954, Reprint of

Paris, 1912), 226.

132. According to sura 4:10, that is the punishment for the greedy, who steal from orphans.

133. Translator's note: The Hebrew *tefillin* is derived from the Aramaic word for "attachments," referring to Deuteronomy 6:8, which calls for the wearing or "attaching" of God's word during prayer. The rendering in the New Testament (Matt. 23:5) by the Greek word *phylacteries*, or "protection," is thus inaccurate and inappropriate, the misinterpretation of which, however, is not apparent in the English language, which just as inaccurately regards *tefillin* and *phylacteries* as synonymous.

134. Because of the destruction of the Temple (Tor Andrae) or God's response to the complaints of the people in the desert (Num. 11:23) (W. Rudolph); cf. Paret, commentary to 5:64.

135. As claimed by Speyer; cf. Paret, commentary to 5:78.

136. On this and other agreements, cf. Antoine Fattal, *Le statut légal des non-Musulmans en pays d'Islam* (Beirut: Imprimerie Catholique, 1958).

137. On 9:29, cf. Meir J. Kister, "'ʿAn yadin' (Qurʾān 9.29). An Attempt at Interpretation," *Arabica* 11 (1964), 272–278; also in: *Der Koran,* 295–303.

138. Cf. also Watt, *Muhammad at Medina*, 219.

139. This is cited in the Koran several times as a characteristic of the faithful; cf. Paret, commentary to 3:104. Commanding that which is right and forbidding that which is reprehensible soon became a basic principle of the Muslims.

140. For details, cf. Räisänen, *Das koranische Jesusbild,* 31ff.

141. Abraham, Joseph, Idris, etc. had the same epithet; cf. Paret, commentary to 5:75.

142. Paret, commentary to 2:216, deals with the question whether this and similar passages are part of the discourse with the pagans or the Christians; the author tends to assume the latter.

143. The prayer here has the function of an oath; see Paret, commentary to 3:61 (with reference to Wellhausen, Goldziher, and Pedersen).

144. M. J. Rouët de Journel, *Enchiridion Patristicum* (Barcelona and Rome: Herder, 1981), 773 (No. 3053): Mary is "partner to his [Jesus'] immortality in all eternity" (sýssomos en aphtarsía eis aiōnas). Jesus awakened her from the grave and took her with him up to heaven. The text of the sermon by Modestus about Mary's returning to her Maker in: Migne, *Patrologia Graeca* 86/2, 3312. Cf. also Joseph Henninger, "Mariä Himmelfahrt im Koran," *Neue Zeitschrift für Missionswissenschaft* 10 (1954), 288–292; also in: *Der Koran,* 269–277.

145. Paret, commentary to 3:18 and 13:43, however, suspects that "men possessed of knowledge" refers to the "People of the Book."

146. Speyer, *Die Biblischen Erzählungen im Qorān,* 443, refers to Deut. 14:1: "Ye *are* the children of the Lord your God." There is frequent mention of the children of God in the New Testament; cf. Matt. 5:9 (seventh blessing); Rom. 9:26, etc.

147. Cf. Paret, commentary to 9:30 (with a reference to Speyer, Horovitz, and Künstlinger). English trans: James H. Charlesworth, ed., *The Old Testament Pseudepigrapha* (Garden City: Doubleday, NY, 1983), especially: B. M. Metzger, "The Fourth Book of Ezra," 517–560; M. E. Stone, "The Greek

Apocalypse of Ezra," 561–580.

148. Cf. D. Künstlinger, "ʿUzair ist der Sohn Allah's," *Orientalistische Literaturzeitung* (1932), col. 381–83.
149. On the etymology of *al-djibt* and *aṭ-ṭāġūt* (the expressions are presumably derived from Egyptian), cf. Paret, commentary to 4:51 and 2:256.
150. For a clear comparison of Bible and Koran texts, including post-biblical works, cf: Johann-Dietrich Thyen, *Bibel und Koran. Eine Synopse gemeinsamer Überlieferungen* (Cologne and Vienna: Böhlau Verlag, 1989). The book has excellent indices.
151. Muslim theologians distinguish between *nabī* (prophet) and *rasūl* (apostle): The *nabī* is someone who has received the word of God and preaches it; the *rasūl* is a prophet who is the leader of a community *(umma)*; cf. A. J. Wensinck, "Rasūl," *Encyclopedia of Islam,* new ed., (Leiden, 1995), VIII:454 f. In the Hebrew Bible, the following are including as books of the Prophets: Joshua, Judges, Samuel (1 & 2), Kings (1 & 2), Isaiah, Jeremiah, Ezekiel, and The Twelve; see Rabbi Aryeh Kaplan, *The Handbook of Jewish Thought* (New York and Jerusalem: Maznaim Publishing Corporation, 1979), 168f.
152. Additional passages on Creation: 7:54/52–58/56 (creation of the world in six days); 15:16–25; 16:3–16; 41:9–12; 55:1–30.
153. God pardoned Adam after he had sinned. This means that the notion of original sin from which human beings must be redeemed is unknown in Islam; cf. section on the Crucifixion of Jesus, pp. 132–137.
154. Nöldeke and Schwally, *Geschichte des Qorāns,* I:79, assumed that this is a revised form; they felt that especially verse 6 is much too long and was probably added later. This is affirmed by Angelika Neuwirth, *Studien zur Komposition der mekkanischen Sure* (Berlin and New York: Walter de Gruyter, 1981), 230.
155. In stories of the prophets taken from the Bible or post-biblical sources, the story is told in its complete form, including names; cf. *The Tales of the Prophets of al-Kisaʾi,* translated from the Arabic with notes by W. M. Thackston (Boston: Twayne Publishers, 1978), 77ff. (al-Kisāʾī lived in the eleventh century).
156. Abraham Geiger, *Was hat Mohammed aus dem Judentum aufgenommen?,* 102f.; Norman A. Stillman, "The Story of Cain and Abel in the Qurʾan and the Muslim Commentators: Some Observations," *Journal of Semitic Studies* 19 (1974), 231–239.
157. Cf. sura 2: 178/173, 179/175, 194/190, and 5:45/49.
158. A mountain in Arabia is meant. Muslims later localized the mountain in the Kurdish highlands; cf. M. Strack, "Djūdī," *Encyclopaedia of Islam,* new ed., II 573–574.
159. An alphabetical list of the old-Arabic gods can be found in: Toufic Fahd, *Le Panthéon de l'Arabie central à la veille de l'hégire* (Paris: Geuthner, 1968), 38–201.
160. Cf. the list of references in Paret, commentary to 7:184.
161. A shrine of Nabī Ṣāliḥ is located on the Sinai Peninsula, near the St. Catherine Monastery. A tomb of Ṣāliḥ can also be seen at Akko (see Guy Le Strange, *Palestine under the Moslems* (London, 1890, reprinted Beirut: Khayats, 1965),

329, 332) and Ramla (see Avraham Lewensohn, *Israel Tourguide* (Tel Aviv: Tourguide Ltd., and A. Lewenson Ltd., 1978), 461. On the tomb in Hadramaut, cf. Harold Ingrams, *Arabia and the Isles,* 3rd ed. (London, 1966), 182ff. On Hūd, see A. J. Wensinck and C. Pellat, "Hūd," *Encyclopaedia of Islam,* 2nd ed., III:537f.

162. Cf. Ulrich Hübner, "Frühe Araber im vorhellenistischen Palästina," *Christiana Albertina* 43, n.s. (1996), 5–17; and C. E. Bosworth, "Madyan Shuʿayb in Pre-Islamic and Early Islamic Lore and History," *Journal of Semitic Studies* 29 (1984), 53–64.
163. On the identity of the two, cf. A. D. L. Beeston, "The 'Men of the Tanglewood' in the Qurʾān," *Journal of Semitic Studies* 13 (1968), 253–255.
164. The "cities that We have blessed" in 34:18 are the cities in Palestine. Abraham and Lot came into the "land that We have blessed"; cf. 21:81 and other Koran passages which clearly show that Palestine is the land that has been blessed.
165. For a detailed discussion of this see W. Montgomery Watt, *Bell's Introduction to the Qurʾan,* completely revised and expanded (Edinburgh: University Press, 1970), 127ff.
166. The list in sura 26 is preceded by the stories of Moses (vv. 10/9–68) and Abraham (vv. 69–104). The similar closings of these passages and the narratives that follow indicate that they are to be considered a unit.
167. The "people of Abraham" are mentioned here. They were unbelievers, but no reference is made to any punishment.
168. This brings to mind 2 Cor. 3:15: "But even unto this day, when Moses is read, the veil is on their heart."
169. Hieronymus, *Quaestiones in Genesim 11:28,* Migne, *Patrologia Latina* 23, col. 1005; and ———, *Commentarii in Isaiam 65:8,* Migne, *Patrologia Latina* 24, col. 636; cited in Speyer, *Die biblischen Erzählungen im Qorān,* 143.
170. According to Islamic tradition, this king is identified with Nimrod, which is actually anachronistic, since Nimrod, the first "mighty one in the earth," appears in the Bible as Ham's grandson (Gen. 10:8).
171. Cf. *Babylonian Talmud, Tractate Pesahim* 118a; and Louis Ginzberg, *The Legends of the Jews* (Philadelphia: The Jewish Publication Society of America, 5728–1968), I 198–203.
172. Speyer, 163, is familiar with neither Jewish nor Christian scriptures that this could have been based on.
173. Paret, commentary to 2:124, discusses the question without deciding which of the two interpretations he prefers.
174. The word is used in this context in the Koran relating to believers (e.g., the Jews in Egypt, 28:5) and unbelievers (the dwellers of the Thicket, 15:79), as well as in reference to the Scriptures (11:17/20; 46:12) or the record, the register of good and bad deeds that must be presented at the Judgment (17:71/73; 36:12).
175. This is the interpretation offered by Ṭabarī (early tenth century) in his extensive Koran commentary on this passage.
176. Ṭabarī cites the respective justification for each of the interpretations.
177. Bekka is another name for Mecca. It can be assumed that switching the initial let-

ter served an apotropaic function, i.e., it was intended to mislead evil spirits. A Valley of the Weeper *(ᶜemeq ha-baka)* is mentioned in Psalm 84:6/7. As they pass through it, the pilgrims make it a place of springs [*"Who* passing through the valley of Bā'câ make it a well" (Ps. 84:6)]. Mecca is situated in a barren valley *(bi-wādin ghairi dhī zarᶜin,* 14:37/40).

178. The most important source for the early history of the Kaaba is the history of Mecca by al-Azraḳī (died 222/837), see above note 89.
179. For a detailed analysis of the narrative, see Anthony H. Johns, "Joseph in the Qurᵓan: Dramatic Dialogue, Human Emotion and Prophetic Wisdom," *Islamochristiana* 7 (1981), 29–55 (with a complete English translation of sura 12 at the end).
180. According to the Bible, Joseph went out to meet his father (Gen. 46:28–30); that is not what is meant here. Cf. Paret, commentary to 12:99.
181. Cf. Herbert Donner, *Die literarische Gestalt der alttestamentlichen Josephsgeschichte* (Heidelberg: Carl Winter, 1976), 48.
182. Gerhard von Rad, cited in A. H. Johns, *Joseph in the Qurᵓan,* 39.
183. A. H. Johns, 44f.
184. Watt, *Bell's Introduction to the Qurᵓān,* 110.
185. The meaning of this name is not known. Cf. also Horowitz, *Koranische Untersuchungen,* 125.
186. The location of the Burning Bush was already known to Egeria/Etheria (fourth century); cf. *Egeria's Travels to the Holy Land,* newly translated with supporting documents and notes by John Wilkinson, revised ed. (Jerusalem and Warminster: Ariel Publishing House, Avis & Phillips, 1981), 97, and Herbert Donner, *Pilgerfahrt ins Heilige Land* (Stuttgart: Katholisches Bibelwerk, 1979), 83 and 89.
187. Hāmān was actually the vizier of the Persian King Ahasverus (cf. Esther 3:1). He is seen as the archetypal enemy of believers, and his name no longer refers to the individual alone, but to such enemies in general.
188. Cf. Acts 5:34–40.
189. Noah's Ark also remained as a sign of warning for future generations; sura 54:15. For a full discussion of the Pharaoh's belated conversion, see Roberto Tottoli, "Il Faraone nell tradizioni Islamiche: Alcune note in margine alla questione della sua conversione," *Quaderni di Studi Arabi* 14 (1996), 19–30 (with a summary in English).
190. See above, chapter 3.3.
191. The narrator might have been referring to the idols at the Egyptian temple in Serabit al-Chadim on the Sinai peninsula, approximately 100 km (as the crow flies) southeast of Suez.
192. The saying was *ḥiṭṭa*; see Paret, commentary to 2:58, which includes a comprehensive discussion of explanations offered by western scholars. According to traditional Islamic sources, *ḥiṭṭa* means "remission of sins" ("unburdening," as translated by Arberry), the gate is that of Jerusalem: "Enter this township, and eat easefully of it wherever you will, and enter in at the gate, prostrating, and say, Unburdening; We will forgive you your transgressions, and increase the good-

doers" (2:58/55). As a result of this interpretation, one of the gates of the north wall of the Ḥaram al-sharīf in Jerusalem is called Bāb Ḥiṭṭa; cf. Guy Le Strange, *Palestine under the Moslems*, 173ff.

193. For a comprehensive discussion, see Paret, commentary to 20:85 (with a reference to Horovitz, Speyer, etc.); and the more recent article by B. Heller and A. Rippin, "al-Sāmirī," *Encyclopaedia of Islam,* new ed., VIII:1046; and Ferdinand Dexinger, "Die Samaritaner in der Kreuzzugszeit," *Hallesche Beiträge zur Orientwissenschaft* 22 (1996), 94–115 (with an expanded bibliography of works on the Samaritans in general).
194. Elliptical temporal clauses are introduced by the conjunction "when" and consist solely of an initial clause, excluding the usual second clause, cf. Paret, *Der Koran,* 3f. Such sentences often mark the beginning of a new section or topic in the Koran.
195. Cf. also the comparison of sura 17:22–25 with the relevant sections from Exodus 20, etc., in: M. S. Seale, *Qurʾan and Bible: Studies in Interpretation and Dialogue* (London: Croom Helm, 1978), 74ff.
196. The only relevant passage is sura 62:9–11.
197. Birket Qārūn is a lake in Fayyūm, indicating that the story took place in Egypt.
198. Cf. also "Sinbad the Sailor," the wealthy merchant, and Sinbad the poor carrier of burden, whose names are identical, since they are both creations of God, though the social circumstances of their lives are very different.
199. Speyer, *Die biblischen Erzählungen im Qoran,* 367f.
200. Cf. Louis Ginzberg, *The Legends of the Jews,* IV 101–104.
201. See John Wilkinson, *Jerusalem Pilgrims before the Crusades* (Jerusalem: Ariel Publishing House, 1977), 83; and Herbert Donner, *Pilgerfahrt ins Heilige Land,* 281. Another site of David's penitence after the census, which was his other sin, is the Holy Rock (al-Ṣakhra) on the Temple Mount, the Ḥaram al-Sharīf of the Muslims. David prayed there, repenting his sin (2 Sam. 24:10–17). For the Muslim tradition see al-Musharraf ibn al-Muraddjā, *Faḍāʾil bait al-maqdis,* ed. Ofer Livne-Kafri (Sfraram: Almashreq, 1995), 14.
202. For a thorough examination of the subject, see Neal Robinson, *Christ in Islam and Christianity. The Representation of Jesus in the Qurʾān and the Classical Muslim Commentaries* (Basingstoke and London: Macmillan Press, 1991).
203. For an explanation of elliptical temporal clauses occuring in the Koran in many passages, see above, note 194.
204. See Ṭabarī's commentary of 3:34. Arberry's translation "the seed of one another" is colorless, as is that of other modern translators; cf. Paret: "Nachkommen, die zueinandergehören"; R. Blachère, *Le Coran* (Paris: G. P. Maisonneuve & Larose, 1966): "en tant que desendants les uns des autres."
205. See Robinson, *Christ in Islam* 18. The question as to how much typologically influenced biblical texts determined Muhammad's understanding of scripture has been virtually ignored in the past.
206. For the actual text, cf. Agnes Smith Lewis, trans. and ed., *Apocrypha Syriaca* (Studia Sinaitica No. XI) (London: Clay, 1902).
207. "Who hast received food from the hand of an angel" (ch. 13.2) is not included in

Joseph's question in the edition and translation by Agnes Smith Lewis (though it does appear in a virtually identical question posed to Mary by the priest in ch. 15). It is indeed part of ch. 13.2 in one of the earliest extant handwritten manuscripts of the *Protevangelium,* the Papyrus Bodmer V (ed. M. Testuz, 1958), cf. Edgar Hennecke, *Neutestamentliche Apokryphen in deutscher Übersetzung,* 4th ed., Wilhelm Schneemelcher, ed., vol. I: *Evangelien* (Tübingen: J.C.B. Mohr (Paul Siebeck), 1968), 277 and 285. It also appears in the English translation by William Hone, *The Apocryphal New Testament*, 2nd ed., (London: Reeves, ca. 1820), ch. 10.9.

208. Cf. Luke 1:29: "she was troubled at his saying, and cast in her mind what manner of salutation this should be," i.e., the salutation: "Hail, *thou that art* highly favored, the Lord *is* with thee" (1:28).
209. Cf. H. Räisänen, *Das koranische Jesusbild,* 17, note 4 (sura 2:87/81, etc.; there are a total of 22 instances where Jesus is referred to as "Son of Mary").
210. Cf. Hennecke, *Neutestamentliche Apokryphen,* I:305f. According to the Infancy Gospel of Thomas (Hennecke, I 293ff), every word uttered by the child Jesus was a deed and became a miracle.
211. Ibid., 293ff. (Infancy Gospel of Thomas).
212. Henninger, *Spuren christlicher Glaubenswahrheiten im Koran,* 22.
213. The "sign" is one of the main theological terms of the Koran; cf. Räisänen, *Das koranische Jesusbild,* 23, with an analysis of the term that is used almost 400 times in the Koran.
214. This statement will be discussed in detail in chapter 5.6.
215. See above, ch. 3.3.
216. This is what Ṭabarī said in his commentary to 3:37 (the passage deals with Mary being given into Zachariah's care. An English translation of the Ṭabarī text is cited in: Abdelmajid Charfi, "Christianity in the Qurʾan Commentary of Tabari," *Islamochristiana* 6 (1980), 105–148; here: 113.
217. Ṭabarī, commentary to 19:16 (not cited in Charfi, see preceding note).
218. Cited in Paret, commentary to 19:16.
219. Cf. Paret, commentary to 19:17.
220. Räisänen, *Das koranische Jesusbild,* 24ff.
221. Cf. Hennecke, *Neutestamentliche Apokryphen,* I:307. Paret, commentary to 19:23–26 (with additional references).
222. Muslim authors such as Muhammad Hamidullah attempt to deal with the problems arising from the fact that Mary is called "the sister of Aaron" by interpreting it in a broader sense, i.e., that Mary is a descendant of Aaron; cf. Paret, commentary to 19:33f.
223. The wording is controversial for dogmatic reasons; the Greek text has *pais,* which means "child, son" as well as "servant." The *Authorized (King James) Version* of the Bible has "son of God," as does Franz Eugen Schlachter, *Die Heilige Schrift des Alten und Neuen Testament* (Geneva and Zurich: Das Haus der Bibel, 1951). The *Jerusalem Bible* (London, 1968) has "servant Jesus," with reference to Ex. 3:6 and Isa. 52:13.
224. This corresponds to the interpretation by, for example, Baiḍāwī in the commentary to 43:61, in: Helmut Gätje, *Koran und Koranexegese,* Zürich and Stuttgart:

Artemis, 1971), 175f. Sura 21:89–94 includes the narrative about Zachariah and John, and Mary and Jesus in a very condensed form.

225. Paret, commentary to 5:112–115, presumes that this was also influenced by Peter's vision (Acts 10:10ff.) On the typological relationship, cf. Gräf, *Zu den christlichen Einflüssen im Koran,* 189 (influence of liturgical texts). Cf. also Abd al-Tafahum, "The Qurʾān and the Holy Communion," *The Muslim World* 49 (1959), 239–248.
226. On the deification of the mother of Jesus, see above, page 23.
227. *Babylonian Talmud, Yoma* 67b, cf. Aryeh Kaplan, *The Handbook of Jewish Thought*, 70. This division also existed in Luther's *Small Catechism,* book 3, chapter 1: "The Holy Ten Commandments."
228. Paret, commentary to 61:6. See also W. Montgomery Watt, "His name is Aḥmad," *The Muslim World* 43 (1953), 110–117.
229. Cf. Heribert Busse, "Das Gleichnis vom Sämann im Koran," *pro Memoria. Das Studienjahr der Dormition Abbey auf dem Berg Sion in Jerusalem,* ed. Laurentius Klein and Immanuel Jakobs (Jerusalem: Dormition Abbey, 1983), 177–197.
230. Rudi Paret, "Sura 57:12f. und das Gleichnis von den klugen und den törichten Jungfrauen," *Festgabe deutscher Iranisten zur 2500 Jahrfeier Irans*, ed. Wilhelm Eilers (Wiesbaden: Otto Harrassowitz, 1967), 387–390; also in *Der Koran,* 192–196.
231. H. Räisänen, *Das koranische Jesusbild,* 65ff.
232. English translation in Charfi, *Christianity in the Qurʾan Commentary of Tabari,* 123f.; similar texts can be found in Ṭabarī's *Annals,* cf. the French translation by A. Ferré, "La vie de Jésus d'après les Annales de Tabari," *Islamochristiana* 5 (1979), 7–29.
233. Cf. Gätje, *Koran und Koranexegese,* 174.
234. The text can be found in Hennecke, *Neutestamentliche Apokryphen,* I:181. The Pistis Sophia is extant in a handwritten Coptic version from the second half of the fourth century.
235. Cf. the chapter entitled "tawaffā" in Robinson, *Christ in Islam,* 117–126.
236. A good example of this is the war between Iraq and Iran. From the Iranian perspective, it was a war of defense and as such legitimate, thus not requiring recourse to the rules of djihād. Saddam Hussein was called "Yazīd" by Iranian propaganda. Yazīd, the second Umayyad caliph (reigned 60/680–64/683), was made responsible by the Shiʿites for the death of al-Husayn, ʿAli's son, who was murdered at Kerbala; he was on his way to Syria to assert his claim to the throne.
237. Monika Tworuschka, *Allah ist gross. Religion, Politik und Gesellschaft im Islam* (Gütersloh: Gütersloher Verlagshaus Gerd Mohn, 1983), 96.
238. There has been much controversy on the meaning of the expression "out of hand." M. J. Kister translated it as "fight them . . . until they pay the djizya (poll tax) out of ability and sufficient means," in: Rudi Paret, ed., *Der Koran* (Darmstadt: Wissenschaftliche Buchgesellscahft, 1975), 295–303.
239. Al-Māwardī's work has been translated into French by F. Fagnan, *Les status gouvernementaux ou règles de drout public et administratif* (Algiers, 1915). See also Henri Laoust, "La pensée et l'action politique d'al-Māwardī," *Revue des Études*

Islamiques 36 (1968), 11–92.

240. See Ibn Ishaq, *Sirat Rasul Allah,* 499–507.
241. This is the site where the conquering emir, ᶜAmr ibn al-ᶜĀṣ, pitched his tent, now a southern suburb of modern Cairo.
242. See Eliyahu Ashtor, *Korot ha-Yehudim bi-Sefarad ha-muslemit* [The History of the Jews in Moslem Spain (Hebrew)], 2 vols (Jerusalem: Magnes, 1966).
243. For details about Eastern Rite Christians past and present, cf. Julius Assfalg and Paul Krüger, *Kleines Wörterbuch des christlichen Orients* (Wiesbaden: Otto Harrassowitz, 1975), with references to sources and dissertations.
244. Cf. "Algeria," *Encyclopaedia Judaica* (Jerusalem: Keter Publishing House, 1972).
245. For a large selection of early agreements and a detailed discussion of the legal questions, see Antoine Fattal, *Le statut légal des non-musulmans en pays d'Islam.* For a more recent work, cf. Albrecht Noth, "Die literarisch überlieferten Verträge der Eroberungszeit," *Studien zum Minderheitenproblem im Islam* I (Bonn, 1973) (Bonner Orientalistische Forschungen, n.s., vol 27:1); and regarding another aspect, cf. ———, "Abgrenzungsprobleme zwischen Muslimen und Nicht-Muslimen. Die 'Bedingungen ᶜUmar's (aš-šurūṭ al-ᶜumariyya),'" *Jerusalem Studies in Arabic and Islam* 9 (1987), 290–315.
246. The subject is dealt with comprehensively in: Peter Kawerau, *Amerika und die Orientalischen Kirchen. Ursprung und Anfang der amerikanischen Mission unter den Nationalkirchen Westasiens* (Berlin: Walter de Gruyter & Co., 1958).
247. For a basic discussion, see B. Braude and B. Lewis, eds., *Christians and Jews in the Ottoman Empire: The Functioning of a Plural Society;* vol I: *The Central Lands,* vol. II: *The Arabic-Speaking Countries* (New York and London: Holmes & Meier, 1982).
248. See Steven Runciman, *The Great Church in Captivity: A Study of the Patriarchate of Constantinople from the Eve of the Turkish Conquest to the Greek War of Independence* (Cambridge: University Press, 1968).
249. For a survey of the constitutions of the Islamic countries, cf. "Dustūr," *Encyclopaedia of Islam,* new ed., vol. II 638a–677a (with bibliography).
250. For information on the subject, cf. Seymour Gray, *Beyond the Veil: The Adventures of an American Doctor in Saudi Arabia* (New York, Cambridge, etc., 1983), esp. 228f. The author spent several years in the country starting in 1975.
251. His work, *Arab-Christian Scholars under Islam 622–1300* (in Arabic), was published in a revised edition as vol. 5 of the series "The Arab-Christian Heritage" (Aleppo, 1984).
252. On the situation for Christians, especially in Egypt, cf. Sami Awad Aldeeb Abu Sahlieh, *Non-musulmans en pays d'Islam (Cas de l'Égypte)* (Freiburg, 1979); a review by Maurice Borrmans in: *Islamochristiana* 7 (1981), 290–294.
253. See Abūʾl-Aᶜlā al-Maudūdī, "Les droits des Ḏimmīs dans l'État islamique (in Arabic and French)," *Pontificio Istituto di Studi Arabi e Islamici* 45 (Rome, 1975), 56–67.
254. For a list of Mawdūdī's 138 works, see Khurshid Ahmad and Zafar Ansari, eds., *Islamic Perspectives: Studies in Honour of Mawlana Sayyid Abul Aᶜla Mawdudi*

(Jidda: Sauda Publishing House, 1399/1979), 3–14.

255. On the position of minorities in the Iranian constitution, cf. René Klaff, *Islam und Demokratie. Zur Vereinbarkeit demokratischer und islamischer Ordnungsformen, dargestellt am Beispiel der Staatsauffassung Khomeinis* (Frankfurt/M., Bern, etc.: Peter Lang, 1987), 89–91.

256. Cf. Michael Lecker, Zayd b. Thābit, "'A Jew with two Sidelocks': Judaism and Literacy in Pre-Islamic Medina (Yathrib)," unpublished paper presented at the 7th International Colloquium "From Jahiliyya to Islam," Jerusalem 1996.

257. Bernard Lewis, *The Jews of Islam* (Oxford: University Press, 1984).

258. See Fazlur Rahman, "Islam's Attitude toward Judaism," *The Muslim World* 72 (1982), 1–13.

259. Cf. Bat Ye'or, *The Dhimmi: Jews and Christians under Islam* (Rutherford, NJ: Fairleigh Dickinson, 1985), 304, 317.

260. Ibid., 228ff.

261. Ibid., 279.

262. Cf. Hans Leuschner, *Friedrich der Grosse. Zeit, Person, Wirkung;* with an essay by Erich Born (Gütersloh: Gutersloher Verlagshaus Gerd Mohn, 1986), 185 (with a fascimile of the King's remark on the petition of a Catholic for citizenship rights in Berlin).

263. There is a the wealth of literature on this subject; cf., for example, Gerd Nonneman, Tim Niblock, and Bogdan Szajkowski, eds., *Muslim Communities in the New Europe* (Reading: Ithaca Press, 1996).

264. On this subject, see Johannes Reissner, "Internationale islamische Organisationen," in: Werner Ende and Udo Steinbach, eds., *Der Islam in der Gegenwart,* 4th ed. (Munich: C.H. Beck, 1996), 539–547.

265. See "Notes on the Quarter," *The Muslim World* 58 (1968), 267.

266. Cf. Christine Schirrmacher, *Mit den Waffen des Gegners. Christlich-muslimische Kontroversen im 19. und 20. Jahrhundert, dargestellt am Beispiel der Auseinandersetzung um Karl Gottlieb Pfanders 'Mīzān al-ḥaqq' und Raḥmatullāh ibn Ḫalīl al-ʿUṯmānī al-Kairānawīs 'Iẓhār al-ḥaqq' und der Diskussion über das Barnabasevangelium* (Berlin: Klaus Schwarz, 1992) (Islamkundliche Untersuchungen, vol 162), based on archival materials, with a comprehensive bibliography.

267. On Ghulam Ahmad and his teachings, see Yohanan Friedmann, *Prophecy Continues: Aspects of Ahmadi Religious Thought and its Medieval Background* (Los Angeles and London, 1989).

268. The name is taken from the Koran, sura 2:265/267: "a garden on a hill" and 23:50/52: a height, where was a hollow and a spring."

269. For an example of the polemics published against this wing of the Ahmadiyya, cf. Ehsan E. Zaheer, *Qadyaniat: An Analytical Survey* (Lahore:Idara Tarjuman Al-Sunnah, 1973).

270. A good summary and description that applies for Islamic missionary activities in general appears in the first issue of the *Al-Fadjr* (The Dawn) newspaper, published by the Islamic Center in Hamburg (est. 1403/1983).

271. *Christ in der Gegenwart,* 5 August 1984. On the "Islamic World Congress of the

da^cwa" that took place in 1981 in Khartoum, cf. *Islamochristiana* 7 (1981), 258–259.

272. *Mélanges de l'Institut Dominicain d'Études Orientales du Caire* (=MIDEO) 11 (1972), 447.
273. MIDEO 1 (1954), 188f.; 3 (1955–56), 470. For further information about other dialogue circles in Egypt, cf. *Islamochristiana* 5 (1979), 250–258; MIDEO 14 (1980), 385–395. On Charles de Foucauld, cf. Ali Merad, *Charles de Foucauld au regard de l'Islam* (Paris, 1975); on Louis Massignon, cf. Giulio Basetti-Sani, *Louis Massignon (1883–1962)* (Florence: Alinea, 1985) [Italia, Oriente, Mediterraneo 2].
274. Cf. Jean Corbon, "Le Cénacle Libanais et le dialogue islamo-chrétien," *Islamochristiana* 7 (1981), 227–240.
275. The Latin text, "Declaratio de Ecclesiae habitudine ad religiones non-Christianas," has been published in: *Acta Apostolicae Sedis* 58 (1966), 740–744. For an English translation, see W. M. Abbott, ed., *The Documents of Vatican II* (New York: Guild Press, 1965).
276. Cf. "Constitutio dogmatica de Ecclesias," *Acta Apostolicae Sedis* 57 (1965), 20. For an English translation, see previous note.
277. First published in 1970, it is now available in a revised, French edition as: Maurice Borrmans, *Orientations pour un dialogue entre Chrétiens et Musulmans* (Paris: Les Éditions du Cerf, 1981), with an appendix including a calendar of events and a bibliography.
278. Ahmad von Denffer, *Dialogue Between Christians and Muslims,* vol I: *A Survey. The Islamic Foundation* (Leicester: The Islamic Foundation, 1980/1400), 12ff.; and John Renard, "Christian-Muslim Dialogue: A Review of Six Post-Vatican II Church-Related Documents," *Journal of Ecumenical Studies* 23 (1986), 69–89.
279. Ahmad von Denffer, *Dialogue,* vol III: *Statements and Resolutions,* 11. See also the survey in: *Christians Meeting Muslims* (WCC Papers on 10 Years of Christian-Muslim Dialogue) (Geneva: World Council of Churches, 1977); also: *Islamochristiana* 9 (1983), 299–300.
280. I have a copy of the Arabic text from an unidentified publication.
281. Cf. the summarizing presentation by Youakim Moubarac and Guy Harpigny, "Der Islam in der theologischen Reflexion des zeitgenössischen Christentums," *Concilium* 12 (1976), 343–348 (with bibliography).
282. Cf. the report in: *Islamochristiana* 11 (1985), 238–240.
283. On this subject, see Abdullah Siddiqui, *The Henry Martyn Institute of Islamic Studies. An Attempt to Christianise Muslims in India* (Leicester: The Islamic Foundation, 1984) (The Islamic Foundation, Study Paper No. 8). Cf. also *Islamochristiana* 5 (1979), 129–133.
284. The reply was published in the Meccan newspaper *Akhbār al-^cālam al-islāmī* (News from the Islamic World), no. 65 (1387/1968), 2, 7.
285. According to a report published in the German weekly *Christ in der Gegenwart* 52 (1974).
286. Ibid., 18 April 1982.
287. *Christ in der Gegenwart,* 16 May 1965. For the text of correspondance and let-

ters of protest addressed to the Vatican see *Proche Orient Chrétien* 14 (1964), 355–359.

288. On the British section founded in 1972, cf. *Islamochristiana* 7 (1981), 195f.
289. Cf. the report in *Islamochristiana* 4 (1978), 223–225.
290. Ibid., 225–230; 9 (1983), 295f.
291. *Islamochristiana* 4 (1978), 236–242.
292. *Journal of Ecumenical Studies* 19 (1982), 197–200. See also *Islamochristiana* 8 (1982), 250–252.
293. After Sadat's violent death on October 6, 1981, the idea of a mausoleum was abandoned. His grave is near the tomb of the unknown soldier in Cairo, not far from the site of his assassination.
294. *Christ in der Gegenwart,* 7 September 1986.
295. Reuel L. Howe, *The Miracle of Dialogue* (New York, 1963), cited in Ray G. Register, Jr., *Dialogue and Interfaith Witness with Muslims: A Guide and Sample Ministry in the U.S.A.* (Fort Washington and Toronto: Dialogue and Interfaith Witness with Muslims, 1979).
296. The Arabic text with an English translation by A. Mingana appears in ᶜAli Tabari, *The Book of Religion and Empire: A Semi-Official Defence and Exposition of Islam Written by Order at the Court and with the Assistance of the Caliph Mutawakkil (A.D. 847–861)* (Manchester, London, New York, etc.: University Press, Longmans, Green & Co., Bernard Quaritch, 1922–23).
297. Cf. Raif Georges Khoury, "Quelques réflexions sur les citations de la Bible dans les premières générations islamiques du premier et du deuxième siècles de l'hégire," *Bulletin d'Études Orientales* 29 (1977), 269–278; and Sidney H. Griffith, "The Gospel in Arabic: An Inquiry into its Appearance in the First Abbasid Century," *Oriens Christianus* 69 (1985), 126–167.
298. For a Spanish translation of Ibn Ḥazm's major work, cf. M. Asín Palacios, *Abenházam de Cordoba y sua historia crítica de las ideas religiosas* (Madrid: Tip de la "Rivista de archivos", 1927–32).
299. Ibrāhīm b. ᶜUmar al-Biḳāᶜī, *Naẓm al-durar* (String of Pearls) (Beirūt, 1314/1995), II: 350–363.
300. For a French translation, cf. Rahmatullah, *Idh-har-ul-haqq ou Manifestation de la vérité,* trans. P. V. Carletti, 2 vols (Paris: Ernest Leroux, 1880).
301. David Benjamin, *Muhammad in der Bibel* (Munich: Bavaria Verlag & Handel GmbH, 1992); and Muhammad ᶜAta ur-Rahim, *Jesus, A Prophet of Islam,* 3rd ed. (London: MWH London Publishers, 1983).
302. For a partial English translation, cf: Thomas F. Michel, ed. and trans., *A Muslim Theologian's Response to Christianity: Ibn Taymiyya's Al-Jawab al-Sahih* (New York: Caravan Books, Delmar, 1984).
303. Cf. Camilla Adang, *Muslim Writers on Judaism and the Hebrew Bible: From Ibn Rabban to Ibn Hazm* (Leiden, New York, and Cologne: E.J.Brill, 1996).
304. Cf. Erdmann Fritsch, *Islam und Christentum im Mittelalter. Beiträge zur Geschichte der muslimischen Polemik gegen das Christentum in arabischer Sprache* (Kirchhain N. L.:Max Schmersow, 1930).
305. Cf. Louis Massignon, "Le Christ dans les évangiles selon al-Ghazali," *Revue des*

Études Islamiques (1932), 491–536. Others question the authenticity; cf. Maurice Bouyges, *Essai de chronologie des oeuvres de al-Ghazali (Algazel),* edited and updated by Michel Allard (Beirut: Imprimerie Catholique, 1959).

306. Muhammad b. Saᶜīd al-Būṣīrī, *Manẓūma fī r-radd ᶜalā n-naṣārā wa l-yahūd* (Didactic poem about refuting Jews and Christians), (Cairo, 1979).

307. As an introduction to such works, cf. Arthur Jeffery, "A Collection of Anti-Christian Books and Pamphlets Found in Actual Use Among the Mohammedans of Cairo," *The Moslem World* 15 (1925), 26–37; 16 (1926), 25–427; 17 (1927), 428–429; and with a notable change in title, cf. Hugh P. Goddard, "An Annotated Bibliography of Works About Christianity by Egyptian Muslim Authors (1940–1980)," *The Muslim World* 80 (1990), 251–277. See also the regular report "Textes arabes anciens édités en Égypte," under the heading "Polémique et apologétique," published in MIDEO, Cairo; 1954–1988: Georges C. Anawati, ed.; since then: Claude Gilliot, ed. (with brief commentary). For a thorough analysis of texts pertaining to the twentieth century, see Maurice Borrmans, *Jésus et les musulmans d'aujourd'hui* (Paris: Desclée, 1996).

308. For a short discussion of the subject see W. Montgomery Watt, "The Christianity Criticized in the Qurᵓān," *The Muslim World* 57 (1967), 197–201.

309. Cf. Mikel de Epalza, "Cordova Welcomes its Muslim Friends," *The Muslim World* 65 (1975), 132–136. For the complete text of the declaration, see Ahmad von Denffer, *Documents on Christianity and Christian-Muslim Relations,* No. 1: *Dialogue between Christians and Muslims* (Leicester: The Islamic Foundation, 1980), 13f.

310. The Arabic text appears in: *Islamochristiana* 2 (1976), 164–170. For an English translation, cf. Ahmad von Denffer, *Dialogue* III:27–34.

311. For example, a discussion took place in 1983 in Tashkent; cf. *Islamochristiana* 9 (1983), 274.

312. Cf. *Islamochristiana* 11 (1985), 219–20.

313. This was said at a meeting of Jewish, Christian, and Muslim representatives in Jerusalem, in the Centre Notre Dame de Jérusalem on August 16, 1995; cf. *Proche-Orient Chrétien* 46 (1996), 208f.

313. Cf. *Acta Apostolicae Sedis* 87 (1995), 621–626.

Index of Proper Names

Index of Koran Verses